RETIRED

WHAT HAPPENS TO FOOTBALLERS WHEN THE GAME'S UP

ALAN GERNON

First published by Pitch Publishing, 2016

Pitch Publishing
A2 Yeoman Gate
Yeoman Way
Worthing
Sussex
BN13 3QZ
www.pitchpublishing.co.uk

ISBN 978-1-78531-138-3

Typesetting and origination by Pitch Publishing
Printed by Bell & Bain, Glasgow, Scotland

Contents

Foreword

by Niall Quinn

ALAN GERNON'S *Retired* is a stark reminder for all football fans that our on-pitch heroes are often hopelessly prepared for life after the final whistle.

As the lights start to dim on even the most brilliant careers, the pain of letting go and the failure to seek early transition intervention has led to carnage in the 'afterlife' of many top players. Lacking basic life skills, education and wealth of mind, an alarming number of former greats face identity crisis, depression, addictions, bankruptcy, divorce, jail and even suicide instead of a happy retirement.

Today's footballers are portrayed as overpaid, spoilt and out of touch, while public sympathy is scarce for those who 'had it all' only to lose everything. But not long into reading *Retired* a bleak reality unfolds – footballers are a vulnerable breed and need serious help adjusting to the outside world.

The depth of research is evident and culminates in numerous harrowing tales of destruction. By recording so many sad plights Alan has sent a much-needed wake-up call to the conscience of the business of football. *Retired* lifts an uncomfortable lid on an age-old problem and as a result football, if not all sports, can no longer ignore the 'afterlife' suffering of its previous, current and future stars. This makes *Retired* one of the most important sports books of recent times.

Niall Quinn, Retired Footballer (still married)

Acknowledgements

THERE are numerous people from the football world to thank, without whom this book wouldn't exist. Many thanks to the likes of David Bentley, Pat Nevin, Lee Bowyer, David Busst, Geoff Thomas, Jody Craddock, Mark Ward, Shane Supple, Espen Baardsen, Matt Holland, Steven Caldwell, Mikele Leigertwood, Richie Sadlier, Gordon Watson, Gary Stevens, Paul McGregor, Steve Walsh, Jon Newsome, Richard Leadbeater, Paul McVeigh and several others, who did not wish to be named, for their insights into life as a retired professional footballer. Their honesty and experiences were crucial in piecing together the life of a retired footballer.

Others to thank include Geoff Scott of XPRO, Mark Sands of Baker Tilly, Professor Chris Brady, Sam Sloma of First Wealth LLP, Robert Segal at Impact Sports Management, Dan Clay of Clay & Associates, Dr Philip Hopley of Cognacity, Dr Vincent Gouttebarge of FIFPro, Dr David Blakelock, John Duncan of Coach 24/7, Michael Bennett of the PFA, Mark Hands of Irwin Mitchell, Dr Steven Ortiz of Oregon State University, Simon Green of BT Sport, Dr Eric Nauman of Purdue University, Simon Taylor of the Professional Players Federation, Dr Andy Turner of Coventry University, Michael Kinsella of Onside Academy, James Hall at Anthony Collins Solicitors, Gregor Robertson, the amazing Laraine Astle,

Dawn Astle, Claire Astle and The Jeff Astle Foundation, Jim Hicks of the PFA, RTÉ's Ryle Nugent, ITV's Mark Demuth, Brian Barwick, Dr Gwen Fernandes of the University of Nottingham, Dr Michael Grey of University of Birmingham, Dr Dorian Dugmore, Kevin Harris-James at Harrison Clark Rickerbys who was an enormous help, and many, many more.

Again, I'd also like to thank those that contributed but didn't wish to be named. I was overwhelmed by the willingness of everyone to assist me with their expertise and experience in diverse subjects. I sincerely apologise if I've forgotten anyone.

I'd also like to offer my thanks to the likes of Gavin Hoey, Rory Callan, Aidan Homer, Colin Howard, Jim Burke, Paddy Faul, David Moran, Paddy McDonnell, James Wogan, Nigel Seeley, Eamonn Murphy, Michael Wogan, Duncan Olner and Martin McGahon for their various assistance. Also, a special thanks to Will Reilly for his diligence and great help in the final few weeks of the writing process.

I'd like to thank my parents, Tom and Eileen, for developing my love of books and football. Saturdays as a kid meant a visit to Dundalk Library with my mother, Sundays meant a trip to Dundalk FC with my dad. Those weekends, along with my parents' love of course, were the best parts of my childhood. I simply couldn't have wished for better parents. I had also better mention my brothers, David and Thomas, who don't really like football so might only read this bit.

Most of all, thanks to my amazing wife Tracey. She's been a rock for me for many years and her patience and support during this project has been immense. I'd need another 80,000 words to adequately convey my love and respect for her. Finally, thanks to my three kids Daisy, Noah and Joel, who have seen a lot less of me for the past few months. I love them all dearly and am so grateful for my life with them.

1

Introduction

ON 16 April 1977 the population of a small Swedish town called Vittsjö increased by one. The new arrival's proud parents – Roy Alve Erling, a civil engineer and owner of a construction business, and Elisabeth, a Swedish Labour Department worker – decided to name their firstborn Karl. Karl Fredrik Ljungberg.

The same week, over 2,000km away in Drogheda, Ireland, I also entered the world. Both of us would harbour fierce ambitions to become a professional footballer but, alas, only one had the talent and perseverance to succeed. As a kid, I may have possessed rudimentary technical ability but my tactical awareness was non-existent. Put it this way, if you ever met me at an airport or train station, there's a fair chance I would have been returning from an offside position. I still play indoor football but often the matches are imbalanced, with five against six or six against seven. Although they do say in football that 'sometimes the extra man makes no difference at all'. Like in The Corrs.

Due to the proximity of our birth dates, I've always kept a close eye on Freddie Ljungberg's career. I rather unwisely benchmarked his life against mine as he was the highest-profile professional footballer closest in age to my own. This proved to be a foolish decision for my self-esteem. While the highlight of my football career was hitting the bar for Glenmuir Under-12s, Ljungberg went on to amass three league titles and three FA Cups at Arsenal and was a key component in their famous Invincibles season. While the Swede was the face, and body, of Calvin Klein, the only six-pack I was modelling in my underwear came in the form of cans of Harp Lager.

However, Ljungberg provided hope. Every football fan retains a dream of playing the sport they love for a living, and while a player the same age as me was still performing, a deluded part of me maintained some belief that I could still make it as a footballer.

And then he retired. He'd originally hung up his boots in 2012 but dusted them down for a cameo in the newly-formed Indian Super League in 2014. However, after just four appearances for Mumbai City FC, his comeback was brought to an end through injury and, with it, any faint, irrational hopes I had of ever playing professional football. He announced, 'It's still fun to play the big games, but when you no longer have the motivation for training then it's time to call it quits.'

And yet still I envied him. 'Retired at 37? Lucky sod,' I thought to myself. I daydreamed about retiring, with millions accumulated from a successful football career. He probably had the beautiful wife, the fleet of luxury cars and the penthouse apartments in the world's nicest cities. What a time to be alive for Freddie, I thought. Until I discovered there was possibly an alternative fate awaiting him.

His retirement sparked a curiosity in me as to what exactly happens to professional footballers when they hang up their boots. Yes, I'd fantasised about retiring at the same age, but what would I do to fill my remaining days? It seemed like a simple question, with a simple answer. Ask many people and they'll presume that retired footballers live off their vast millions while managing a club or sitting comfortably on the *Match of the Day* panel pretending to laugh at Mark Lawrenson's jokes.

It transpires that it's not all champagne lifestyles and glamour.

The American author Roger Kahn wrote in *The Boys of Summer*, his acclaimed 1972 book on baseball, 'Unlike most, a ball player must confront two deaths. First, between the ages of 30 and 40 he perishes as an athlete. Although he looks trim and feels vigorous and retains unusual coordination, the superlative reflexes, the *major league* reflexes, pass on.

'At a point when many of his class-mates are newly confident and rising in other fields, he finds that he can no longer hit a very good fast ball or reach a grounder four strides to his right. At 35 he is experiencing the truth of finality. As his major league career is ending, all things will end. However he sprang, he was always earthbound. Mortality embraces him. The golden age has passed in a moment. So will all things. So will all moments.'

This quote may as well have been written about the experience of a newly-retired footballer. Ljungberg's old boss at Arsenal, Arsène Wenger, echoed Kahn's sentiments when he stated that retired players experience difficulties because they 'lose passion, fame and income at a very young age. To replace that is nearly impossible.'

Wenger has always maintained that he is keen to look after players upon retirement but his compassion seems uncommon in the modern-day, affluent game. According to Geoff Scott, chief executive of XPRO, a charity established to help, support and advise former professional footballers, Wenger's concern is all too rare.

'The clubs don't care about what happens to players when they retire. Once the footballer has got his 30 grand a week and his Range Rover, the clubs wash their hands of them. It's a similar attitude from the Football Association, and certainly from the Premier League, who don't even call it football any more. To them it is a product,' the 59-year-old says.

Scott is certainly speaking from experience. After 176 appearances in the Football League during the 1970s and 80s for the likes of Stoke City, Leicester City and Birmingham City, the defender's career ended prematurely at 26 through injury. He had very little assistance in figuring out what to do next.

The idea for the charity first came about following a chat between former Northern Ireland striker Derek Dougan and his friend Bob Runham, a West Midlands businessman. The latter was organising an event to honour the European Cup-winning Celtic team of 1966/67 but was shocked to discover that one of the victorious Lisbon Lions was unable to afford a pair of shoes for the occasion. Runham bought the footwear himself, but questioned Dougan as to whether there was anything they could do to help former professionals who had fallen on hard times. It was then that the seeds for XPRO were sown.

Despite having no support mechanism in place when he was forced to retire following a cruciate ligament injury, Scott forged a successful second career away from the game – gaining a Business degree and holding directorships with several global telecommunications companies. He forgot about football and hadn't watched a live game for over 25 years before being invited by a former team-mate, Terry Conroy, to attend a Stoke City match. Amazed at the lack of support and contact from the football world for former players, Conroy put Scott in touch with Runham, and the former took over as CEO of XPRO in 2007.

His first objective was to establish a national database of former professionals, with an estimated figure of over 60,000 living former players across the UK and Ireland. To put that total into perspective, it's enough men to fill Arsenal's Emirates Stadium or Celtic Park in Glasgow. If I merely typed the name of every ex-footballer living in the British Isles, it would fill this book one and a half times over. While high-profile modern-day footballers garner little sympathy from fans, the majority of these ex-pros spent their careers in English football's lower tiers, earning modest amounts and were offered little or no support upon retirement.

Ernest Hemingway said 'retirement is the ugliest word in the language', and that can certainly be the case for many ex-footballers. Research from XPRO on the effects of retirement on professional footballers in the English game is startling. It suggests that two out of every five Premier League players – who earn an average of £42,872 per week – face the threat of bankruptcy within five years of ending their careers.

Let that figure sink in. When you're watching *Match of the Day* next Saturday night, around nine of the 22 players on the pitch could be bankrupt within 60 months of retiring. The next time you're choosing your starting XI for your fantasy football team or playing FIFA, consider that almost half of your team could face financial ruin in the coming years.

It seems absurd that young men with so much earning power could possibly fall on such hard times, and these are just the figures for the Premier League. Yet even if an ex-footballer is financially secure, there are a myriad of other difficulties to overcome.

In recent years, TV shows such as *Footballers' Wives* and *The Real Housewives of Cheshire* have glamorised players' marriages to such an extent that British teenage girls would rather become a WAG than a politician or charity campaigner. It is clear that the lavish lifestyle of a WAG is an aspiration for thousands of young females across the UK, whose motives may not be entirely inspired by romance.

When asked what he'd be if he wasn't a footballer, Peter Crouch once quipped 'a virgin'. While he was obviously joking, he was making a pertinent point about the wannabe WAG culture. There are certainly cases where footballers' spouses have married the player, the lifestyle, the image rather than the man. Despite this, XPRO's figures on divorce rates for retired footballers are still staggering.

They estimate that a third of footballers will be divorced within just 12 months of retirement. Marriages in the United Kingdom last, on average, 32 years, according to the Office for National Statistics.

It's not just lower league players who are affected. When I spoke to Geoff, he'd just got off the phone to a recently-retired former England international. The player had enjoyed a great career, had earned great money and had cash in the bank, but realised his marriage was splitting and that he was 'getting more and more divorced every day'. We will investigate the reasons for this staggeringly high rate of failed marriages later, but it is clear that they can also have a detrimental effect on a retired player's financial situation.

There may be some ex-players who are financially secure and remain in happy marriages, but they will have other problems to navigate upon retirement.

Physical and mental health issues can be acute. XPRO estimate that 80 per cent of retired players will suffer from osteoarthritis, a degenerative joint disease that will typically affect ten per cent of males over 60 in the general population. Taking the figure of 60,000 retired footballers, that's up to 48,000 ex-players who could be suffering with a debilitating condition that will impinge on their daily lives. However, football is one of the few professions where the UK government does not recognise osteoarthritis as a prescribed industrial disability, meaning retired pros do not qualify for state benefits. This is something XPRO has been eager to remedy, conducting extensive research into the effects of the disease on its members.

While footballers will also suffer from many other career-related injuries for the rest of their lives, the hidden effects of retirement on mental health are also a key issue. Recent research by world players' union FIFPro revealed that 35 per cent of former players faced problems with depression and anxiety, particularly if they had suffered serious injuries during their playing careers. This compares to a rate of between 13 per cent to 17 per cent in the general population.

Despite high-profile cases of depression involving the likes of Clarke Carlisle and Stan Collymore, it sadly remains something of a taboo subject within the game.

It's not just injuries that can lead to bouts of depression, but the actual transition from playing days to a life without football. Scott says that players can become 'depressed within the first week of retirement. Addiction can creep in and depression follows.' The adjustment to a new life can be huge and players can find it difficult to let go of a career that, for some, is all that they have known.

In a 2012 column with *The National*, former England and Manchester United striker Andrew Cole vividly portrayed many players' experiences upon retirement. He wrote that few people outside the game realise how tough 'normal' life can be when they have never been a part of the football world. He likened the world of football to military life, where soldiers spend '15 or 20 years with the same group of people, an organised life in a regiment. They are told what to do and where to go. Every day is planned for them and their identity is shaped around their profession. And then it stops. Suddenly you are at home alone. You don't get paid, you don't keep fit and you don't know what to do with all your time.'

Unfortunately, some turn to a life of crime. This is more prevalent in young footballers that have failed to make the grade, left on the scrapheap by their clubs in their late teens and early 20s. With many clubs signing boys as young as seven years of age, attrition rates in academies are extraordinarily high, with just two per cent of scholars signed at 16 still playing the game when they turn 21.

Many of these young men leave the game with little or no qualifications or life skills and enter a competitive labour market where job prospects are incredibly low. It comes as little surprise that some turn to crime to subsidise their income. Figures as of October 2015 intimate that 141 former players are in the British prison system. Almost 90 per cent of these offenders are under the age of 25, with a similar percentage incarcerated for drug-related offences. Many more are believed to be in the young offenders' system.

Again, XPRO is at the forefront of schemes to assist these players, conducting prison visits to encourage education and helping offenders find employment upon release. Another scheme called On Sport Intervention Development and Education (Onside) has been established by former Liverpool schoolboy player Michael Kinsella, who himself was given a ten-year sentence for drug offences in 2007. Thirteen members of his schoolboy side joined professional clubs, with only two enjoying long-term careers. Six ended up in prison.

These are the first wave of retirees, abandoned by the game by the time they hit their 20s. For many, it's a crushing blow as they've often never even contemplated the possibility of not making it. The former Republic of Ireland striker Richie Sadlier recalls being brought into a room when he joined Millwall and being told, 'Lads, do the maths. Two or three of you might get a first-year contract. Maybe one or two of those three will get a contract the second time.'

He remembers thinking, 'The odds are massively stacked against us. And there was like 20 or more of us in the room.' If you get to the stage where you're signed by a professional club, a sense of invincibility can creep in.

'You're not really used to any kind of knock-backs,' says Richie. 'You, and all your family members, can very easily fall into the trap of thinking you're different from all the rest. But, if you do get to England, the competition is ferocious. There are the best kids from Africa, Paris, Belgium, Australia, wherever. It's perceived as being a failure if you've dropped out. Often, with some lads, there's not even a token effort at an education or any kind of grounded development.'

He regularly speaks to parents of youngsters currently with English clubs and asks them what will happen if their son doesn't make the grade. They often don't even entertain the notion. 'They even reject answering the question because they haven't contemplated it,' he explains. 'Actually in the world of football, discussions around what your plan B is, in my experience, are not really encouraged that much, because it can sometimes be perceived as a lack of focus, or a lack of self-belief, or a lack of drive, or a lack of ruthlessness that sometimes people think you need to make it. Hopefully, that's changing and I think it is. In my day there were no discussions.'

He believes that, due to the pressures of the game, looking ahead to the day you retire is often frowned upon when the focus is literally 'taking each game as it comes'.

'There's a certain amount of focus and commitment required to make it as a footballer,' he says. 'It's kind of necessary to be fully focused but it's unhealthy if that's your sole focus, which for me it kind of was and, for other lads, even more so. When I was 23 or 24, 35 seemed a lifetime away. You kind of have this dream that "maybe I'll have made enough money by 35 that I won't have to work again or I'll go into coaching or something". It's not something I gave all that much thought to. When you're in it, it's a weird little world. There's a huge amount of focus on the next game. And even if you talk about the game that's coming up after that, someone will reprimand you, "Don't get ahead of yourself." It's how that world operates, because your training is focused on the next opponent.

'So if you start talking about what you're going to do in ten or 12 years, or which college course will I go on, or what skill I should better myself with, someone in the club will say, "Well, listen, if this is interfering with your football in any way, drop it. We're paying you 'X' amount of thousands. You don't have the right to go off and do something which jeopardises what you bring to the table for us." In the world of football, football is all that matters. The result the next week matters. Nothing else matters. You can easily be kidded into thinking that that's the reality, that this is the most important thing I'll ever do.'

While career options can be limited for jettisoned young footballers, those who have enjoyed a long-term career in the sport can find their job opportunities similarly restricted when they finish playing. While punditry work and coaching roles are often the Holy Grails for retired footballers, these avenues are highly competitive with media companies often favouring high-profile ex-players to provide analysis and commentary. Sky Sports's pundits for the 2015/16 season were mostly made up of highly decorated retired players with the likes of Gary Neville, Thierry Henry and Jamie Carragher their star attractions. BT Sport's panel is equally stellar with the likes of Paul Scholes, Rio Ferdinand and Michael Owen preferred over lesser-known names. The increasing global appeal of the Premier League and openings in radio, online and with third parties such as bookmakers have increased opportunities but, again, they are dominated by the same old faces. Quite simply, there aren't enough jobs to go round.

For many retired players a future in coaching and management appeals, but earning the necessary qualifications can be time-consuming, challenging and prohibitively expensive. Players must start at Level 2 of the UEFA pyramid, studying for a Certificate in Coaching Football. Even if a footballer has won Premier League titles and Champions League medals, they must complete this course, which allows them to work in Football in the Community schemes, with local authorities and in US soccer camps. They have two years to complete this level but it can be achieved in six months.

Another two-year period is then allotted to completing the UEFA B Licence, which allows graduates to work in Centres of Excellence and Academies. The next step is the two-year UEFA A Licence, which finally allows graduates to work as a manager, coach or academy manager in the professional game. Finally, the UEFA Pro Licence, which most candidates complete in a year, is by invitation only and is mandatory for managing in the Premier League and UEFA competitions.

The English game is often criticised for preferring foreign coaches and managers to indigenous options but the completion rates for the UEFA A Licence and Pro Licences across Europe appear to hint at a dearth of English talent. At the time of writing, there are only 203 Pro Licence holders in England, compared to 2,140 in Spain and over 1,000 in Germany. Similarly, there are just 1,173 A Licence holders in England, with Spain boasting ten times that figure and Germany over 5,000. It's apparent that cost can be a factor – although courses are subsidised by the Professional Footballers' Association (PFA) – with the A Licence costing almost £6,000 in England, as opposed to just over £500 in Germany.

It is clear that not every former footballer will be lucky enough to stay in the game. Brian Deane, who scored the first Premier League goal and now works as a sports consultant, doesn't feel there's enough help for retiring players and feels there's a lot more careers advice required for players approaching retirement. Deane was one of 23 goalscorers on the Premier League's opening day in 1992. While some of the others, such as Alan Shearer and Mark Hughes, have remained as high-profile figures in the game, many have had to seek a life away from football and have forged diverse careers as teachers, chefs, car salesmen, travel agents and solicitors.

Deane has outlined in the past his own struggles with finding coaching work in the English game, where he applied for jobs but didn't even warrant a reply, despite earning his UEFA A Licence. Retired players of black and minority ethnic (BAME) seem to find it harder than most to break into coaching and management. The Football League has introduced a version of the 'Rooney Rule' – which requires American Football's NFL teams to interview ethnic minority candidates for head coaching and senior football operation jobs – where shortlists for first-team managers must include at least one BAME candidate. Nevertheless, research from the Sports People's Think Tank suggests it will take 30 years to achieve parity between coaching roles and the proportion of BAME players. As of September 2015, just over four per cent of coaching roles in the English game were filled by BAME candidates, as opposed to a 25 per cent representation among players and 14 per cent in the general population.

The PFA provides some support and guidance for former and current players to prepare for a second career. The PFA spends the vast majority of its £8m education budget on training players for new careers, with the most popular courses including sports science, physiotherapy, sports management and journalism. However, it has assisted players in forging more unusual career paths such as airline pilots, doctors, oil-rig workers and even a clergyman.

With 60,000 former players scattered across the UK and Ireland, it is inevitable that the majority have had to establish a life beyond the game. My parents recently cleared out their attic and dumped boxes of my childhood memorabilia with me. Among the dozens of copies of *Shoot!* magazine, team tabs and broken Subbuteo figures were several Panini sticker albums from the late 1980s and early 1990s.

Randomly opening my tattered copy of one from 25 years ago, the Crystal Palace squad of 1990 stared back at me. As a kid I had an encyclopaedic knowledge of all these men. Some familiar faces smiled back at me. Ian Wright and Mark Bright are TV pundits, while I'm still aware of Geoff Thomas through his charity work after he was diagnosed with chronic myeloid leukaemia. But the rest? I hadn't heard or read their names in over 20 years.

Some, it transpired, had managed to stay in the game in various capacities. A 13-year-old me would have known Perry Suckling always insisted on putting his right boot on first, now I hadn't a clue of his whereabouts. Google did though, and I was pleased to see he was probably still carrying out his pre-match superstition as academy manager of Queens Park Rangers. Fair play on the UEFA A Licence, Perry.

Further perusal of the sticker album, and some research, revealed how diverse players' lives had become once their playing days ended. QPR's spread includes a cheerful-looking Kenny Sansom, a consistently excellent left-back who won 86 caps for England. I was saddened to learn of problems he's encountered post-retirement. After his marriage broke up, Sansom had battled alcoholism and ended up homeless, relying on his monthly £622 PFA pension to fund his drinking and gambling addictions. Thankfully, at the time of writing, he'd begun to put his problems behind him.

Nottingham Forest's 1990 vintage included several England internationals of the day. While the likes of Stuart Pearce, Nigel Clough and Steve Hodge have gone on to enjoy managerial and coaching careers, others like Des Walker withdrew from the game on retirement. A pacy centre-back, Walker became the fastest player in history to win 50 England caps and earned a big-money move to Sampdoria in 1992, but when he retired from football, he turned his back on the game for his own sake.

'When I retired my way of dealing with it was just to stay away from it. I didn't want to watch it, judge it, be around it, see it,' he told journalist and former team-mate Gregor Robertson in a *Nottingham Post* interview. Anxious about his future and with a 'big black hole' in front of him, he became almost a recluse. He's spent much of the last few years working 15-hour days as a lorry driver but has recently begun his UEFA A Licence and returned to the game in February 2016 as an academy coach with Derby County. Walker also likened the life of a footballer to that in the military and suggests, 'I don't think you leave football behind, it leaves you behind.'

For him, like many other retired players, 'football never existed'. For others, the transition to a new life is often their most difficult opponent. Here are their stories.

2

A Crippling Career

IT was a balmy March evening in Columbus, Ohio, when it finally ended. The perimeter advertising promoting ESPN's Major League Soccer coverage flashed from 'Unstoppable' to its French translation 'Imparable' as the Toronto FC central defender pulled up with an injury. He tried to return to the field of play and run it off but had torn his calf muscle in three places and was substituted at half-time. The number 13 emblazoned on the back of his shirt proved poignantly apt. Bad luck had brought an unstoppable 17-year career to an abrupt conclusion, 6,000km and over 400 appearances from where it had begun.

'There are times I will be watching a game and I could cry, such is my urge to be back out there on the park. I miss the feeling of doubt, the butterflies in the stomach and the elation and comfort of all that going away as soon as the match kicked off.

'I miss sitting at my locker after a victory feeling so satisfied and elated as if nothing else in my life mattered for that small length of time.'

Of all the ex-players I've spoken to, Steven Caldwell is the one who put the feelings experienced by footballers upon premature retirement most eloquently.

His story had begun 17 years earlier at Newcastle United before he went on to enjoy a career that saw him play for nine clubs, including Sunderland, Burnley and Birmingham City, as well as win 12 Scottish caps.

I've always found the old saying 'live every day as if it's your last' a bit odd. I guess it's supposed to mean you should pack each day with fun and excitement, but there's got to be a certain section of society who'd spend it making funeral arrangements and saying goodbye to loved ones. After speaking to Steven, it could certainly be amended for professional footballers. They should play every game as if it's their last, because it might well be.

'I was cognisant of that reality in my later days. I often said to guys in the huddle immediately before a big game to "play today like it might be the last time you step on this field",' explains Steven. 'Unfortunately, I didn't have the opportunity to know it was my last match. I had picked up the injury and hoped I would come back from it, but it wasn't to be. I believe I will regret that for the rest of my life. Even with all the relative success I've had in my career, that thought will haunt me forever.'

The reality that it could all end at any time did make the twilight of Steven's career more special though. 'The enjoyment I got from playing in the last four or five years of my career was immense,' he continues. 'I completely appreciated what I had experienced and how lucky I was. I tried to enjoy it all the more and relished the process. It's actually what makes it all meaningful. The relationships, effort and hard work that goes into success. It's that process that's satisfying. Of course, the thing that I truly miss is matchday, but it's what it takes to prepare you for that moment that truly matters.'

The link between retirement and death that Roger Kahn alluded to is a constant theme among players. 'Retiring from the game is a very difficult decision and one that weighs heavy on most footballers' minds,' admits Steven. 'The meaning of the word "retirement" itself adds to the problem. I am a 35-year-old man and yet I somehow feel like my life is coming to an end. I'm a healthy middle-aged man but there's a realisation that the life I've known – the only life I've known – will be changed forever.'

He believes that this emotion is the major reason why most players strive to get into management or coaching. Of course, not everyone can, which can exacerbate the negative experiences involved with retirement.

'They take comfort in the routine and the normality of that. They don't want to contemplate another way of life that is so alien to them. They have not thought about anything other than the complex facets of the game for so long that the mere notion of something different scares the life out of them! They take the easy way out because it's all they know.'

The media is another avenue many pursue but it doesn't suit everyone. 'Only a handful can go into the media. You must have a certain personality type to be successful in that profession,' continues Steven. 'But, again, there is a certain comfort to be found with staying involved in the game. The reason most people make it in professional football at all is through the sheer discipline and dedication they have to the sport. It takes great sacrifice and, indeed, love to make it as a professional. There are thousands and thousands of kids along the way who fall by the wayside because they don't have the same determination.'

For those who do land a coaching or punditry role, it can prove to be merely a stop-gap. 'I think inevitably with both coaching and media, people fall by the wayside because a very specific skill set and personality type are required that excel in each respective field.'

It's apparent from speaking to former players that the mental scars of retiring can be just as damaging as the physical injuries picked up during their careers.

'The effects on mental health are obvious and far-reaching,' admits Steven. 'The psychological impact of retiring from the game you love at such a young age is serious and not to be underestimated. Players can lack direction after they retire. They have lived in such a cocoon of unique pressures and support since adolescence. The vulnerability they feel is all too real and many can't cope. There is a legitimate sense of loss and lack of direction to their future. It can be compared to a young adult unsure about where they envision their career going. Although, this time, the person has very real concerns and responsibilities in their life, such as kids, financial and mental issues. These are all very real thoughts and emotions that go through most players' heads, especially mine.'

David Beckham jokes that he knew it was time to retire when 'Messi was running past me'. For those with career-ending injuries, like Steven, there comes a time when they also have to draw a line.

'The moment I realised I was going to retire was when I stopped making the required sacrifices to be the best player I could be,' continues Steven. 'My thoughts had moved elsewhere and I was thinking of what I would do after football. I had lost my energy to keep fighting back from an injury, loss of form, selection issues and the overall politics of making a team work. I work every day to embrace my new life. It's exciting and different and I am truly fortunate for the opportunity. But nothing will ever replace football and the emotions the game gave me. I focus on the fact that I was in a small minority who lived his dreams and experienced something magical for almost 20 years.'

He didn't know it at the time, but that match against Columbus Crew on 14 March 2015 in Ohio proved to be his last as a professional footballer. An attempted comeback was stymied by constant niggles and, in the end, he decided enough was enough. After almost two decades as a pro, Caldwell retired in July 2015.

Former Crystal Palace and Queens Park Rangers defender Mikele Leigertwood is another who has found it tough to come to terms with retiring through injury. The Antiguan international hung up his boots after sustaining a hip injury in 2014.

'After the incident I knew straight away that quite a bit of damage had been caused but I was always confident I'd be able to make it back playing,' recalls Mikele. 'That was even after being told by medical experts that it would be a tough ask. The main issue for me when going through my rehab was dealing with the pain. I'm of the mindset, "No pain, no gain!" It was only when I began to step up my running programme that the pain became too much to bear. That is when I started to become increasingly frustrated as I'd always been able to deal with things both physically and mentally. When my body would no longer respond the way I wanted it to I felt let down by it. Being quite physically strong I never thought I'd have a problem like this. Prior to the injury I was probably in the best shape I had been during my whole career.'

He once scored against Nottingham Forest to clinch promotion to the Premier League for Reading, but a meaningless pre-season friendly for Forest was to prove his final match as a professional. He, like many, has found it difficult to deal with. 'My home life suffered, I was angry and sad which leads to more frustrations. I became short-tempered and just wanted to be alone most of the time, which I know is unfair because I have a loving wife and two young boys. I know I wasn't great to be around and sometimes am still not.

Being a footballer is all I've known since the age of 16 and to have that gone in one seemingly innocuous incident is hard to come to terms with. I wasn't ready to retire from the game I love so much. I would have played well into my late thirties. I know there's always a risk and I'm grateful for the career I had but I wasn't ready for it to end. I wasn't prepared for life after football just yet.'

It has always been Mikele's ambition to become a manager after retiring as a player and he's continued to take his badges, while training to be a personal trainer. 'I wanted to be back in football in any capacity. I spent a lot of time at home and I needed to be doing something. Being at home feeling sorry for myself wasn't helping anyone. I know there's extreme difficulty getting into management, especially for black managers. It's been an issue within football for a long time but that doesn't put me off.'

Despite his first forays into coaching, nothing has come close to playing the game he loved. 'It's been nearly a year since I retired and it's still a tough pill to swallow – all I want to do still is play football. I miss the competition, I miss the training, the banter, the travelling, the changing rooms, the tunnels, the walk on to the pitch, the nerves you get just before kick-off, the feeling that you've given everything for your team-mates, manager, coaches and the supporters.'

He carries a daily reminder of what brought his playing career to a close. 'I still struggle with the pain in my hip. I love keeping fit and pushing myself to the limit but I'm very restricted in what I can do. Simple things like standing up from being seated for a short time brings on discomfort. This also has an effect on my coaching as I'm not always able to demonstrate what I'm after.

'I've been lucky in the fact that I have a very supportive family and very supportive friends,' he concedes. 'I know retiring early from football is not the end of the world and realise there are a lot of opportunities out there. Footballers are always being pushed towards coaching and punditry; more should be done by clubs, the FA, agents and advisors to prepare players for life away from football.'

Jon Newsome also retired prematurely, at 30, but is pretty sanguine about his lot. A Sheffield Wednesday fan growing up, he scored against Sheffield United to help Leeds United clinch the final First Division title in 1992 before going on to captain the Owls. 'There's two ways of looking at it. I was 30 years of age and had a decent career, albeit cut short a little bit prematurely,' says Jon. 'But if someone had offered me that at 14 or 15 years of age, I'd have absolutely snapped their hand off. As a 30-year-old guy with a family, I'd got a reasonable start in life and tried to look at it positively.'

He also tried to come back from his injury but, again, it wasn't to be. 'I damaged my knee playing in a game and, unfortunately, it was one of those injuries where there was no remedy or repair for it. It was hang-your-boots-up time. I had a couple of operations and at the time we thought there was some form of remedy for it. I had surgery again three years ago and the surgeon told me that the procedures I had back in the day don't work anyway. I was trying to get back, I was training, but as soon as I started doing anything excessive, the knee just started breaking down. It was around March or April time and the surgeon sat me down and told me it was time to call it a day.'

Like Caldwell, he found it hard to deal with the immediacy of his forced retirement. 'I had some idea of when I would carry on playing until – you hope you're going to get to the 35 years of age milestone, and anything over and above that I would have deemed a bonus. Suddenly, it's cut short. It was probably six months since I'd injured my knee and it was just an innocuous injury really, it wasn't a massive impact injury. I had gone from thinking I'd be back playing in a few weeks to suddenly being confronted by my career ending. You've got to look at doing something else and you've got to get your head around the fact that you're no longer going to be a professional footballer.'

The financial implications of retiring through injury can also be difficult to deal with, reveals Jon. 'Initially it's tough. I did have insurance, which I had hoped would soften the blow financially somewhat. Unfortunately, it didn't really work out that way. I think there'd been a high number of players who were finishing with career-ending insurance and the insurers were becoming a bit more hardened to payouts. It becomes a bit of an uphill struggle, really.' A two-and-a-half-year battle with the insurance company followed which concluded with a settlement for an amount well below the figure for which Jon had been insured.

Like many of his peers who plied their trade at the beginning of the Premier League era, retiring from the game meant looking for a new career. 'Someone once said to me, "When you're saving money, you think you're putting too much away, but when you come to call on it, you realise you didn't put enough away," recalls Jon. 'I think that's a very true statement. Back then, in comparison to if I'd got a "normal job", I was earning pretty good money but, compared to what the lads are earning today or in the last ten years, I was earning very small amounts of money really. So I didn't have enough to retire.'

He still lives with his career-acquired injuries but is upbeat about them and feels they're an acceptable trade-off for the life they afforded him. 'My knee never repaired. I got bone damage and damage to the kneecap. I lost the back of my kneecap and lost a chunk out of the head of my femur so, unfortunately, even to this day there's no repair for that kind of injury. I still suffer with it, can't do any running or that kind of thing. But it's a small price to pay to be lucky enough to live your childhood dream of playing football professionally.'

Terrace chants have become a lot more contrived in recent years. When Sunderland signed Senegalese midfielder Alfred N'Diaye in 2013, fans took an old Whitney Houston hit and serenaded him on his debut with 'N'Diaye, Will Always Love You'. Bobby Zamora, whenever suffering a barren spell in front of goal during his career, has had to endure chants of 'When you're sat in Row Z, and the ball hits your head, that's Zamora, that's Zamora' to the tune of Dean Martin's 'That's Amore'. The 1980s were simpler times. Confusion reigned when England met Scotland in 1986 as Tottenham's Gary Stevens was joined on the English side by his namesake, Everton's Gary Stevens. Fans proceeded to chant, 'There's only two Gary Stevens'. The former won the UEFA Cup with Spurs but a Vinnie Jones tackle in 1988 triggered injury problems that culminated in his retirement before he hit 30.

It was a blow that was hard to accept for a player who felt he had many more years left in the game. He was still just 28 when he played his last game, and just 29 when he received his last pay packet from football as a contracted player at Portsmouth. Despite struggling with injuries for a while, he was still ill-prepared for packing in the game he loves. 'I think when you're still that age you still believe you're invincible, you still believe your career will never end. But, of course, it does end for everybody at some stage. Was I prepared for it? Absolutely not,' Gary admits. 'I would say it was very difficult to deal with. Undoubtedly.

'It probably took me the best part of a decade to get over it,' he recalls. 'And that was because I had retired at 29 years of age. Physically I was super fit, structurally in a muddle. I'm still physically very fit. And I think I was one of those people who, without injuries, could have played until pushing towards 40. By the time I got to 39 I was thinking, "If I'd avoided injuries I would probably be retiring now." I had a very difficult ten years.'

He'd suffered with a knee injury for a few seasons, but when he collapsed in a heap one Saturday afternoon for Portsmouth at Plymouth, he presumed he'd recuperate as he always had done. 'I thought I'd go and see the surgeon and we'd get it sorted and I'd recover,' says Gary, 'because that's what I'd done with previous injuries. Even when the club physio came and met me many months later, after surgery, and said, "I think, really, Gary, you're going to have to call it a day," my answer was, "No." You go into training because you believe you can recover, work with the rehab physio and get yourself back out there. It just takes a period of time for it to sink in.'

He still has a constant reminder of the toll his playing days have taken on his body. 'If you ask me do my injuries still bother me – absolutely yes. I've just had my right hip re-surfaced because it was arthritic so I'm actually rehabbing from major surgery at the moment. I'd my left hip done 12 years ago. Neither of my knees are particularly good. But I wouldn't swap the career that I've had, that's for sure. Arguably, though, I'm paying the price now for the career that I did have.'

Like Jon, Gary's financial cover proved inadequate. 'When I lost my career I was grossly under-insured,' he says. So much so that he established a company providing career-ending insurance for professional footballers.

Again, he likens retiring prematurely to a grieving process but is conscious of possibly offending those who've suffered much greater losses. 'When a player does retire – and it's more difficult if you retire prematurely through injury – you almost have to go through a process of bereavement,' he continues. 'I don't have the words to describe it other than it's like a bereavement, and you have to be careful how you use that word because somebody who's just lost a family member will look at that and say, "Well, actually your career ending or you losing your career is nothing like the fact that I've just lost my son," for example. But I think you do have to go through a bereavement process and say goodbye.'

Like others I spoke to, he's quick to warn current players about the brevity of a playing career and the importance of preparing for the inevitable. 'I think there's a responsibility from the individual to prepare himself,' believes Gary. 'And I didn't prepare myself particularly well. The PFA is there and has done great work and has grown and grown in the services that they provide. It's developed a long way since I retired and lots of other bodies have developed and I think there's probably more assistance to prepare players than there's ever been. But back in my day it was risible, to be honest.

'I think you need a number of strings to your bow. When you are a player you do have a good amount of time on your hands which most players, myself included, do not utilise for their benefit and to prepare for the future. Steven Gerrard recently said he spent a lot of time in hotels with Liverpool and England watching films and television programmes rather than preparing himself for life after his playing days. You don't believe it will ever end. It's just such a fabulous life, such a fabulous career and you're young and think the end is never going to happen. In reality, it does.'

While the above players that I spoke to all retired prematurely through injury, they did enjoy a decent career in terms of longevity with most hanging up their boots in their late 20s. When forced retirement comes early on when a career is on an upward trajectory, it can be devastating. Richie Sadlier was impressing up front for Millwall and had just won a call-up to the Republic of Ireland squad in the run-up to the 2002 World Cup when fate intervened. He recalls a match on New Year's Day in 2002 when his strike partner

Neil Harris made his return from successful treatment for testicular cancer. Harris scored a last-minute goal in a 4-1 win over Gianluca Vialli's Watford and the celebrations commenced.

'We lifted him up, it's a famous moment in Millwall history,' smiles Richie. 'I remember at the time, weirdly, saying to my mum on the bus outside the ground, "If my career ended in the morning, that's the memory I'd remember." About nine weeks later I got the injury that eventually ended me. For years, that celebration was the only football photo I had in my house.'

He may no longer have memorabilia in his home to take him back to his football career, but he does have the physical reminders. After three operations on his right ankle, three on his right hip and one on his right hernia, he admits that his 'right-hand side is a little bit botched. If I don't run around I'm fine. But there's little things. I can't stand at a festival or concert. If I go for a long walk, it'll hurt, stuff like that. It is a bit of a downer for anyone if you have to pull out of certain things because you're physically incapable of doing them. In addition to this, you've come from a background where your physical prowess is what set you apart from everyone else and then you have to adjust to being someone who is actually behind most people in terms of what you can physically do.

'If your self-worth or self-esteem has been wrapped up in your job and what your body can do for you, you can imagine how crushing it is. In the early months and years, in addition to all the psychological stuff, I was in physical pain 24/7. There's a real grating effect. You're going to be in a bad mood at some point. It's going to affect how you interact with people. So, I had constant back pain and hip pain to go through on top of all the mental anguish.'

At 37, he is of an age where he would probably be retiring from playing around now if he had steered clear of injuries.

He admits that the thoughts of what might have been were difficult to overcome.

'I'm really, really grateful for where I am now. I love how things are in my life these days,' he says. 'But everything about my life would be different if I hadn't got that hip injury when I got it. That kind of shaped everything that has happened since. The later in your career that you retire, you've had more years to find your level. I got injured when I was on quite a steep up-curve. For the injury to come then, I was left with, "Well, how far would this have gone? Would I have been at Millwall? Would I have gone to the World Cup?" You're left with all the "what ifs".

'Now if you want to start any thought process with the question "What if?" you can go for miles, you can go for days and years with those kind of thoughts. So, you add all that in on top as well, and I was tormenting myself. And I started resenting lads who could still play when I couldn't.'

When the decision to retire was made, he couldn't cope with speaking to anyone, instead sending a text message to close family and friends announcing his decision. The last line read, 'Don't ring me, I'll ring you; I can't be arsed. I just can't talk about it.'

'I sent a text as I was crying through the morning anyway and I knew I wouldn't be able to hold it together in a conversation,' he explains. 'But I also didn't want to repeat the same conversation 28 times. That was my way of dealing with it at the time, thinking, stupidly, that if I decided that I didn't want to talk about it then people wouldn't ask me about it. I did have a little thing where this was a crushing blow to my ego, because I wasn't strong and tough enough to overcome this injury. Because the culture at Millwall at the time was, "Tough lads play with injury, tough lads overcome an injury, and whatever obstacles there are you clear them. That's how you know you're a man, you're tough, you're a

Millwall player." So when I retired, I went, "Right, I failed, I'm weak.""

Richard was thrown a lifeline when an American surgeon developed a new procedure that had given Sunderland striker Kevin Kyle another chance. He attempted a comeback, with a three-year contract with the Black Cats on the table. He had wondered first time around if there was anything he could have done differently, so gave it his all for 16 months. However, it wasn't to be, but he felt he could finally remove those 'what ifs'.

'I always had it in my head that the crushing blow that happened first would never be repeated,' he says. 'I know absolutely that there's nothing else I could have done. It was kind of a bit of closure.'

Nevertheless, his footballing ambitions haven't totally disappeared. He reveals that 13 years after being forced to retire, 'I still regularly have dreams of where I'm recalled to the Irish team or where I sign for a big club. It still happens all the time, so it's still there.'

* * *

Nobody knew it at the time but it was to be Eric Cantona's final match in a Manchester United shirt. The brooding, brilliant Frenchman bagged a brace in his swansong, but it was another goal that proved more poignant for the sell-out Highfield Road crowd on 16 May 1997. An uncharacteristic, some say deliberate, handball by Gary Neville gave United's opponents Coventry City a last-minute reprieve. The Sky Blues brought on a substitute to a rapturous reception from the crowd and he converted the penalty with aplomb. It was a fitting end to his testimonial for David Busst and, indeed, to his football career.

Cantona shocked the football world two days later, retiring from the game at just 30 years of age. Busst had already retired at the same age, seven months earlier, but in very different circumstances. Mention gruesome sporting injuries to me, and indeed to many football fans of a certain age, and the first name that springs to mind is David Busst. The former Coventry City defender suffered an horrific leg injury in a 1996 game against Manchester United, during a collision with Brian McClair and Denis Irwin. It was so bad that Peter Schmeichel reportedly vomited at the sight of it and it took 12 minutes to clear blood from the pitch. The Danish keeper admitted that he thought about the incident every day for the following two years.

While Busst admits the nature of his injury was a shock, his late start as a professional footballer enabled him to cope better when it ended so abruptly. 'I was 28 and was late coming into the game; I didn't sign professionally until I was 24. I always knew I wouldn't have long in the game. I'd planned to play until 30 and slide down the leagues, into non-league and stuff like that,' says David, who is now a director of the club's Sky Blues in the Community programme.

'The game at Man United, I didn't know at that time I'd have to retire through injury. It probably took around six months before I'd had all my operations and seen all the experts. I was told that the damage to the tendon in my left foot, which left me with a dropped foot, was what stopped me from playing, not the actual leg break. And you sort of reflect back then, the highs and lows, "Why me? Why that split second? Why were the other two players tackling me at that particular time?" I always had the sort of outlook that I knew I was only ever going to be in professional football for a short time, and knew it wouldn't be something that would set me up for the rest of my life and that I'd have to go back to something else. I was glad to have played for five years in the Premiership, and if you're going to go out, what better place than to go out at Old Trafford.'

His injury was so bad that he was told, had it happened 20 years earlier, his leg may have had to have been amputated. He points me towards some photos of his leg as it is today, which is still heavily scarred – something 'that will never change'. He's also 'still left with a dropped foot' but has used his injuries as a talking point in his new career.

The Sky Blues in the Community programme employs two directors, who oversee approximately 20 coaches that go around the Coventry and Warwickshire area delivering health, sport, inclusion and education projects. 'Every single football club has a community scheme attached to it and they're doing similar stuff up and down the country, supported by funding from the Premier League, the Football League and the PFA. Doing the job I do, the injury is a conversation starter,' David says. 'People remember the injury and where they were that day, and ask me how it is. It's just a good way of opening doors and being able to speak to people.'

Despite a background in financial services, upon retirement David was eager to remain in the game. 'I spoke to the PFA, worked out what my options were. I was out for two years with operations and during that time I started doing my coaching qualifications. And then an opportunity just arose at Coventry City to work in their community scheme so I took that and I've been here ever since, from about 20 years ago.'

However, he was conscious of the subliminal effect his injury may have had on his former team-mates. 'I probably had to stop going into the ground every day,' he recalls. 'When I got injured I was away from the club for three months anyway. I was still under contract and hadn't officially retired then. But I just found it too hard to be in and around the players. I think it was more from their point of view as well, as I was conscious that it was a constant reminder that my injury had finished me and it could happen to them. I went to the games and would pop in every now and again to the training sessions just to say hello. I just decided that this isn't fair on them, seeing me and being a constant reminder of what could happen. Because, obviously, it's everyone's biggest fear that that sort of thing might happen. They were all brilliant and supportive and wanted me to be around and tried to keep me involved, which you'd expect with any team.'

I ask about career-ending injuries being every player's 'biggest fear' and wonder if it's something they're always conscious of when taking to the pitch. 'If you went into it like that, you'd be jumping out of tackles and things like that. There were plenty of players before me who had cruciate injuries and hadn't played for two years and hadn't come back. At the back of their minds, players know it's there. They've got that attitude that it could happen, but they're not going to be constantly thinking about it or it will affect your performance,' responds David.

He looks back fondly on the night of his testimonial which he sees as a celebration of his career. 'It was a chance for the supporters of Coventry City to come out and appreciate what I'd gone through and what I'd done for the club. It was a very humbling experience for the game to be sold out prior to the actual matchday. It was a celebration for everyone who had done everything for me and supported me through my professional journey. It was a great way to celebrate my career rather than be a benefit match because I'd had to finish. What a way to go out,' he continues. 'It was a great evening, there were loads of stars. George Best had come down and played in the game as well. Les Ferdinand and Paul Gascoigne, they both joined the Coventry City team to play against the Man United side.'

He also has another reminder of his testimonial night – Eric Cantona's final shirt as a professional footballer, which the Frenchman gave after the match to David, who jokes the shirt is 'locked away in the vaults'. I ponder whether he felt envious of Cantona, who had retired around the same age as him through his own choice. 'I never realised the similarity until you just mentioned it so no, I've never resented anything. Shit happens, life goes on,' he concludes.

We learned earlier in the book that up to 48,000 former footballers across the UK and Ireland could be living with the daily effects of osteoarthritis. Quite simply, it's a condition where the surfaces of joints become damaged and don't move as smoothly as they should. A team at Nottingham University is leading research into the condition among former footballers, which hopes to lead to greater awareness of how to prevent and avoid it. The five-year study, 'Osteoarthritis Risk of Professional Footballers', aims to determine the actual prevalence of knee pain and arthritis defined by pain and radiographs, and compare this with the general population to see if footballers are really at greater risk. Collaborators include FIFA, the FA, the PFA and Arthritis UK.

The project is on a much larger scale than any previously undertaken and is the largest study in the world to focus on ex-professional footballers. Existing literature on the subject shows a wide variation between the prevalence of osteoarthritis in former footballers, with figures ranging from 40 per cent to 80 per cent. However, these studies – mainly from overseas – have involved relatively small samples. For example, a 2014 Brazilian study, 'Early osteoarthritis and reduced quality of life after retirement in former professional soccer players', only involved 27 former professional soccer players. The project at Nottingham University is a lot more ambitious.

It has involved 1,300 former footballers and a control group of 3,440 men, with the latter age-matched to the former. Most statistics regarding osteoarthritis in the general population includes females, so this control group by gender is crucial in determining the prevalence of the disease in ex-players compared to the 'man on the street'. The research is scheduled for completion in June 2016, but even if it concurs with the lowest figures already detected of 40 per cent, that will still represent around double that of the prevalence in previous general population studies.

XPRO recently referred its 300th player for medical treatment, with the most common procedures being knee and hip replacements. Their experience suggests that former players are being diagnosed with osteoarthritis ten to 15 years before the average male. This means that many ex-footballers are deemed too young to undergo replacement knee surgery. As mentioned earlier, football is one of the few professions where osteoarthritis is not recognised by the UK government as a prescribed industrial disability, meaning state benefits that are available to other professions are not available to former footballers.

Players often retire in the knowledge that career-related injuries will come back to haunt them later in life. One player I spoke to was warned, at the age of 33, by a surgeon that if he didn't retire he'd end up in a wheelchair by the time he was 40. He took his advice but, now 50, he still requires walking aids to get around. His disability has also led to alcohol and weight issues.

Dr Andy Turner of Coventry University co-authored a qualitative study sponsored by the British Medical Association titled 'Play Hurt, Live Hurt: Living With And Managing Osteoarthritis From The Perspective Of Ex-Professional Footballers'. He authored the study after being diagnosed with the condition himself in his late 20s. It found that participants often used idealised accounts of their playing careers to enable them to 'accept their current health problems as a part and parcel of playing and a price worth paying for having had the opportunity to enjoy a fantastic and unmissable experience'. This tallies with some of the experiences we've already seen.

Many spoke of the pressure from managers and physiotherapists to play through injury, but also self-imposed pressure prompted by the fear of losing their place in the starting XI. Pain was a constant feature of everyday life and something that led to the loss of a range of work, social and leisure activities. Some participants were concerned that more should be done to make current players more aware of the potential long-term health risks involved in playing professional football. One said, 'You never thought about arthritis or the effect that it could have on you in years to come. It may be something that young footballers of today should be warned about – what could lie ahead for them.' Another felt, 'I think that the warning from this study is actually to those in control of players, to have respect for their future. That's where I think the warning goes and that medical teams, coaching people, the managers, the boards of directors give respect to the players and their future well-being.'

Osteoarthritis may affect the bulk of former footballers but there are many other conditions that are prevalent among ex-players. A previous study by Dr Turner entitled 'Long term health impact of playing professional football in the United Kingdom' looked at the effects that playing the game professionally can have on players during retirement.

Almost 300 former professional players took part, over half of whom had represented their country at senior international level. Some 63 per cent of the respondents had played in the English top flight. Of those who took part in the study, 32 per cent had undergone surgery since hanging up their boots. The vast majority of these had either knee or hip surgery. Nearly 30 per cent were taking medication to relieve symptoms associated with injuries incurred during their playing careers. A further 15 per cent were registered disabled. Finally, approximately three and a half per cent reported neuropsychological problems such as memory complaints, dizziness and headaches, hinting at the cumulative effects of heading a ball and sub-concussive events during a footballing career.

Brain conditions are more common among footballers than the general public, with heading a football being blamed for neuro-degenerative problems such as chronic traumatic encephalopathy (CTE). In the United States, fears around concussion have become so great that children under ten years of age have been banned from heading a ball by the US Soccer Federation. The regulations came about following a lawsuit filed by young players and their parents in 2014, accusing governing bodies of negligence concerning the treatment and monitoring of head injuries.

The FA has yet to follow suit, but it has appointed an independent panel of experts to advise them on the subject. However, in November 2015 it launched new guidelines that ensure all players – from grassroots to the Premier League – must be immediately removed from the pitch if they suffer a suspected concussion during a match or training.

Concussion has been the subject of fierce debate in recent years with incidents involving Tottenham's Hugo Lloris and Chelsea's Eden Hazard generating headlines. New regulations were introduced by the Premier League in 2014 following a storm of criticism when the Spurs keeper, Lloris, continued playing after losing consciousness in a match against Everton. Players with head injuries must now leave the pitch, with the final decision on whether they can continue to play resting with the team doctor. The change in protocols led to the furore over José Mourinho's clash with Dr Eva Carneiro, who subsequently left Chelsea following an incident involving Hazard. The Blues were already down to ten men when Carneiro treated the Belgian in stoppage time. Mourinho was furious as he was 'sure that Eden didn't have a serious problem'.

However, under the guidelines the referee had signalled for medical attention, meaning she would have breached a doctor's duty to the patient if she had not gone to the aid of Hazard. The Football Medical Association fully supported her actions and Mourinho was roundly condemned for his behaviour.

Dr Michael Grey is a Reader in Neuroscience at the School of Sport, Exercise and Rehabilitation Sciences at the University of Birmingham and one of the UK's leading experts in sport-related concussions. He believes the game in England still has a long way to go when it comes to dealing with concussion. 'Personally, I don't think they have done enough. I think they've been denying this was a problem for a very long time. There has been a belief that this was rugby's problem rather than football's problem, and two years ago when I was speaking with rugby folks, I was hearing things like, "Well, this is not our problem, this is American football's problem." We know now that this is something we're going to have to deal with in football as well.

'We have to be clear when we're talking about head injuries, that we do not categorise them all as the same thing,' he continues. 'We can look at the problem in three areas. First is immediate danger to the player who is suspected of having a concussion on the pitch – this player needs to be removed from play and this is potentially where we have the biggest problem in the sport. Next is the return to play decision in the days following the injury – we need to be following accepted return to play guidelines and we need to be extra cautious with the player who has had repetitive concussions. A third issue is the idea of repetitive sub-concussive events – where a blow to the head is minor but still causes some damage. We believe over the lifetime of play this may lead to accelerated neuro-degeneration later in life.'

I got the feeling that the FA were beginning to act mainly due to the couple of aforementioned high-profile events in recent years. Dr Grey concurs, 'In my opinion, that's certainly what caused rugby to change their ways. The NFL lawsuit has really made people aware. To be fair to football, I think people just weren't aware previously.'

The lawsuit he refers to is a $1bn settlement in 2015 between the NFL and thousands of former players who suffered from neurological disorders during retirement. Many players, not happy with the deal, are taking individual cases against the NFL. Of the 91 former American football players who donated their brains to research after their deaths, 87 of them tested positive for CTE.

'It used to be that you got a knock on the head and just shook it off. Many people would say, "Just play on, it'll go away." Others would come off the pitch, shake it off and get back on. Now we realise this isn't something that players should just be shaking off,' says Dr Grey. 'A brain injury and disruption of brain function is something we actually need to deal with. After a concussion the brain will heal itself, but only if we allow it to rest and recover.'

It sounds to me like it should come to a point where players are ruled out for a certain period with concussion-related injuries as they are with, for example, leg or groin injuries. Dr Grey agrees but believes it's not as simple as that, with a footballer's self-preservation often kicking in. 'Players should be out of action until the brain recovers. The challenge is that we all recover at different rates. This has to do with genetics, the level of damage, and the number and severity of concussions previously experienced. For example, we know that people who get concussions repeatedly are more susceptible to them. With a leg injury, you can see it, you can feel it, you know something is not right. With many concussions you just don't know there is a problem unless the player admits to it. And that in itself is a massive problem because many players, by and large, won't tell us. First, we're all taught at a young age to "man up, play on, take one for the team". Second, there is a widespread perception that we're only as good as our last game, but if we're only as good as our last game and we're at risk of not playing the next game because we speak out, then we're less likely to do so.'

I suggest there is clearly a change in mindset needed among players but Dr Grey would go further. 'And officials, coaches, parents, everybody that's connected with the game. For me, that is fundamentally the crux of the issue. We have to educate and change the mindset.

'The ones we worry about are the ones that aren't really clear where there is that difficult judgement call – do we let the player play on or not? In my opinion, the guidelines are very, very clear.' These guidelines have been established by a concussion group, who have been meeting since 2001, and as recently as 2014 have published consensus statements on concussion in sport.

'If a player is suspected of having a concussion, they should be removed from the field and not allowed to return that day. This is through all levels. Now, we know this is not being followed, but the guideline is crystal clear. Then we move on to the issue of whether we know they are concussed. There are tests that we can do. On the field there is something called the SCAT3 assessment tool. It's quite good but does rely quite a lot on the player answering the questions truthfully and it does take some time to administer properly – so frequently corners are cut. FIFA have signed up to it and all the team doctors know of it. Whether or not they use it is unclear.'

Dr Grey would welcome the English game adopting the same approach as their US counterparts in relation to the banning of heading for young children. 'I'm on record as saying I do welcome it, but with a caveat. I welcome it because there is a clear mechanism for children that they're more susceptible to concussion than are adults. And the truth is we just don't know the extent to which sub-concussive events in children from repetitive headers are leading to neuro-degeneration. So, from my point of view, I do welcome the ban until we have the answers. I think we should be removing it from the game for young children and phasing it in in a better way than we do now. I think we should be erring on the side of caution.'

He doubts we'll ever see a ban on heading through the whole game and doesn't believe this is necessary. 'It makes more sense to me for children. I do think we need to consider how we can teach heading, at what point we should bring it into the game, and then the extent to which it should be practised. There's a lot of work to be done in that area and a lot we need to better understand.'

So, is it safe to head a football? What are the long-term effects of heading a football? Or have they even been established yet?

'Unfortunately, the answer is we don't know, ' concedes Dr Grey. 'Our big challenge is that we know there are cumulative effects from repeated head injuries and this is believed to accelerate neuro-degeneration. The problem is that we all degenerate as we age, with some statistics suggesting that, by the time we reach 80 years old, more than one in six of us will have dementia. We know this is accelerated with repetitive head trauma. The issues with respect to football are two-fold. First is the issue of players who get repetitive concussions, and second are these sub-concussive events that are never actually diagnosed. And it's with the sub-concussive events in particular where we don't really know the extent to which they may be leading to neuro-degeneration.'

The problem with CTE is that it takes many years to manifest. 'That's the challenge,' explains Dr Grey. 'What we see though, with people with head injuries, is accelerated neuro-degeneration.' Michael discusses a number of cases of former footballers that were diagnosed with dementia at a relatively early age in relation to the general population.

'That's why we call it early-onset dementia. But the challenge is that other people who are not exposed to sub-concussive events also get early-onset dementia, although this is really, really rare. So, we can't say conclusively that heading the ball leads to neuro-degeneration. When I talk to some of the professional sporting bodies they say, "Well, there's no conclusive evidence." I liken this very much to the argument over smoking in the 1950s, where the tobacco companies were saying, "Well, there's no conclusive evidence."'

I wonder if the modernisation of the game may have improved things when it comes to head injuries. 'The heavy, wet, leather balls were an issue but that's a bit of a red herring,' explains Michael. 'That doesn't mean we can't have the same issues now. We have coated balls now that don't really get wet, and they're lighter. But, we're also kicking the ball a lot harder than we were before. When the ball strikes the head it moves because the kinetic energy is transferred from the ball to the head. In physics, the formula for kinetic energy is ½ Mass * Velocity^2. So if we're kicking the ball faster, it can impart significant kinetic energy to the head and this is still sufficient to damage the brain.' It's potentially just as dangerous now as it was in previous generations.

Michael says, 'Most of the concussions we see are not coming from ball-to-head contact. It's actually coming from head-to-head, head-to-arm or head-to-ground contact associated with the challenge for the ball. With children who are learning the sport, you've got unskilled players jumping up and smacking each other on the head. They're more susceptible to concussions, their neck muscles are weaker so their heads are moving more when they collide. That's why I support the idea of stopping young children from heading the ball – at least until we have evidence that this is not a problem.

'What is the FA doing? What is FIFA doing? Where are the studies that are sponsored by them? You have to question how much are they really doing. The FA are a multi-million pound organisation; why are they not sponsoring any independent research?'

Research from Purdue University in Indiana suggests that heading a football can carry as much force as a tackle by an American football player. Dr Eric Nauman, the director of the Human Injury Research and Regenerative Technologies Laboratory at the university, also supports the ban on heading a football by under-tens in America.

'Most kids at that age don't have the skill, neck muscles or wherewithal to head the ball well and with proficiency,' agrees Dr Nauman. 'There really isn't much need for them to be heading a ball at that young an age. It is a good step. Soccer players at a high school level in the US are heading the ball almost every day so their brains don't get a chance to heal and recover. There just doesn't seem to be the need to do that until they're older and better able to handle the forces involved.

'We definitely see that the sub-concussive events add up. Sometimes when we call them sub-concussive it makes them sound like they really aren't that big of a deal. The real problem is that they accumulate and each one adds to the damage.'

He suggests a number of recommendations to limit the current levels of concussions and sub-concussive events. 'There's lots of little things than you could do – decrease the pressure of the ball a little bit, that would help tremendously. And I think it would take very little effort to legislate the head-to-head hits out of the game. Honestly, one of the big things I would do to prevent a lot of the catastrophic stuff that happens to keepers would be to make the posts out of rubber instead of metal. That would be a small step to take forward but would help quite a bit.'

His team's research mostly involves high school soccer players and how their experiences compare to those of

American footballers. 'We do pre-season MRIs and we can see changes from the pre-season to the in-season that are very dramatic. It's not just concussions. We're seeing somewhere between 50 per cent and 70 per cent of a team that exhibit changes in brain physiology that are worse than the concussed players. We're desperately trying to figure out what are safe levels of contact, what crosses the line into becoming unsafe. That's been our goal for quite a while.'

Their methodology isn't limited to headers, but the likes of elbow-to-head, knee-to-head and head-to-head hits. 'After we do the pre-season MRI, we tape a sensor behind each player's ear. Every day we go out to practice we glue the sensors on the players and rip them off afterwards. Then we take MRIs during the season and after the season to try and look at the relationship between how their brain changes and how many hits they take and what kind of hits they take.'

He reveals that headers aren't necessarily the most dangerous factor in football-related brain injuries. 'When somebody kicks a goal-kick, we usually see a 10G to 20G shockwave that goes up and arrives at the head. But then we've seen head-to-head blows that have been in the 220G range.'

Dr Nauman agrees that it's incredibly difficult to determine the long-term effects of concussions until it's too late. 'A lot of those things don't show up until many years down the road. And that's because something like CTE really results in blockages around all the blood vessels, and once you get enough of those blockages from head impacts then the nutrient transport becomes fouled up. And we think that's a big part of why it takes so long for these things to manifest. You do the damage, and you get the plaque, and then they shut off the transport around the blood vessels. And then you start to see cells dying and cells not working correctly long-term. The best thing is to really just limit how many times you hit your head.'

Due to managers' attitudes it may be down to the players themselves to self-regulate. 'Most coaches in most of these sports don't really seem to look at the data. I think getting them to play safer is going to be a very difficult thing. I'm willing for one of them to prove me wrong but I don't think it will happen. The NFL Players Association, as a result of a lot of the data that we have collected and others have collected, actually bargained for fewer contact practices, particularly at the beginning of the season. So, if you look at it broadly, the players took it on themselves to limit how much contact they'd get in pre-season. The NFL side of it hasn't really done a whole lot.'

I'm too young to remember Jeff Astle's playing days but I do recall his comedy interludes on David Baddiel and Frank Skinner's *Fantasy Football League* in the mid-1990s. However, I was always aware of his legendary status at West Bromwich Albion, where he plundered 174 goals in 361 appearances – including the winner in the 1968 FA Cup Final – and was renowned as an excellent header of the ball. To put his goal tally into context, at the time of writing Wayne Rooney has scored 177 goals in 362 league appearances for Manchester United, who have won five Premier League titles during his time at the club. Affectionately known by Baggies fans as 'The King', Astle's prowess in the air, however, led to his death in January 2002 at just 59 years of age. A coroner concluded that he had suffered neurological damage from heading a football. His illness was later diagnosed as CTE which, as we have learned, can take effect years after a sportsperson's career comes to an end.

The late player's family established the Jeff Astle Foundation, with the help of the PFA, in 2015 to raise awareness of brain injuries in sport and to offer support to those affected. His widow Laraine and daughters Dawn and Claire are at the forefront of a long-term plan to provide support for sportspeople living with the effects of dementia or chronic neurological impairment. Laraine told me that Jeff's condition first became apparent during rehearsals for Baddiel and Skinner's show.

'We'd done it for several years and when we used to get there we were always given a song to learn. Even if you'd never heard of it, you'd rehearse it all day from a tape. I used to help Jeff to learn it. The last one we did in 1998 was a real struggle,' reveals Laraine. 'He would know it while we were in the dressing room. And then in the short space of time that we went into the studio, which was only a matter of a couple of minutes' walk down the corridor, he'd more or less forgotten what we'd rehearsed. We used to go every other day and it was live, which hardly any television programmes were then. Although Jeff didn't normally worry, I just wondered if it was because it was live and we'd been getting up really early to get over there. I just thought, "Is he just tired? Is it just the strain of it?" If it was a song that he knew he had no problem with it. If he didn't know it, it took longer and it was a real struggle. Never in a million years did I think it was anything serious.'

When the series ended the couple spent a 'holiday from hell' in Spain, where Jeff insisted on pacing the promenade in over 100-degree heat and couldn't relax. Laraine's worries were eased when he got back to normal upon their return home, where he 'didn't feel threatened, he felt safe. It was when he was somewhere that he hadn't been before, that's when he was at his worst. Everything was strange to him, so, in a way he was frightened of it,' recalls Laraine. 'I didn't know anything at all about short-term memory loss or about dementia. I thought Jeff was having, although it's still serious, a little bit of a breakdown because of all that he'd been doing.'

Another holiday to Spain was planned for a few months later but Laraine still felt there was something wrong and, despite Jeff's protestations, rang a doctor who called them in immediately.

'I just got a bit worried about him. He'd forget things. If he'd gone to the shops for something, he wouldn't remember it all,' says Laraine. Some days he was fine while others he tended to struggle with his memory.

'Bear in mind he was only 55,' she adds. Jeff believed that they were wasting their time as he felt 'as fit as a fiddle' but agreed to go along for his wife's sake. 'I told him, "Just go for me Jeff, because I'm worried about you. If I'm wrong and nothing's a problem, then you can curse me all the way home."'

It was there that Laraine realised her husband was very, very seriously ill and was never going to get better. 'The doctor did a test where she gave him a pencil and said, "I'll tap twice, you tap twice, I'll tap once, you tap once,"' she explains. 'And Jeff gave me a look as if to say, "Is she all right?" He did it perfectly and she said, "I'm going to give you a name and address and, in a bit, I'm going to ask you what it is." And it was something like, "Peter Smith, Blackpool Street, Bolton." And he did all these other tests, went through them with flying colours and she said, "Right Jeff, what was that address?" And he said, "Oh yeah, isn't that funny, now what did you tell me? What was it Laraine?" The doctor said, "No, no, no, don't ask Laraine, I'm asking you." He couldn't remember one word.'

The doctor told them that she thought Jeff's brain cells were dying and that nothing could be done. 'Literally, in that one sentence, everything in our lives changed,' says Laraine.

Subsequent MRI scans led to doctors concluding that Jeff was suffering from the onset of dementia but Laraine instinctively knew what had caused his condition. 'Straight away when I heard it was his brain, his frontal lobe, I knew it was from heading a ball because he was the best header of a ball in the game, there was no one to touch him anywhere in the world. He scored more with his head than his feet, and I don't think another footballer has ever done that. A phenomenal header of the ball.'

She recalls a vacation when a comedian welcomed Jeff from the stage and joked, 'He can head a ball further than I go on holiday!'

'When they were training, everything was aimed at Jeff. Every game, all the corners, all the free kicks, everything was aimed at Jeff. I knew in my heart, I said it straight away, that it was from heading the heavy leather ball,' she adds.

Jeff Astle passed away on 19 January 2002. 'It was very quick, very vicious,' remembers Laraine. 'And when he died he was thin, he was stooped over, he was grey. He was 59, but looked 159.' Jeff's daughter Dawn adds that while many may presume he died peacefully in a care home, due to his illness he literally 'choked to death' in front of his loved ones.

Despite the new regulations in the game surrounding concussion, there still seems to be a lack of awareness among current players as to the potential gravity of head injuries. Laraine believes that if they'd seen her husband in his final days, they wouldn't hesitate in taking it seriously. 'I've often thought if a camera had shown the various stages of Jeff and shown how he was at the end, I promise you every player that goes down who doesn't want to leave that pitch would have left it if they'd seen how it ravaged my Jeff,' she insists. 'Every one of them. None of them would argue about coming off the pitch, they would be off like a shot.'

A Home Office pathologist carried out the post-mortem 'as the hospital realised that Jeff had headed a ball and that he was a young man to have this' and at the inquest stated that Jeff's brain resembled that of a boxer's. The verdict was industrial disease. 'Or, in other words, his job killed him,' adds Laraine.

The FA promised to 'look into it and do some test cases', but the family were contacted by the *Mail on Sunday* a couple of years ago to inform them that nothing had been done. Jeff's brain had been donated for research – 'as he believed in organ donation' – and Dr Willie Stewart, a leading world expert in CTE, sought permission for Jeff's brain tissue to be examined. 'It was then we learned about CTE,' says Laraine. Dr Stewart visited the family's home and told them that it was the worst case of CTE that he had ever seen. 'He said that if he hadn't have known Jeff was 59, he'd have thought it was a man of 89 or well into his 90s,' recalls Laraine.

'It was very distressing at the beginning,' she remembers, 'because a lot of people thought we were compensation-chasing. It was never about that. Never about that. I have proof now it killed him. Have I gone after anybody? No. We were accused of scaremongering, we were accused of trying to ban heading in football. It was never about any of that. What we were saying was to watch for the signs of a clash of heads, a boot to the head, concussion. The brain can't repair, once the brain is damaged it doesn't regenerate itself. It's not like a broken leg or a metatarsal or a pulled muscle.

'This is the brain, it rules the body. And, when your brain is damaged, you're on a slippery slope, there's no going back, there's no happy ending. If there's one thing you have to protect, you have to protect your brain. And now, of course, if there's a clash of heads they're off the pitch. It was never about banning heading. It was about making people aware of the dangers. And instead of when Jeff used to play – "Clash of heads, go off, have a few stitches, go back on, how many fingers am I holding up? That's right." Thank God that's gone now.'

Jeff was the first professional footballer confirmed to have died from CTE and the family were soon inundated with phone calls and emails from former players' associations whose members were also suffering with some sort of dementia.

'It was very, very moving,' says Laraine. One player's son described his father's symptoms to Dawn and 'it was the mirror image, exactly, of how our Jeff was. Everything about it was identical to Jeff. And he was a big centre-forward, big lad, headed a ball.'

Dawn adds that many of those affected played as centre-halves or centre-forwards, positions traditionally associated with heading the ball.

Laraine also believes that there's a misconception out there that just because the heavy leather ball has been removed from the game, problems can no longer occur. 'It was heavy, it soaked up the water. In the winter, when it was frozen, you got the ice in it and I remember my Jeff saying, "It was like heading a bag of bricks." Nowadays the ball doesn't soak up the water, it's lighter but it goes through the air quicker. It doesn't have to be a ball. It could be a boot, it could be a clash of heads, it could be an elbow. Don't think because we haven't got the heavy ball now that it isn't going to happen. It will. We know players that have never played with the leather ball – they played for West Brom after Jeff – that are suffering from it. And they've never headed the heavy leather ball.'

She's pleased that some people in the game seem to be taking things more seriously. She attended a match recently, where Neil Warnock insisted that a concussed player leave the field, despite the player's protestations. 'It's good to know they're not all like Mourinho!' she laughs.

'The brain is in trauma when there's a clash of heads. You have to come off, sit quietly and let the brain calm down,' she reasons. 'And you don't train again until the doctor feels that it's safe for you to do so. Even if you're unconscious for just a few seconds, it's because your brain is in trauma.'

The 'Justice for Jeff' campaign quickly gathered momentum, with a banner raised aloft at every West Brom game – home and away. Laraine says the family are eternally grateful to Baggies fans for their support. 'Nobody listened to us. Thank God for the West Brom supporters, who didn't back away when news broke that we'd been let down and nothing had been done. We'd waited very patiently, very quietly, very politely for ten years. I thought, 'Well, where has it got us?' Jeff died, football killed him and nobody gave a damn. We got the banner and the Albion fans supported us 100 per cent. Without their support, make no mistake about it, none of what has happened would have happened. It would have been swept under the carpet again. But those fans, on nine minutes every game home and away, that banner went up, and every game they applauded. My Jeff isn't the first and he won't be the last. We need to get justice, not just for my Jeff but for the others.'

The Astle family are also quick to acknowledge the 'incredible support' from the wider football community for their campaign. Beginning at Hull City, the campaign gained traction among Premier League clubs, who allowed the 'Justice for Jeff' banner to be held aloft in their grounds on the nine-minute mark – as a tribute to Jeff's shirt number. Even some of West Brom's biggest rivals, including Aston Villa and Birmingham City, paid tribute to Jeff by displaying his image on their big screens when they hosted the Baggies.

The Jeff Astle Foundation has become a focal point for former players suffering from head injuries in sport, along with their families. 'It's for them and their relatives to have someone to talk to,' Laraine explains. 'When Jeff was poorly, because then it was an isolated case, we had nobody to talk to. Because, now it's been acknowledged what killed Jeff, we've had lots of families in touch with us. Their husbands, their brothers, their uncles, their fathers who have played football and have got dementia/Alzheimer's but could be, like Jeff, CTE. A lot have said that when anything happens to them that their brain will be donated and they'll look to see if it is CTE. We help them financially, give them support and educate them and let people know what it's about. It's a very frightening thing and it's a lonely illness. Although you're there with them you're lonesome because they don't remember anything. Jeff's face lit up when he saw his daughters but he couldn't name them.'

She mentions the honours Jeff won during his career but 'at the end of the day, he gave his life getting them all and he had no recollection of ever doing it. Yet it cost him his life. He remembered nothing, had no idea. And he was 59.'

Laraine often used scrapbooks and mementoes from Jeff's career to test his memory. 'We've got a huge photo on the wall of him scoring the FA Cup-winning goal for West Brom. Every day I'd say to him, "What's this, Jeff?" and at the beginning he'd look at me as if to say, "Are you crackers keeping asking me this?" He'd say, "It's the cup final."'

Then one day the conversation changed.

'What's this, Jeff?'

'Oh, I don't know.'

'That's you there.'

'Is it?'

'Yeah. Don't you remember?'

'No.'

'You scored the winning goal in the cup final.'

'Did I?'

'Yeah. Do you remember who you played for?'

'Did I play for Fulham?'

Laraine explains, 'And that was his answer. "Did I play for Fulham?" And I think that sums everything up.'

Jeff Astle died not knowing he was a footballer, not knowing he was a hero, not knowing his legacy would be a campaign to help save the lives of future footballers. 'The King' may be dead, but long live 'The King'.

3

How Do Retired Footballers Go Bankrupt?

SINCE you started reading this sentence, Wayne Rooney has earned about a fiver.

Anyone who has seen the 1985 Richard Pryor movie *Brewster's Millions* will understand just how difficult it is to blow exorbitant amounts of money. Pryor's titular character had never earned more than $11,000 a year yet struggled to splurge $30m in 30 days. So spare a thought for poor (okay, not so poor) Wayne Rooney whose £300,000-a-week contract until 2019 should be difficult to fritter away, considering he's already England's richest footballer with an estimated net worth of £45m. So, what could the Manchester United and England striker splurge his weekly wages on?

Despite currently residing in a £12m luxury Cheshire home, he could theoretically splash out on a house above the average UK property price every single week. With average prices hovering around the £250,000 mark, he'd still have cash left over to kit it out.

Nappies, baby wipes, multiple trips to *The Lego Movie* – it all adds up. The cost of raising a child in the UK, and supporting them through university, has risen to £227,266, according to the Centre of Economic and Business Research. This encompasses the total outlay on your progeny from birth until they receive the key of the door at 21. So, with just seven days' salary, Rooney could pay for his five-year-old son's upbringing and have almost a hundred grand left to splash on Kai's 21st birthday party. And then do it all over again in the following weeks for Kai's little brothers Klay and Kit.

The most important man in the free world, that's Barack Obama rather than José Mourinho, would take about 15 months to earn Rooney's weekly wage. While dealing with domestic issues like Medicare and international problems in Syria and Ukraine are obviously not as onerous as nabbing a meaningless third goal away at Everton, it seems bizarre that Rooney's annual salary would pay for the next 15 US Presidential terms. Closer to home, the United striker could pay British Prime Minister David Cameron for two years and still have change left over for an entry-level NHS nurse. Okay, forget about Cameron, Rooney's annual wage packet could employ around 700 new staff nurses.

Incredibly, Rooney's weekly wage would pay for 400 entry-level season tickets at Old Trafford, which are around £700 a pop. While that might not seem great value based on some of the team's performances since Sir Alex Ferguson retired, it seems absurd to realise that United would have to sell 20,000 season tickets a year – or just under a quarter of all seats at Old Trafford – just to pay Rooney's salary.

Just 44 miles from Old Trafford lies Rimington, a picturesque little village in Lancashire. The parish, and its surrounding area, contains about 600 inhabitants, meaning

Rooney could employ all of them – men, women and children – on the average UK industrial wage of around £590 every week.

With such an outrageous weekly stipend the general public can find it difficult to comprehend how professional footballers can get into financial difficulties. But Rooney is an outlier – one of the highest-paid sports stars in the world. The striker was 34th on *Forbes*' list of the world's highest-paid athletes in 2015, beating off the likes of Serena Williams, Andy Murray, Wladimir Klitschko, Usain Bolt and Jordan Spieth. Rooney's wages from Manchester United are also topped up with lucrative endorsements with the likes of Nike, Samsung and EA Sports.

The situation in League 2, English football's fourth tier, is a lot more pragmatic. The most recent figures suggest this division's average weekly wage is £747, with a mandatory salary cap in operation that restricts clubs' spending on players' wages to 100 per cent of turnover. This means Rooney's wages could pay just over 400 League 2 players every week. Basically, England's record goalscorer could almost cover the wages of every League 2 player who makes their club's matchday squad next weekend. While marquee brands are willing to pay the likes of Rooney millions every year, local car dealerships and retailers can sponsor a player in the lower leagues for a couple of hundred quid a season.

Move up a division and players' earnings are still relatively modest. With a Salary Cost Management Protocol in place in League 1, limiting clubs' spending on players' wages to 60 per cent of turnover, the average weekly wage is estimated be to around £1,400. This means that Rooney could pay over 80 per cent of the starting line-ups in the next round of fixtures in England's third tier.

It wasn't always so. Before the advent of the Premier League in 1992, there was a much more level playing field across England's divisions. In the final year of the old First Division, average player earnings were about £60,000 per annum, compared to £22,000 in the third tier and £16,000 in the fourth tier. Theoretically, players in Liverpool's side which dominated the 1980s earned less than three times that of men playing for sides like Newport County, and just under four times that of players plying their trade for the likes of Aldershot.

It all changed when 22 clubs broke away from the Football League in 1992 to form what was originally called the Premiership, rebranded as the Premier League in 2007. Backed by a £305m BSkyB deal, it wasn't long before clubs were splashing their newly-found wealth. Players had threatened to strike if they didn't receive a greater say in how the game was run – and a larger cut of TV income – and their average earnings began to spiral. Within five years of the new breakaway league being formed, players in the top flight were averaging £175,000 per year – an almost 300 per cent increase on the final year of the old First Division. Lower-league players weren't so lucky. Basic pay in the third tier rose just 30 per cent – roughly in tandem with the average UK worker's wage – with a similar increase recorded in the fourth tier.

By 1997, top-flight players were earning six times that of those in the old Third Division and over eight times that of those in the Fourth Division. In 2010 the disparity between divisions was staggering – literally leagues apart. Basic pay for Premier League players had risen to £1,162,350 compared to £73,320 in the old Third Division and £38,844 in the old Fourth Division. Elite players were now earning vast multiples of their lower league counterparts – just under 16 times those of players two divisions down and 30 times those of players in the fourth tier. Lower-division players were being priced out of the sport.

Sam Sloma was Dagenham & Redbridge's first scorer in the Football League but took the drastic decision to retire at 26 as he simply wasn't earning enough money from the game.

Sloma left school at 16 to join Wimbledon, then in the Premier League, and completed a three-year scholarship before being released by the Dons. He began to realise that life as a footballer might not be as lucrative as many believe.

'I needed to get a job – not so much for the money, as I was living at home, but more so to get in touch with the real world,' he admits. 'I went into property lettings while playing semi-professional football. I was lucky in that I worked my way back up through the leagues until I went into the Football League to where I had to give up working. I earned less in professional football than I did playing part-time and working.'

In his mid-20s, he understood that if he wanted to get married and start a family, the cost of living meant he wouldn't be able to do this playing professional football in League 2.

'To a degree I had achieved something in football by playing, scoring and living the football lifestyle – however, I needed to progress financially. When I stopped the second time I was 26 and it was time to get a serious career. The financial implications were that I knew I had to work and I knew that to buy a house and live in London – I had to stop playing professionally and get working – I wouldn't earn enough playing. Some say it was a brave decision but I'm pleased I took it.'

Seven years later and Sam is an associate partner with First Wealth, where he assists several footballers with financial management. Having been on both sides of the fence he's in the ideal position to assess why so many players get into financial strife when they retire.

'Footballers' earnings go from extreme highs to nothing – if the club stops playing you, you have no income. Usually, while they have been earning large sums, they replicate this in their spending habits. Now this is a large generalisation – which I hate doing – however, it gives you an insight. If they haven't prepared properly for this then it is easy to see how they will run out of money. Likewise players will yearn to pay off their mortgage prior to finishing their career. A large portion of their income is gone into the house, however, even if you are mortgage-free you need to pay for cars, the bills, school fees etc. so being mortgage-free isn't the Holy Grail. It is better to have, say, £200,000 on a mortgage and £200,000 in cash that can actually be used during the period of re-adjustment.'

He also believes that divorce, childcare and maintenance all play a large part in financial and mental issues post-retirement. 'It is hard to quantify to anyone who has never played professional football but there is a feeling of superiority or invincibility while you play – you are generally pretty young, fit and healthy and earning your money from the world's most popular sport. Therefore some kudos comes with the territory. Similarly to the earnings fall-off, players are quickly forgotten, unless you are a Steven Gerrard or a Thierry Henry type. This can affect the home life and therefore financial issues can arise from the amount of free time players have.'

Sloma suggests that financial problems have increased in the Premier League era, although concedes there is no general rule of thumb. 'Pre-Premier League, most players knew they wouldn't have been able to retire from their earnings so finances would have been more in their mind. This ensured a lower percentage of financial issues. However, the mental aspect hasn't changed dramatically – players are more in the spotlight now than they were years ago but the feeling of what to do with yourself now that football is finished is a difficult one to overcome.'

Furthermore, drastic changes to pension legislation on 5 March 2006 – known as A-Day – have been 'extremely detrimental to footballers', according to Sloma.

'Anyone with a pension prior to A-Day has a protected retirement of age 35, anyone post- has a retirement of 55,' he explains. 'Footballers do retire at around age 35 and need funds then. The government has recently changed the legislation again and anyone earning over £210,000 per annum can only put a max of £10,000 in per year – again this is going to mean most footballers won't bother building up a pension fund in their most profitable earning years. I understand the logic that people earning at that level shouldn't be given large amounts of tax relief as well. However, for footballers it has been a double whammy in recent years.'

Sloma adds that for players at the elite level, earning millions every year, a pension becomes irrelevant. 'It is more a case of the middle and lower levels of players that have been adversely affected. The top-level players don't really need pensions. The middle-level players need funds at 35 and the lowest-level can't afford it anyway.'

These changes to pension legislation just add to the financial minefield awaiting retired players, but Sloma hints that there is little assistance from within the game on financial planning and management for players.

'There is a small amount given by the PFA – and from some of the clubs. However, Barclays were sponsoring the Premier League and as part of this had first refusal. Clubs don't want the issues of players being misadvised by people they have recommended so they have steered clear. I do understand the clubs' viewpoint – there is a need to help younger clients but, again, who do they bring in? Can the clubs trust the advisors?'

Sam has two pieces of advice for young footballers regarding their finances, and they hark back to his playing days. 'Keep it simple and get into good habits. They should be able to out-earn any financial advisor so all they need is someone to help, guide and structure for them.'

A 2015 report by Sporting Intelligence suggests that average earnings in the Premier League are now a whopping £2,229,374 per year, or £42,872 per week. Wages are expected to accelerate even further in the next few years, with Sky and BT Sport paying a combined £5.136bn for UK live television rights for the Premier League from the 2016/17 season. All 20 2013/14 Premier League clubs ranked among the 40 highest-earning globally, a situation that is unlikely to change with the advent of the new TV deal. This means Premier League clubs will be able to compete with European rivals for even better players – resulting in even bigger salaries among the elite.

The enormous gulf between earnings across English football is only going to get worse according to Professor Chris Brady of Salford University, who is in an ideal position to comment. Chris played semi-professional football as a young man and even then the riches on offer in the lower leagues were not sufficient to support a young family.

After being released by Leyton Orient at 16, Chris juggled non-league football with the likes of Harlow, Romford and Wealdstone and a job as a surveyor before being offered a professional contract with Southend United. The terms would have meant a 45 per cent drop in income, so with two children and a wife to support he turned it down and has never regretted his decision. He has gone on to have a varied career, including a return to Southend, where his son owned a share in the club, authored several sports management books and – an A Licence coach himself – has contributed to the Football Association's senior Pro Licence management course. As well as being a professor in Salford's Centre for Sports Business, he's recently co-authored a book, *Quiet Leadership*, with Bayern Munich manager Carlo Ancelotti.

Chris envisages the Championship becoming a Premier League 2, with the remaining two divisions becoming almost an afterthought. 'The latest Premier League TV deal has seen a 70 per cent increase on the previous one. Compare that to the last Football League deal, which was down 24 per cent. When that comes up for renewal next time around, I can see broadcasters offering "X" amount for the Championship and saying, "We're not really interested in the other leagues, let Leagues 1 and 2 go to another channel,"' he predicts. 'We're the only country in the world with 100 full-time football clubs. In a country of 60 million, that doesn't make economic sense.' This, of course, would have a detrimental effect on players' earnings in the bottom two divisions.

Chris reveals that earnings in the lower tiers of English football are still relatively modest, with many players still not able to afford the jump from non-league football to a full-time career in the Football League. 'Players won't go from non-league to League 1 or 2, they can't afford it. You'll probably earn half the average wage in non-league, and then you can add on your wage [from your day job].'

For those who do play in the lower divisions, there are some who think they should have the footballer lifestyle – 'the Range Rover Evoque and all the rest' – despite earning maybe £300 a week. It's not hard to see how that type of standard of living can't be sustained. However, Chris says that lower league players 'get it' more and are 'very aware of where they are after a few years, putting money away etc'.

So, where is it all heading? Will we eventually see a £1m per week footballer while lower leagues struggle? Chris believes this player already exists – Lionel Messi. 'If Manchester City, for example, were to buy Messi now they'd have to pay him £1m a week. It's only around £50m a year. There are top CEOs and hedge fund managers that earn two or three times that and nobody bats an eyelid.' He concedes that Premier League wages are only going to increase and can't see it ever stopping.

Nevertheless Chris admits that XPRO's startling figures on retired footballers' financial struggles don't surprise him. I ask if even the likes of Wayne Rooney could lose it all. 'Why not?' he replies, before listing some sports stars who have suffered financially.

Chris has been asked on a couple of occasions by the PFA to put on courses in financial planning and awareness for young players, and would give one simple piece of advice, 'There's no point going in doing presentations. We need to get these players one-on-one and if a player is asked to invest in something, the answer should be "don't". Ninety-nine per cent of the time, I'm going to be right.'

Even experienced players who've enjoyed glittering careers would do well to heed his advice. In November 2015, the *Sunday Times* claimed that up to 100 retired players faced financial ruin – with total losses of up to £100m – as a result of investing in film schemes and property ventures. It was reported that the likes of Rio Ferdinand, Robbie Savage, Martin Keown and Danny Murphy were among those affected. Some people I spoke to suggested that as many as 300 players may have become embroiled in these schemes.

The former Leicester City captain Steve Walsh is one of the players who has been affected by the fall-out from these film schemes but is quick to accept some responsibility for the problems that followed. 'I've only come out of it in the last month. It's been 15 years of torture,' admits Steve. 'Finding the right things and being careful with what you do was something where I made a few errors. I guess I could have been misadvised, albeit it I took a cash amount out of that in the early stages, which I had been promised. It was a bit of both really, my own fault as well as a bit of bad advice. But, looking back it was a scheme that came back to haunt me.'

As a former PFA chairman, Pat Nevin examined many complex financial arrangements but even he is perplexed by the nature of these film schemes. 'There was no way that they, or indeed their accountants, could have known those schemes,' he says. 'I studied accountancy and economics and I've had a look at some of those things and, bloody hell, they're absolutely incredible. More complicated than actuarial valuations of pension schemes, which is the most complicated thing I've ever got involved in looking at for the union. So, they've had to trust those advisors and those advisors have let them all down. As, I believe, the government did as well to be honest.'

His advice to footballers regarding their finances is fittingly concise. 'I'd advise them to keep their accounts as simplistic as possible. If you understand something then you're not going to be scammed by it,' he concludes.

Brady, however, believes young professional footballers are not stupid. 'They're uneducated. Like in American sports, most come from a working-class background, don't understand money and suddenly it's there. There's a lack of financial literacy, which is much more damaging in a sport where money is available. Players think it's always going to be there. At 20 or 21 years of age, you never imagine a day when you won't be playing. You could end up not playing again tomorrow. That youthful vulnerability is another factor.'

Footballers' earning powers have clearly driven a gulf between them and fans. 'Tom Finney ran his father's plumbing business while he was playing for England,' says Chris. 'You'd see players on the bus going to games. They were more in touch.'

With eight years being the average duration of careers in English football, it's not hard to fathom how footballers that spend their time in the lower divisions can get into financial difficulties upon retirement. While the bumper contracts of elite players such as Rooney and big-money TV deals will generate the headlines, the general public doesn't get to read about a journeyman midfielder's pay-as-you-play contract at Luton Town.

Mark Sands, an insolvency expert with London accountancy firm Baker Tilly, has dealt with several bankruptcies involving well-known Premier League footballers. Growing up, Mark could hear the roars from Portsmouth's Fratton Park whenever Pompey scored, but never fell in love with the game. However, it's become a large part of his professional life. In spite of the huge gulf between earnings across the divisions, Sands has rarely had to deal with insolvency cases involving players who've spent the majority of their careers in the lower tiers. 'If you don't have much, you don't borrow much, so there's less chance of getting into difficulty,' he concedes.

Of course, this does not mean than retired players who've spent years in the lower echelons of the English game are financially secure. As many affected by the recent recession throughout the British Isles can attest, it is possible to struggle day to day, week to week, without having to resort to the bankruptcy courts. Thankfully, I've never been declared bankrupt but I've often had to scramble under the sofa cushions for loose change as pay day looms. As Sands suggests, the less you've earned the less debt you're likely to have accrued. Just because you're not bankrupt, doesn't mean you're not under financial stress.

Despite his vast wealth, it's unlikely that Rooney will add a World Cup winner's medal to his impressive haul of club honours before he retires. But he could buy one. Or two. Manchester United legend Nobby Stiles sold his 1966 gold medal for £188,200 in 2010 – to the Old Trafford club. The fact Stiles had to resort to selling his precious garland, and wept as he did so, while Rooney could snap it up with about four days' wages displays a lot of what's wrong with modern football. Rooney would still have change to buy Gordon Banks's 1966 medal – which was auctioned for £125,000 in 2001.

Stiles and Banks are just two examples of stars of yesteryear who have had to resort to selling off their prized memorabilia to provide for their families. Of the 11 players who appeared in England's World Cup-winning side in 1966, just three still own their medals. George Cohen, once described by George Best as 'the best full-back I have ever played against', was first to sell his due to financial hardship in 1998. Even the late Bobby Moore and hat-trick hero Sir Geoff Hurst sold theirs, while fellow West Ham alumni Martin Peters offloaded his after being made redundant from an insurance company in 2001.

Should England pull off an unlikely World Cup triumph in Russia in 2018 – they are tenth favourites with the bookies prior to the qualification process – it's highly doubtful that the likes of Joe Hart, Raheem Sterling and Harry Kane would ever have to resort to selling off their winning medals to provide financial security for their families.

Or is it? Despite the lavish salaries doled out to modern-day Premier League stars, some still contrive to get themselves into financial bother. Sands concedes that it's not beyond the realms of possibility that current elite stars, despite their vast stipends, could end up insolvent.

'I would hope that anyone playing at the top level now would have sufficient funds to support themselves during retirement,' says Mark, who is also president of the Insolvency Practitioners Association. 'But insolvency is not impossible. It really depends on how you go bust. It's one thing to lose everything with extravagant spending. It's another to lose it all on an investment. If you guarantee the debts of a business, and you haven't had that money, you could end up with a huge liability. You could lose the shirt off your back.'

One player who literally did lose his shirt – and plenty of them – was David James. Football fans were bewildered in 2014 when news broke that the former England keeper was auctioning off personal possessions after declaring himself bankrupt.

The BT Sport pundit enjoyed a highly successful career, with the likes of Liverpool, Manchester City and Aston Villa among his ten clubs. Indeed, a two-year stint at Bristol City in the twilight of his career reportedly earned him around £1.5m. How had he resorted to auctioning off his possessions including dozens of signed football shirts, chainsaws, a Vauxhall Astra van, 1,800 vinyl records and even his footballs?

Quite easily, it seems, when we consider the aforementioned research by XPRO, which indicates that 40 per cent of Premier League players face the threat of bankruptcy within five years of retirement.

James, who won 53 England caps, not only earned an estimated £20m from his footballing career, but enjoyed many lucrative sidelines including modelling for Armani. It's been cited that a costly divorce in 2005 contributed greatly to his financial downfall, but his extravagant spending must have been a factor.

James's former Liverpool team-mate Stan Collymore wrote in his 2004 autobiography, 'If he [James] had a new car and he pranged it, he would just go and buy a new car...Too easy to spend money like you're going to be earning that kind of money for the rest of your life.' Much of James's spending, however, was far from selfish. He established the David James Foundation in 2005, with the objective of funding improved agricultural practices in Malawi. He'd visited the country a few years earlier with fellow England internationals and was moved by the plight of many of the country's inhabitants. However, even his altruistic nature was taken advantage of with many getting involved to profit themselves. He also donated his fee for a regular column with *The Observer* newspaper to charity.

Sands doesn't agree with XPRO's figures but has seen plenty of cases involving professional footballers caught up in the perfect financial storm. 'Most of the footballers' bankruptcies I've been involved with have been down to a combination of bad investments and not adjusting to a change in income. Many involved buy-to-let properties, which were badly affected by the crash in 2008.'

The likes of Robbie Fowler are famed for their buy-to-let empires, with the former Liverpool striker now running 'property academy' courses at around £1,000 a head. Such is the extent of Fowler's property interests that terrace wags often sang, 'We all live in a Robbie Fowler house' to him to the tune of 'Yellow Submarine'.

He even made the *Sunday Times* Rich List in 2005 as one of the wealthiest 1,000 Britons. The course promises to teach participants how to build a property portfolio without a footballer's salary. Sadly, they've come too late to teach some of Fowler's former fellow players how to build a property empire *with* a footballer's salary.

The former Aston Villa midfielder Lee Hendrie once earned £40,000 a week but was declared bankrupt two years ago after racking up debts of £200,000. Hendrie, who broke up from his ex-wife one day after their wedding, has admitted he lost £10m after the property crash and that his financial woes led to him twice trying to take his own life.

He suggests that retirement from the game and the financial pressures it brings are not uncommon. He's been quoted in the past that people would be surprised at the amount of former players he's spoken to who have sat in every day and not got dressed, having got to the stage where they don't want to do anything.

Hendrie has turned his life around since his financial woes, establishing a football academy that also aims to help young players with life skills away from the football pitch.

Failed investments play a huge factor in star footballers' financial problems. Allied with misplaced trust, it can lead to financial Armageddon. A former holder of the British transfer record, Chris Sutton formed a formidable partnership with Alan Shearer – the so-called SAS – during Blackburn Rovers' title-winning campaign in 1994/95. The Nottingham-born target-man was joint-top scorer in the 1997/98 Premier League season, and his exploits earned him a move to Chelsea – and international recognition.

Sutton was declared bankrupt in 2014, blaming bad financial advice on his malaise after he and his wife became embroiled in a multi-million pound fraud. He admits that he didn't fully understand the investment scheme he got involved with, which he'd been reassured he had been making a profit on. However, it came to light that advisor Simon Grinter was misleading him and other investors and Grinter was subsequently jailed for fraud.

It's all a world away from the events of January 1961. Footballers, aggrieved at a maximum wage of £20 per week compared to the average industrial wage of £15, threatened to strike. A meeting of players was called to vote on industrial action, where someone felt it was unfair to earn more than miners. Tommy Banks, a former Bolton Wanderers defender and previously a miner himself, said he 'admired people in the mining community, but it didn't mean they could cope with marking Stanley Matthews on a Saturday afternoon'.

The decision to strike was almost unanimous, with many players voting against their club's wishes. The Football Association finally acceded to their demands and abolished the salary cap. Almost immediately, Fulham's Johnny Haynes – a predecessor of David Beckham as the Brylcreem

Boy – became the first £100-per-week footballer, a five-fold increase on his previous salary. Within ten years George Best was earning £1,000 per week and the disparity between footballers' earnings and those of the fans was getting ever wider. Best, of course, was no stranger to extravagant living, famously stating, 'I spent 90 per cent of my money on women, drink and fast cars. The rest I wasted.'

By 1985, the average annual salary of a footballer in England's top flight was around £25,000 – 250 per cent of the average UK worker's wage. Twenty-five years later the percentage had risen to approximately 3,500.

The rising gulf in income has led to many fans being unable to identify with the modern-day elite footballer. How could they when even the most average player on their team is probably earning more in a week than the supporter does in a year? It's no surprise then when fans show little compassion when a footballer falls on hard times.

Elite footballers aren't the only highly-remunerated sportsmen who get themselves into financial difficulties. Professional sports stars face an opposite income cycle to most people, earning their peak returns early in life, but retiring young and not hitting those income levels again. Consumption smoothing is a model which many professional sports stars – with a relatively short peak period of earnings – find hard to master. It is an economic concept whereby people balance their income and spending to ensure sufficient funds for a comfortable retirement, usually by 'smoothing' their consumption levels during their earning years.

Research from the National Bureau of Economic Research (NBER) in the United States in 2015 suggests that one in six NFL stars declare bankruptcy within 12 years of retirement. It found that initial bankruptcy filings begin very soon after retirement and continue at a substantial rate through at least those first 12 years. Surprisingly, the report indicates that bankruptcy rates weren't really affected by the length of career or player's earnings. A previous piece by Pablo Torre in *Sports Illustrated* was even more damning, suggesting that a jaw-dropping 78 per cent of former NFL players have gone bankrupt or were under financial stress due to joblessness or divorce within just two years of retiring from the sport.

Gridiron football stars have an even shorter career than their soccer counterparts, with an NFL player only in the league for an average of three and a half years. Despite this short earning period, American football stars are renowned for their lavish spending, with peer pressure in the locker room a key influencer. Some of their expenditure is extraordinary.

Warren Sapp enjoyed a 12-year NFL career, earning over $80m in the process, but filed for bankruptcy in 2012, declaring $6.45m in assets and $6.7m in debt. At the time he had $826.04 in his bank account.

Vince Young earned around $26m during a six-year career but the 2006 NFL Rookie of the Year filed for Chapter 11 bankruptcy in 2014. Among his many reckless spending habits was regularly dropping $5,000 a visit at restaurant chains such as TGI Friday's and the Cheesecake Factory – the equivalent of Wayne Rooney blowing his fortune at Nando's.

And it's not just American footballers that splash the cash. Allen Iverson was an 11-time NBA All-Star, but regularly travelled with a 50-strong entourage and managed to blow his $200m career earnings. Former NBA star Rod Strickland, whose father was his business manager, once shelled out a reported $4m on a lifetime supply of Kool-Aid.

As retired basketball star Danny Schayes once explained, 'Guys go broke because they surround themselves with people who help them go broke.' Professor Chris Brady had suggested I watch a scene from the HBO show *Ballers*, which perfectly portrays this phenomenon. Dwayne 'The Rock' Johnson plays Spencer Strasmore, a former NFL player turned financial advisor, who targets current star Vernon Littlefield as a potential client. Littlefield's current business manager is a childhood friend, but he's already in debt despite having signed a $12m deal. Strasmore calls to Littlefield's mansion to loan him $300,000 only to find dozens of people wandering around. 'Who the fuck are all these people?' asks Strasmore. 'I don't even fucking know,' admits Littlefield. 'You better start knowing,' warns Strasmore.

This is a problem that's becoming ever more prevalent in English professional football. Chris feels that the background of professional footballers could be a major factor. 'Maybe it's a working-class thing. They do feel, "Well, we've got money, we need to look after our mates." I know because that's where I'm from and I still think that way.'

One retired player told me that young players need to cut out any 'so-called friends' that are sucking money out of them, which he said is a common problem with some players from certain backgrounds who are new to earning lots of money. He also warned that these burgeoning entourages can also prove to be a distraction from the footballer's playing career.

Most Manchester United fans would agree that Eric Djemba-Djemba was one of Sir Alex Ferguson's worst signings during his reign at Old Trafford. However, the Cameroonian, once lauded as a successor to Roy Keane, seemed to waste more money than Ferguson did when buying him from Nantes for £3.5m in 2003. The midfielder was on £75,000 a month at United but his former agent claimed he was quickly resorting to win bonuses and appearance fees to get by.

Agent Christophe Mongai suggested that Djemba-Djemba had 30 bank accounts, a fleet of ten cars and had no hesitation frittering away money on numerous hangers-on. The player has refuted many of the claims but admits he was too young when he joined United and too naïve and trusting.

It's no surprise then that the former Aston Villa midfielder was declared bankrupt, despite earning around £4m in the Premier League alone.

Richard Rufus and Jason Euell played together for three seasons at Charlton Athletic in the early 2000s, helping the London side to a best-ever finish of seventh in the Premier League in 2003/04. However, despite earning respectable sums from the game they'd both suffer financial turmoil after leaving the club.

Rufus, voted by Addicks fans as the club's greatest ever defender, was forced to hang up his boots in 2004 through injury and pursued a career as a financial consultant. A born-again Christian, Rufus was allegedly given £5m to invest by the Kingsway International Christian Centre, which subsequently went missing. He was declared bankrupt in 2013 and two years later was appearing at a High Court hearing facing allegations of misappropriation of funds, misrepresentation to investors and unregulated taking of deposits.

Euell was forced to file for bankruptcy in 2011 after a property business he'd invested in failed, claiming his signature had been forged on a number of documents.

Legend has it that the late Sir Bobby Robson wasn't great with names. When asked in an interview what the then Newcastle United boss called him, Shola Ameobi once replied, 'Carl Cort.'

So it's no surprise that the former England boss is at the centre of one of the most infamous of transfer mix-up stories, also involving Cort.

Sir Bobby had apparently been impressed by a talented young England under-21 striker at Wimbledon and sent his scouts to run the rule over him. The player in question was the aforementioned Jason Euell, who unfortunately in the game scouted was pushed back to midfield with Cort taking his place up front.

Wimbledon were shocked to receive a £7m bid for Cort, who'd scored just 16 goals in 70 appearances. After a poor return of seven goals in four years with the Toon, it was evident that Sir Bobby had possibly signed the wrong player.

The late England manager may have confused their looks but Euell and Cort were to have something else in common – bankruptcy. Cort, a half-brother of current Chelsea youngster Ruben Loftus-Cheek, finished his career with Tampa Bay Rowdies in the United States but in 2010 his bank and credit card accounts were frozen by court order and he was adjudged bankrupt following a petition by NatWest.

Cort isn't the only player involved in a supposed transfer mix-up to suffer from financial woes. While no one has actually admitted making a mistake in signing Luther Blissett for AC Milan, the rumour persists in Italy over 30 years later that the club had in fact meant to sign Blissett's Watford team-mate John Barnes.

Blissett endured a torrid single season at Milan, scoring just five goals in 30 appearances and supposedly bemoaning that in Italy 'no matter how much money you have, you can't buy Rice Krispies'. The AC Milan owner and president at the time, Giuseppe Farina, never denied the story but did concede that Blissett had been recommended to him by a London gardener.

Barnes went on to sign for Liverpool for £900,000 and became a household name. Despite a highly-decorated playing career, Barnes had several unsuccessful stints as a manager before he was made bankrupt over an unpaid tax bill by a Liverpool court in 2009. The order was quickly overturned as Barnes stressed the tax liabilities were due to an oversight. He'd previously admitted to poor financial management, conceding that he didn't 'like dealing with bills and never have done'.

It can be hard for the general public to comprehend the scale of some professional footballers' earnings, but when it's presented in black and white on an everyday payslip it can make staggering reading.

John Arne Riise was furious in 2007 when a payslip from his club Liverpool, marked 'Private & Confidential', entered the public domain. Relating to his wages in September 2006, it showed he'd earned £82,000 after deductions for the month and paid a whopping £55,000 in tax. His tax deducted for the year to that point was an incredible £304,137.66. Despite these vast contributions to the Exchequer it was still surprising that earlier in 2007 Riise had been declared bankrupt for an unpaid debt of around £100,000.

Riise quickly moved to have the bankruptcy order annulled, which is the only way of reversing the original decision, as Mark Sands explains. 'With bankruptcy, it's a matter of drawing a line in the sand. In return for losing your assets, your debts are cleared. After one year you are discharged from your debts but your credit rating will be affected for six years. Surplus income for up to three years may have to be contributed to a trustee. However, if you pay off the debts in full, you have an annulment. Basically, the bankruptcy goes away.'

James Hall is an avid Aston Villa fan. He is also a senior associate at Anthony Collins Solicitors, where he has advised footballer clients, both during their playing career and post-retirement, on matters associated with their finances.

'Retirement can crystallise a lot of issues, lots of things which are there under the surface when someone's playing that they don't see the negatives with, the problems, until afterwards,' explains James.

'Footballers aren't really unduly special cases. A great analogy often used is people in the entertainment industry generally. A lot of people who go into the likes of music, acting and things like that are exposed to a lot of the same issues that footballers are – which is often around, essentially, a lot of money and a lot of acclaim at a young age with not too much responsibility on people's shoulders. It's that situation where you've got people being told from a young age how wonderful they are and they have the same sort of vultures hanging around who want to take advantage. Money attracts people. If you've got people who are earning a great deal of money, then suddenly there's a lot of people coming out of the woodwork to see if they can get their share.'

With many failed investment schemes involving footballers in the media, Hall believes that players cannot be entirely absolved of blame.

'There definitely seems to be a slant in the reporting of blaming the financial advisors in some cases, and a secondary slant involving a dig at the agents. While those two criticisms may be very fair generally, I note that the press have stood off from having a go at the players. Sometimes people are too happy to let other people just do things for them, and they never actually stop and think. If someone comes to you and says something along the lines of, "If you throw your money into this, you will get this absolutely ridiculous return; oh and by the way you'll never have to pay tax again," then I think most of us, even without a Harvard education, would say, "Well, actually there might be something funny about this. Can I go away and think about this or can I speak to someone else?"

'My concern sometimes is we allow people to be abrogated of their responsibilities. There are plenty of players out there who, because they were willing to take some responsibility, they were willing to think a little bit and ask some questions, they didn't suffer quite as much later on as some of the players did. What we're seeing now is the tip of the iceberg. In the next few years we're going to see far worse than the things that are coming out now.

'Some of the investments that players have been attracted into, particularly in the Premier League era, have been utterly ridiculous – the sort of thing which most independent professional advisors would look at and say, "You can go into that if you want but are you willing to throw your money away, and have HM Revenue & Customs pay you undue amounts of attention long after your support network has disappeared?" It is very much a shared responsibility and I'm not saying people shouldn't be able to rely on their professional advisors or to take professional advice, but there is a temptation for some people – and it's not just footballers – to say, "Ah well, he's dealing with that, I don't have to think about it."'

Dan Clay of Clay & Associates has dealt with tax compliance for several footballer clients during his career. We spoke during the week that former Everton and Newcastle United striker Duncan Ferguson was declared bankrupt and he agrees that plenty more cases will emerge in the immediate future. 'Over the next six months, this is really going to pick up momentum,' he believes. 'The Revenue are placing demands on a lot of people who entered into structured schemes previously. In the last ten years, footballers have gone into over 100 different tax schemes. There's going to be a lot more Duncan Fergusons in the next six months because the Revenue have and are continuing to put those Advanced Payment Notices to the players.'

Unfortunately, many of the players affected by these schemes are no longer playing and no longer have the earning power to deal with the retrospective taxation involved. 'If I said, "This scheme is going to save you £500,000," someone on £50,000 a week is going to look at it and say, "I'll have a bit of that, no real downside. If it comes back, fine." But the problem is the delay until it comes back,' explains Dan.

'Take film partnerships for example, which were done in the main from 2002 to 2005. They're getting a call today to pay, potentially, what they should have paid back then and not many of them will be playing football any more. In addition to this, what they then invested the tax savings into was high risk and lost money as well. So they're now looking down the barrel and saying, "I need to pay half a million quid, which I've no longer got. What can I do?" And they've very little choice really.' Quite often, bankruptcy is the only option available.

Dan hopes that anyone playing in the Premier League today would earn enough to enjoy a comfortable retirement, but it's often not as simple as that. 'If they're sensible with their money during their playing career, their retirement should sort itself out,' he says. 'They all want to do something which is slightly sexy and racy, and gone are the days where sexy and racy are what should be done. If they do safe, structured, pretty boring stuff it's preserving their future. Thankfully there are fewer schemes out there today as many of the providers have closed down.

'There's been a lot of publicity about the fact that these went wrong so you'd like to think that less and less people will get involved in them. But people will get involved, will still have an appetite for them and think, "Well, I earn £50,000 a week and £25,000 of that goes into tax. It'd be nice if I could get some of that back." But, inevitably, not many tax schemes work.'

Like many I spoke to, James Hall is bewildered at the lack of financial education given to young players, particularly with such a high attrition rate among academy graduates.

'Young lads are groomed as footballers from a very young age; they're told that they're amazing, they're told they're very special. For the vast majority, it doesn't work out so straight away you've got your first wave of retired footballers that are on the scrapheap at the age of 18. And they rarely have another plan.

'They maybe didn't think about getting an academic education because in their small schools they were the best footballer and everyone thought they were going to make it. But it turns out they weren't good enough. These lads are truly abandoned; it's a case of, "That's it, off you go, not interested any more." So you've got a guy whose dreams have been crushed who has no other options. Those are just the ones that don't make it.

'Sometimes, in some of the more terrifying cases, it's the parents who see that their little boy is suddenly their meal ticket and they'll never have to work again. Very often, you'll have the situation where the agent comes into the equation and he makes promises that either he can't keep or, frankly, he never had any intention of keeping. I've seen that numerous times where some lad at 16 or 18 has been promised the moon on a stick. There's a commonality here, which is the player's at the centre and there's no one truly independent there to give them advice or help.'

Hall also reiterates the common theme that clubs just wash their hands of players. Some retired professionals I spoke to didn't see anything wrong in this, citing that companies in other industries generally don't take an interest in their employees' financial affairs. But with the game awash with money and careers so short, surely it's in the best interests of clubs to protect their assets?

'Clubs don't get involved. It's been floated in the past about how contracts could be re-modelled to have a percentage of money put into a trust, for example, which would pass to the player at a certain age,' says James. 'There's no appetite for that and even then you have to encourage everyone to get on board. You've got the player who's not that bothered one way or the other because he's just been promised a great new boot deal, the agent's not all that interested because it might affect his income and the club seem to think, "Well, this seems a bit complicated so we're not that bothered."

'Some clubs are much better at this but the majority of clubs just aren't interested in that side of it. As far as they're concerned, as long as they honour their contractual obligations with the player then that's it, they're off the hook.'

Former Ipswich Town and Charlton Athletic midfielder Matt Holland agrees. 'Clubs never really advised us. Agents tend to help players, putting them in front of a financial advisor. The PFA came into the clubs and tried to help and advise but, again, in your early 20s you're not really thinking about retirement, you're thinking year by year. If you've got a two-year contract, you're thinking about those two years, you're not thinking about what it's going to be like when you finish,' he admits.

It's essential that players plan for retirement but of course many don't, unwilling to admit that some day they'll have to hang up their boots.

'When the single greatest income source is the player's contract and that goes, well you've got to rely on that player having kept enough money back and saved up,' says James. 'There's so many problems around that. It may be the player did very well but they didn't preserve their wealth. Maybe they had a profligate lifestyle, maybe they invested in the wrong thing, maybe they were encouraged to invest in things that weren't suitable and that investment has failed altogether or may be locked in for a period.'

Hall is dubious of the widely-publicised film schemes which some players have got embroiled in and is not surprised at what's transpired. 'I spend a lot of my time with financial advisors and dealing with them. I can honestly say I never in my entire career met a financial advisor who was in any way reputable that believes in the benefits of film schemes. They were always seen as extremely high risk, and footballers wouldn't be aware of this. You've got a type of investment which is very high risk, and, in theory, very high return but by nature of that high risk that return is unlikely to be seen. The person selling that investment will earn enormous commission. They will regrettably almost certainly share that commission with the agent. It's the player who loses.'

In many cases agents are not looking after their players' interests as they should.

'Agents don't understand the nature of fiduciary for the most part,' reveals James. 'The vast majority don't understand they're there to represent their player and no one else, they're not there to line their own pockets. Under the old regulations, contracts with agents were fixed at two years. A two-year contract with someone is not going to lend itself to long-term thinking and planning. There are lots of really good agents out there but there are some that are the absolute stereotype. The really terrible ones, you look at some of the things they do and all you need is some evidence of a breach of fiduciary duty and you could then change the world for people. Half the time players suspect something is going on, but the attitude is, "Better the devil I know." That's no way to handle your affairs.'

Duality is also an increasing problem, where agents sometimes act for the player and also a club when negotiating a contract or transfer. 'It's a total conflict of interest. There's always a big question mark over the permissibility of it. The general feeling seems to be that as long as the player and club are fully informed then it's okay. I don't think it ever can be. It's much more prevalent than people believe. How can you possibly do your best by someone if you're being paid by someone else?'

So, what advice would James give to a player starting his career to ensure he doesn't suffer financially in retirement, as many do?

'The first thing I'd always say to a young footballer is to not only get advice but get your *own* advice. Don't rely on everyone doing everything for you. I think that's the most important thing you can ever say. If you want a lawyer, for example, call up the Law Society, get yourself your own solicitor, not someone who was put in front of you by someone else who's already in the frame. If you've got concerns, if you're even vaguely bothered about something, don't just rely on someone put in front of you by someone who you think you can trust. I know this sounds ridiculously paranoid, I appreciate that, but to a degree you have to be like that.'

James reveals that the 'macho nonsense around football' sometimes results in players not including their loved ones in life-changing decisions. 'It's not a sign of weakness to have your wife or your partner go over the papers with you or sit down in a meeting with you. Whenever I act for players, I try and always ensure their other half is with them because everything they're doing affects their whole family.'

He continues that players should 'always ask people to disclose to you if they've been paid any fees or commission, directly or indirectly, to be introduced to you. Players also have to accept there's no magic bullet for them in the financial world. You actually do have to pay some tax, you can't have a miracle. They should never be afraid to change their advisors if they think their advisors aren't keeping their promises. They should always get the basics right before they go for flashy extras or silly investments. Make sure you have a decent, reputable financial advisor, an accountant, a lawyer and actually engage with them, really be involved with them – this is your life you're talking about here.'

As many others have said, Hall agrees that the most important thing is to have a plan. 'If it doesn't work out, what are you going to do? We only need so many coaches, pundits and managers. When you retire, what else are you going to do? And that's not just from the financial perspective, but also doing something with your life and being mentally healthy.

'Pre-Premier League, it always used to be that when a footballer retired, he opened a pub. These days they think they don't have to do anything because they've got so much money but, as we've seen, there's so much that can come back to bite them and that network that was supposed to help and support them has disappeared.'

Peer pressure in dressing rooms is also a major factor with many young players conscious of keeping up with the Phil or Kenwyne Joneses. 'Any agent or financial advisor wants the captain on their books. If they can get the biggest voice in the dressing room, they have got a good chance of winning a lot of the other lads, especially the younger ones. Peer pressure is enormous in football.'

Dan Clay agrees that advisors often target the 'one person everyone listens to' in the dressing room. 'If he does it, everyone will look at it and say, "I'll have a piece of that." An advisor will get to the right person in the club and get him to do something on the basis that he won't charge him a fee, but takes a whopping fee off everybody else that gets involved in it. Purely because the figures are so big. So you'll get financial advisors, banks, accountants and tax advisors trying to put them into tax schemes, by virtue of the fact that they'll be earning fairly hefty commissions off the back of them. And once an advisor is in at a club, it's very easy to filter through to all the players and put everyone into the same schemes.'

Hall and Clay both concede there are many good agents out there. Robert Segal of Impact Sports Management represents several Premier League players and managers and is on the Board of the Association of Football Agents. The impressive young Tottenham and England midfielder Dele Alli counts among his most recent clients. He is 'disappointingly, not surprised' by XPRO's statistics but is staggered by the fall-out from the aforementioned film schemes.

'There's a lot of players who get taken for a ride with mis-advice by independent financial advisors [IFAs],' says Robert. 'This week alone there was the classic case involving the film schemes. It's scandalous.'

Robert agrees with James Hall that it isn't just a problem in football. 'This happens with actors, musicians and generally people in the entertainment business,' he explains. 'They concentrate on entertaining and leave the other side of it to their management. This is rife in all walks of life. It just so happens that when most people are building their businesses between the ages of 30 and 50, for footballers that's when it's all ended.

'They've got to be gathering in their money for their family's future at a very early age, when most people aren't mature enough to even understand that.

'The majority of problems are bad investments, and that can be anything from tax schemes to property. Also, retrospective taxation doesn't help. There are plenty of footballers out there who are very, very wealthy. Wealthier than when they were playing. But, unfortunately, if you add it all up, I think you'll find that more are down than up.'

As aforementioned, many footballers were affected by the property crash in 2008 and have found it difficult to recover. 'A lot of people were caught by that but, whereas you've got property developers that live to fight another day, when a footballer's done it then that's it, he's done. He's got no earning capacity at that level to try and salvage the situation,' says Robert.

His main advice to young footballers to ensure financial stability in retirement tallies with James Hall's. 'Firstly, I would say get independent financial advice with somebody of high standing. Also, invest within your means. When people say you're going to get back so much money, with so little outlay, just be very, very careful. I would sit players down and let them see two or three IFAs, who over the years have proven themselves to be steady and they can decide which one they want. Have an accountant double-check everything is absolutely the golden rule.'

However, he can understand clubs' reluctance to get involved in players planning for retirement. 'It's very difficult for a club to prepare a player for the long term when they know that there's every chance that the player will leave before the end of his present contract anyway,' he explains. 'The days of testimonials and being able to plan like that are long gone. The club aren't going to be too interested in what they do after leaving the club.'

Peer pressure in the dressing room might result in financial losses but social influences of another kind can have even more drastic consequences. Mark Ward enjoyed a relatively successful career, starring for the likes of West Ham, Manchester City and Everton before retiring in 1998. After a nomadic few years taking in outposts in America, Scandinavia and Asia, the Scouser was offered a coaching role in Sydney. And that's when it all went so terribly wrong.

4

How Do Retired Footballers End Up In Prison?

L ESS than two miles north of Everton's Goodison Park lies Walton Prison. A taxi ride between the two takes about five minutes, but Mark Ward travelled a more circuitous route. Eleven years on from marauding down the right wing for the Toffees in the Premier League, he found himself locked up in the notorious prison's B-wing.

How he got there is a salutary tale for young footballers on the benefits of financial planning for retirement. Ward readily admits that, as a player, he was a 'spender rather than a saver'. His peak earnings were £2,000 a week, which worked out at around £1,200 after tax. 'But, even then, you try and live up to that lifestyle of a footballer, the holidays and nice things,' he admits. Even while he was impressing in the top flight and being talked of as an England international, Ward willingly admits he was living beyond his means.

'People say to me, "Would you love to be playing now?" and the only reason I would is that the money is 20 or 40 times more than what I was on,' he admits. 'As regards playing the game, I'd rather have played when I did. The money was never great but, to be honest, when I started playing I never played for money. It was just a thing I wanted to do.'

He discloses that when John Lyall signed him for West Ham, who he helped to a club best league finish in 1986, he didn't even look at the amount he was signing for.

'He came to the house to pick me up, sat me down and there was no agent – I just signed. And that's the way it was. I'd have signed for nothing to play for Everton because I was a supporter. You wouldn't get that now, the game has changed. It's a business. I never treated it as a business, or a job. I only had an agent later in my career, as the game had already changed by then, but even then I never argued about how much I should have been on.' Mark recalls that he was on around £300 a week at West Ham when he first signed. 'You don't say that you're not signing for that, it's just the way it was. That was why agents really became involved in the game, because the clubs were exploiting footballers. But then it just went the other way, where footballers have got too much power now.'

As his playing career neared its end, he was 'clinging on to football, playing as much as I could' and travelling to the likes of Scotland, Iceland and Hong Kong for short spells 'just to get a kick of a ball'.

He'd always planned to embark on a management or coaching career after his playing days ended, and still harbours hopes of going back to it. Ward won the old Second Division as player-coach with Birmingham City, but Barry Fry, their manager at the time, didn't renew his contract. 'I always thought I was the natural successor to take over from him. After six weeks at the club, he'd already accused me of trying to take his job. That wasn't the case as I wasn't ready for management. I was player-coach, I'd just left a big club in Everton and was there to do a job. And I did a great job, we won the Second Division, went to Wembley, it couldn't have gone better for us.'

He felt a lot of managers, for purely selfish reasons, were reluctant to sign a veteran player who'd played at the top level. 'You're always a threat, especially in the lower leagues,' he says, with managers feeling their job may become vulnerable with an experienced, successful pro at the club.

He played non-league football, before getting his break as player-manager at Altrincham. 'That was the start of my managerial career, where I was hoping to do well and progress, but I had a bad experience.' The chairman who'd appointed him resigned shortly afterwards, having been at the club for years.

'Another chairman, who was a director, got involved and wanted his dad in charge. I went to the PFA and it was just a bad experience. I got sacked because I'd sold a player to Leicester City in the Premier League, sold my best player to Macclesfield and sold my captain to Northwich, so I'd brought in about 150 grand to keep the club afloat. But when you're working with people like that, it does make you angry because of the effects afterwards of not knowing the difficulties about getting another job. People would start asking questions about why I was sacked. It was a big blow for me when Altrincham did that to me.'

Ward had been planning to build a young, talented side, bringing in youngsters on loan from Liverpool and Everton. 'In hindsight, I took the job open to a future in management and coaching but there's only so many jobs that go around. There are some great ex-players out there who can't get on to the network.'

He struggled to get another management role after his experience at Altrincham, and agrees with others I've spoken to that it's often a case of who you know, rather than what you know on the managerial and coaching merry-go-round. 'When a manager gets the sack, he'll move on to another club and bring staff along who they've been friendly with during the course of their careers.'

Ward's eventual retirement from the game hit him hard. 'Certain players can't deal with the vast void. I loved training, I was first in and last to go. You don't realise until it's over that it's a big part of your life – the banter in the dressing room, the day-to-day involvement with other players, the sort of discipline that you need to be a footballer. Once that's gone or you're not involved on a full-time basis you start scratching your head and wondering, "Well, what am I going to do now?" If you haven't planned for life after football, which I didn't do financially, it's a major factor in why retired players make the bad decisions like I did.

'It's a difficult life when you finish. Some players go on to do media work or remain in the game coaching or managing, which is great as it's just a natural progression. But sometimes you're not that lucky and you don't get the right breaks. I made some terrible choices. I always feel for Gazza [Paul Gascoigne]. He was a very emotional player and that's why he got into trouble. He misses the game. He finds it difficult to cope without it.'

With this great emptiness in his life upon retirement, Ward admits that he turned to alcohol. 'I bought a pub and starting drinking a lot. And that was just the start of my slide. I hung around with the wrong people, neglected the disciplined approach I had to eating and drinking as a player and it was all a big mistake.'

Like many others of his era he didn't receive much assistance from his employers on the effects of retirement. 'Looking back, football clubs were quite ignorant in that they weren't there to help players when they finished. They should be educating players and telling them this career doesn't last forever.'

A chance encounter with an old school friend, Peter Jones, led to a stay in Sydney and a chance for Mark to turn his life around. He arrived in Coogee Bay with £2,000 given to him by family and friends, the equivalent of his peak weekly wages as a player, and the chance to start afresh.

'I wasn't that interested but Peter said I could run a soccer school over there. I went over and absolutely loved the place. I was 42 at the time and my holiday visa was running out. I went down to Immigration with Peter and the immigration officer turned around and told me, because of my age, I'd need a distinguished talent visa. "If he's good at something we might be interested in keeping him," she said. Peter replied, "He scored the goal in the derby! He scored the goal in the derby! That's how good he is!" She just looked at him blankly as if to say, "What are you talking about?"'

After just three months he returned home to Merseyside to sort out a long-term visa. And that's when it all started to unravel. After a spell in hospital with a suspected bleed to the brain, Ward was desperate to gather the money required to return to Sydney and made a decision that would define his future.

'That's when I was offered some money by people to rent out a property. A couple of them used to go to my brother's pub and they offered me around £500 a week to rent the house for six months.'

He feels he was an easy target, being at a low ebb and in dire need of the money to fund an Antipodean return. They told him they would be using the house as a 'stash' and Ward, regrettably, didn't ask any further questions.

'I gave them a separate key and that was it. But people like that need vulnerable people like me. The people I became involved with had already been under observation by the police. I was worried after a month when I found out what was going on.'

What was going on was a massive operation, with drug-manufacturing equipment littered throughout the house. He knew it was only a matter of time before he was going to be arrested. That moment came on 12 May 2005, the day Malcolm Glazer won control of Manchester United. It would also have been the 69th birthday of Mark's late father, William.

Ward, who was attending a funeral that morning, received a call from the letting agency to inform him that the burglar alarm was going off at the rented property and that police were outside. He realised the game was up. He was arrested on suspicion of possession of a controlled drug with intent to supply.

'People ask me why did I do it? I didn't do it because I was a drug dealer,' he explains. 'They gave me the money to go to an estate agent to rent a property in my name. Who on Earth would rent a property in their own name and then put four kilos of cocaine in it? It was only being let for six months and I thought I'd be out of it then.

'I still think on the day of sentencing the police wanted me to get even more, because I got 12 years originally, and I pleaded guilty at the first opportunity so got one third off the sentence. I got an eight-year sentence, and did four. When they all got arrested, ten months later, there were nine of them – Operation Vatican it was called – the main men got 11-, ten- and nine-year sentences for five seizures of drugs. I got hammered with mine.

'The police knew that the drugs weren't mine because they'd been following the property. They knew whose drugs they were, but they had to deal with me on my own because I wouldn't disclose who I rented the property for. I just had to take it on the chin.'

I asked Mark why he didn't reveal who he'd rented the property for but it wasn't as simple as that. 'If you live in the real world, I wanted to do my sentence and come out without another sentence hanging over me,' he says. 'I didn't want to be looking over my shoulder while I was in prison and out of it.'

His first stay was in Walton Prison. Now known as HM Prison Liverpool, it houses some of north-west England's most notorious criminals, with a damning report in 2015 calling it 'dirty, overcrowded and unsafe'. Ward, associated with the number seven shirt throughout his career, was identified as prisoner number NM6982.

'That is a tough prison. Cockroaches, the food is terrible, the violence. I ended up in the lifers' wing for the first couple of nights and I thought to myself, "Fuck it, I haven't killed anyone!" But it's more disciplined there because everyone has been sentenced.'

There is emotion in his voice when he recalls his fellow prisoners who killed themselves. 'What amazed me more than anything in the place was the amount of suicides. There were six while I was there on the B-wing, including two in a week. I ended up in the cell of a "number one" prisoner, he'd been there for four years and was due to be released. He hung himself the day before he was to be released. I ended up in his cell the next day with my mate.'

Ward quickly decided to keep his head down and not get into any further bother. 'In prison you've got to fight for everything and I was always a fighter all my life, so I thought to myself, "I'm going to do my prison as best I can and not get into any trouble," which is very easy to do. But I wasn't gonna lick anyone's arse, the screws and that.' He stuck by the rules for the most part, aside from securing a £350 old Nokia phone from a fellow inmate, and the rather unpleasant concealment of a SIM card in his foreskin.

He dedicated his spell in Walton Prison to keeping fit and his 'time went quite quickly'. Ward was moved to an open prison and found work in a church and on a building site as part of a community pay-back charity scheme. 'I wasn't a threat to society. But them two years went quite slowly. Even though you're out in the community, you still have to go back to the prison. But I was grateful for it.'

Inside, he wrote the book *Hammered* about his time in prison as 'it gave me something else to do'. He didn't finish it until well after he left prison, after finding work on a building site upon his release.

That release came in May 2009 and Mark made a vow that he'd never return to prison after seeing several fellow inmates repeatedly return after only a short spell of freedom. 'I'd see lads go and then a couple of weeks later they're back in again! I'm just taking the positives from being in prison.'

A lot of people have suggested to him that he should go into clubs and speak to young players about his experiences and the dangers of retirement. 'I'd love to go in and be able to say to them, "This was me and this is what happened to me and these are the pitfalls that can happen to you." Because I've been there and done it all.'

Mark admits his former team-mates were 'gobsmacked and gutted' about his incarceration, but he keeps in touch with many of them, particularly his former West Ham colleagues. He does some work for the club and is involved on the after-dinner speaking circuit but admits he's found it hard to find employment due to his criminal record.

'It's been difficult. When you've been in prison, it doesn't matter if you've been a footballer. The only time I've got a job since prison, whether it be painting or on building sites, is from people who have known me through football. When I apply for a job online, you have to disclose your criminal record. It's so difficult to get a job. When you get out of prison, there's certain things you need. You need a roof over your head, a job and someone to love.'

He sees the victims of his crimes as his family and friends. 'I hurt them so much. You do victim awareness courses and things like that but I still argue the case that, directly, my family were my victims.'

Mark's advice for young players would be to, 'Enjoy your career, work hard, listen to coaches but, first and foremost, have enough money put aside or get into business. There's so many who went the other way from the likes of Robbie Fowler. I see a lot of players from my day who didn't earn enough to retire so they all have to still work and graft. My advice to young players would be to plan financially for when their football careers ends, and it can finish at any time through injury. We all want to be managers and coaches and work for Sky. But it might not happen.'

I felt quite sympathetic towards Mark after speaking to him. It's quite easy to read headlines like 'Ex-Premier League Star On Cocaine Charges' and quickly make judgements. But he's admitted he made a terrible mistake, has served his time diligently and acknowledges the suffering he's brought to his loved ones. It'd be nice to think that his idea of visiting clubs and speaking to young players about the perils of retirement might one day come to fruition.

Joey Barton is another footballer who's spent some time inside Walton Prison, in his case for common assault and affray outside a McDonald's in Liverpool. Indeed, you can compile a pretty handy team of footballers who've served prison time during their playing careers. The likes of Tony Adams, Duncan Ferguson and Jan Molby have all spent time inside for various misdemeanours, but for many like Ward it's when they finish playing that their problems with the law begin.

Peter Storey was an Arsenal legend in the 1960s and 70s, renowned as a hatchet man throughout the Football League.

He won the Double with the Gunners in 1971 and earned 19 caps for England before his career, excuse the pun, petered out at Fulham. Like many players of that era, he initially chose to spend his retirement as a pub landlord but his life soon spiralled out of control. He was charged with conspiracy to counterfeit money and, in order to raise funds to flee to Spain, he decided to open a brothel. Storey was sentenced to three years' imprisonment but his incarceration in Wandsworth Prison didn't halt his criminal career.

He was later handed a suspended sentence for stealing two cars and spent a further month in prison for trying to smuggle 20 porn videos into England, which were hidden in the spare tyre of his car.

The paths of Peter Storey and Robin Friday crossed briefly, in a 1974 friendly match between Arsenal and Reading. Friday's unsung talent was the subject of a biography, *The Greatest Footballer You Never Saw*, and the cover of a Super Furry Animals single called 'The Man Don't Give a Fuck'. And he certainly didn't. The image shows him giving the V-sign to a goalkeeper in celebration of a goal, which landed him a two-match ban and was symbolic of his career.

The maverick player was fond of a drink, as the 'mild' and 'bitter' tattoos on his chest attested, and he spent some time in borstal as a teenager before embarking on a career in professional football that never really lived up to his undoubted potential.

He once celebrated a goal by kissing a policeman but immediately regretted it as he 'hated coppers so much'. His career ended at 25 as he struggled with his demons. After spending time in prison for impersonating a police officer so he could confiscate people's drugs, he died aged 38 from a suspected heroin overdose.

You may have heard of Robin Friday, but Justin Geor-celin's name probably won't ring a bell unless you were a fan of Championship Manager 2001/02. Or, perhaps, a Northampton law enforcer. The talented striker was a must-buy on the management simulation game, becoming a world star no matter what side you captured him for. Championship Manager, and its successor Football Manager, have fine records of predicting future wonderkids long before they make their club's first team with Lionel Messi, Neymar and Vincent Kompany among their many successful predictions of future stars.

Such is their success that many top football clubs use Football Manager's database as a scouting tool. However, even the game's prescient developers couldn't have predicted how Georcelin's career would pan out.

Unfortunately, the striker's potential in real life was cut short after falling in with the wrong crowd while a youngster at Northampton Town. The forward soon developed a £500-a-day crack habit and resorted to getting involved in knife attacks on taxi drivers to fund this. He was sentenced to nine years in prison.

Medi Abalimba was so keen to maintain a footballer's lifestyle that he even resorted to pretending he was still playing – only as someone else. As a once-promising career began to fail, the former Derby County and Oldham Athletic player took to impersonating Hebei China Fortune winger Gaël Kakuta, running up extravagant bills to sustain a lavish lifestyle. A clever choice, considering that even most Chelsea fans probably wouldn't recognise Kakuta, who cost their club a transfer ban following his acrimonious move from French club Lens in 2007.

Passing himself off as the Frenchman, who was then at Stamford Bridge, Abalimba ran up £20,000 shopping sprees, blew thousands on champagne and even hired a helicopter. It all caught up with him in 2014 when he admitted to 12 offences of fraud and dishonesty and was jailed for four years.

Roy Keane revealed in his first autobiography that he didn't have any of his Manchester United team-mates' phone numbers. He did, however, keep in touch with a former Nottingham Forest colleague, whom he helped when he fell on hard times. Gary Charles and Keane roomed together at Forest under Brian Clough and remained in touch despite their careers progressing in different directions. Charles is probably best remembered for being on the end of an horrendous tackle from Paul Gascoigne in the 1991 FA Cup Final that resulted in a lengthy injury for Gazza and almost scuppered his big-money move to Lazio. The defender soon suffered his own injury problems, which began a downward spiral that culminated in several spells in prison.

Charles battled with alcohol during his career and spent six months in prison in 2004 for dangerous driving and failing to provide a breath specimen. He was later jailed for threatening a nightclub bouncer while serving a suspended sentence. While inside, he received a letter from Keane promising his support upon Charles's release. True to his word, the then-Sunderland manager offered his former team-mate a place to stay as he adjusted to life outside the penal system. In sentencing for the latter offence, the judge commented, 'There really does come a time when the police and everyone else have to have a rest from Gary Charles. I hope it knocks some sense into his head.' It seems to have worked as Charles has since completed his coaching badges and taken an Open University degree on substance abuse.

Michael Branch was deemed a special talent as a youngster at Everton but the headlines surrounding him ended up more 'Drugs Squad' than 'Special Branch'. A ten-year-old Wayne Rooney had posters of Branch on his bedroom wall and the striker had a blistering start to his Everton career before having little impact at a series of clubs such as Wolves, Birmingham City and Bradford City. Branch played for the

Toffees in the 1999 Merseyside derby where Robbie Fowler was subsequently punished for mimicking the snorting of cocaine on one of the white lines at Anfield. Fowler had been responding to unfounded allegations of drug-taking, but Branch was to get into much more bother in relation to the same substance.

Aged 37, the striker should be retiring around now and looking back on a glittering career. However, he had descended into a world of crime and was sentenced to seven years for supply of Class A and Class B drugs in 2012. He had been caught with cocaine worth £160,000 in his home, after earlier being seen handing over a bag containing three kilos of amphetamine to a man in a Liverpool pub's car park.

The above stories are all unique, but for the vast majority of the nigh-on 150 former footballers currently residing at Her Majesty's pleasure, there is one unifying factor – drugs. As we saw in the opening chapter of this book, almost 90 per cent of these are under 25 with a similar figure, coincidentally, locked up for drug-related offences.

Branch is just one of over 100 former footballers XPRO's chief executive Geoff Scott has visited in prison. XPRO believes that the salaries doled out by clubs to young players, which are totally out of sync with those of their peers in other walks of life, are a large factor in contributing to this problem. A young player, groomed by their club since childhood, has solely focused on a career in the game. They generally have no education to fall back on, so when they're one of the 98 per cent to be jettisoned between the ages of 16 and 21 panic sets in – remember only two per cent of 16-year-olds on a club's books are still playing professionally by the age of 21. For the 22 players on the pitch in the next match you watch, consider that there are another 1,100 who were churned out and discarded by professional football before getting the proverbial key of the door.

They had been earning a relatively decent salary, but that's no longer there. How can they maintain the lifestyle they've become accustomed to? Sadly, for many, they turn to drugs. This is the common story among those who Geoff Scott and XPRO assist.

Geoff believes it's very simple to understand why so many young players end up in the penal system. 'Boys are taken out of the normal education system at the age of seven. They are embedded into academy systems from that age. So they're exposed from a very, very early age to the possibility that they may become pro footballers. They all probably believe that. And so do the parents, probably even more so. By the time the young guys get to scholar level they've been at the training ground, they've been treated like gods, they're exposed to what young pros and seasoned pros acquire in terms of wealth. They see the clothes, they see the brands, they see the Range Rovers and the Porsche Cayennes in the car park and they believe that some day this is all going to be theirs.

'At a certain age, they go to a school that's chosen by the football club. Manchester City, for example, put all their lads at St Bede's, and they go there three days a week. Which means two days a week, they're not being educated. At that point when they've been given umpteen pairs of boots, they have had their teeth done, they live a very healthy life, they've everything done for them – are they really concentrating on the education that's put in front of them? They're taken out of ordinary life. What damage is it doing to the young person, who's not able to mix with friends or people of the same age who are doing something completely different? They only mix with people from the academy, so they have no experience of life skills.'

What hope have these young players of actually making it? One of XPRO's ambassadors is Kevin Campbell, the former Arsenal and Everton striker. Kevin's son Tyrese is a centre-forward with the Manchester City academy but Geoff is pessimistic about the chances afforded to young English players in the modern game. 'Are City going to develop that boy into their first team? Or is the next foreign manager going to spend £50m on the finished article? Do they have the time to develop these young boys? Probably not. But these lads have the ability, they should be developed. If our English academy players are only ending up in Leagues 1 and 2, what's the point? To be at a Premier League club for ten years and reach the age of 17, and told you're not going to make it and, "By the way, because you've been mollycoddled at a Premier League club you're not ready for the rough and tumble of the lower leagues," it's devastating. It's a massive adjustment to make.'

If they are lucky enough they will be retained as a scholar and then a young pro – young pros aged 15 or 16 in the Premier League now start on a minimum of £2,000 per week. 'If they then don't get retained or lose their contract, their brain is already thinking, "I want this wealth, I want the trappings of it." Most of them then go back to their local environment,' reveals Geoff. 'And a lot of them come from inner-city working class environments, where some of their previous class-mates are already dealing in drugs. So, they're exposed to this drug culture and we've found that for a package of cocaine, for example, delivered from Liverpool to Birmingham you will get paid £1,000–£1,500. You don't even need to know what's in it.'

In many cases these young men aren't really bothered as to what's inside these packages, it's more a case of how many packages they can deliver in a week. 'In working with the Serious Organised Crime Authority [SOCA] and the police, we've found they tend to let any drug dealer accumulate material wealth and, therefore, allow a few deliveries to go through,' says Geoff. 'The more wealth they've got and the more they catch them with, then the bigger the proceeds of crime bond is placed on them and also the bigger the prison sentence. So they get the drug dealer off the street for a longer period.

'The majority of the guys under 25 that we've visited have fallen into this situation. It's exactly the same scenario. There are a few of them who have also got a gambling habit, and they've used the drug industry to pay off their gambling debt. All but one or two have never actually taken drugs at all, they're literally just delivering it. The most common crime is the possession of with the intent to supply drugs. Depending on the amount they're caught with, and the value of that amount, tends to determine the prison sentence. But most of the guys we've seen are serving six to eight years, that seems to be standard, of which they will serve half of that and the rest on licence.'

XPRO has only been involved in this for two years so it's too early to look at figures on recidivism, but the handful who have been released in that time have not re-offended.

'Our role in this is to work with them and the prison service, take advantage of the education programmes available in the prison system and to encourage them to enrol in an education course that's going to result in a job or being able to go on to further education when they are released,' said Geoff.

XPRO has excellent links with blue chip companies who are willing to give a second chance to young former footballers who've been to prison and have already had some success stories with former players who've gone on to be personal trainers and taken psychology degrees.

Geoff feels there's not enough realism among young players and the education that's provided by clubs isn't useful enough. One of the former players he's helped revealed, 'The qualification I got [a BTEC in Sports Media], at the age when I was released, I found I was underqualified in an oversaturated industry. There were people younger than me in the job queue getting jobs so the only job available to me was shelf-stacking jobs in Tesco. So, when I was given the opportunity to earn £1,000 I took it.'

'There's not enough awareness of what happens when you retire,' says Geoff. 'That's where football can help, and that's where we can help football because we've got experience. If you don't make it, you've got to prepare for that as much as you prepare for what you do on the football pitch.'

Geoff believes that the FA and the PFA are spending enough on education but they're not spending it in the right areas. 'Perhaps the money would be better spent working with the individuals to work towards getting a job or getting used to the fact that they might need to re-train if they don't get a professional contract.'

As mentioned earlier, Michael Kinsella was a promising young goalkeeper who was on Liverpool's books as a schoolboy but never made it professionally. He played in Liverpool's youth team with Jamie Carragher before drifting down the lower leagues with the likes of Bury and Tranmere Rovers. Before long, he had turned to a life of crime.

He established Onside Academy four years ago after serving four prison sentences, in Holland, Spain and England. His aim was to prevent other young footballers from pursuing the same path, by aiding the transition from being a footballer into finding a career outside of the game. He accepts that he was responsible for his own downfall but that if an organisation such as Onside had been around when he was playing it may have prevented some of his difficulties. He agrees that the expectation levels of youngsters, signed by clubs at under ten years of age only to be released in their late teens, are sometimes unrealistic. 'There's an expectation of glamour,' he says. 'But it's not always like that.'

He played a lot of semi-pro football and suggests that many of the players at that level were just as good as those at professional clubs but 'they just hadn't been spotted'. He's now also working with several players released by clubs as well as semi-pro footballers to help establish a full-time playing career and feels the success of the likes of Jamie Vardy and Dele Alli may lead to a trend of top clubs taking a punt on lower-league and non-league talents. One of these includes his brother Gerard, who played for Everton's youth team alongside Ross Barkley. He'd been with the club since he was seven but a series of injuries led to David Moyes releasing him at 19. Gerard helps his sibling run the academy, which has already secured professional and semi-professional contracts as well as university places for some of its graduates.

XPRO is also seeing the fruits of its tireless work with young offenders who have been discarded by football. The below is a case study from a player whom XPRO has helped that is sadly typical of the young former players who've been abandoned by football and resorted to crime. However, it also highlights the success of XPRO's work. The player's name has been changed to protect his identity.

* * *

Peter House will never forget the day he was told he would not be offered a professional contract. Rejection, an alien word for a player who had sailed through the age groups, captaining all of his academy teams and representing England at youth level before winning a scholarship, triggered an acute sense of failure that would ultimately see his life unravel. After two suicide attempts, House drifted into a life of crime, dealing drugs until hitting rock bottom when he was given an eight-year prison sentence. 'I just couldn't cope with being rejected,' he reflects. 'Everything I'd worked and lived for, just taken away during the course of a conversation. Eight or nine years, for what?'

A talented defender, House had joined one of the north-east's biggest clubs shortly before his ninth birthday. Training three nights a week and playing matches at the weekend, he went on to represent England at under-14 and under-15 level and by 16 was offered a scholarship. Within 12 months, he had captained the reserve team. A career in football beckoned.

Born into a working-class Catholic family in the Low Fell area of Newcastle upon Tyne, money had always been scarce. House's father, a former coal worker, was long-term unemployed, his mother a nursing assistant at the local hospital. Together they had four children to support. Yet now, with House's prospects of becoming a professional within touching distance, the club was bending over to offer the family financial assistance.

'I'd been courted with football boots and things like that when I was eight by different clubs looking to sign me but now, at 16, 17, my father was being made a scout and put on the club's payroll,' House recalls.

A turning point would come when the club signed another defender from Africa. Accommodation and employment were quickly found for his family and he became a direct rival for House's position in the team. Then, at the end of the season, came the news every aspiring footballer dreads. 'I was told I wouldn't be getting a contract because they'd reached the full allocation of players in my position,' he says. 'I was devastated, felt like a complete failure. Within a month my dad's role as a scout also ended. The club paid me the equivalent of the first year of the professional contract and I tried to find a job but I couldn't even contemplate playing non-league football.

'I'd been around the first team. I'd witnessed first-hand those trappings of wealth and success and had craved the chance of achieving the same. I felt tremendous guilt, like I'd let all of my family down.'

As a youngster, House had excelled at school but his studies had gradually been neglected as he strived to become a footballer and, by his late teenage years, his qualifications were worse than even the poorest of those former class-mates he had once outshone.

'I'd known nothing else but football and before long I was very depressed,' he says. He twice tried to take his own life before resorting to pushing drugs. Each week he would drive from Newcastle to Lincoln to deliver cocaine. Every delivery earned him £1,500. 'Some weeks I'd earn £3,000,' he says.

The life of a drug dealer would soon catch up with him and House was eventually caught and jailed. Prison would prove a sobering experience but his depression was so severe, his sense of guilt so pronounced, that the recovery process was slow and painful. When XPRO learned of House's plight, it was quick to offer support. House was encouraged to take advantage of one of the prison's education programmes as he attempted to rebuild his shattered confidence. By the time he was released from prison he had received his Level 4 accountancy qualifications and, at present, is training towards becoming a chartered accountant. Now 22, he wants to specialise in the sports and entertainment industry. 'It has been a long road to get here,' he says. 'There was a time when I doubted I ever would.'

As for football? 'I haven't kicked a ball since being released,' he says.

5

D.I.V.O.R.C.E.

THE Japanese seem to have a condition for everything. Tourists vacationing in the capital of France sometimes suffer from Paris Syndrome, basically an acute form of culture shock brought about by actually being present in a city that is so idealised in Japanese advertising. It has become so prevalent that the Japanese Embassy has set up a 24-hour helpline for sufferers. This might explain why no Japanese footballer has ever prospered in France, with only one of the five who have played in Ligue 1 lasting more than one season. Even then, Daisuke Matsui played for four sides – Le Mans, Saint-Étienne, Grenoble and Dijon – in just four seasons.

Taijin Kyofusho is another condition peculiar to Japan. Roughly translated as 'the disorder of fear', it's a social anxiety where the sufferer worries that their body parts or functions may displease, offend or embarrass others. This may lead to Hikikomori, a phenomenon where people become reclusive and withdraw from society for periods of over six months. Its main victims seem to be young men, with the Japanese Cabinet Office estimating that over 700,000 are affected.

Another syndrome that originated in the Land of the Rising Sun was first identified in 1991 by Dr Nobuo Kurokawa, who noticed a surge in women reporting to him with similar symptoms. Their illness was characterised by depression, skin rashes, asthma, ulcers and high blood pressure. The patients also had one other thing in common – their spouses had recently finished, or were nearing the end of, their working lives. They were, felt Dr Kurokawa, suffering from Retired Husband Syndrome.

Japanese society is still dominated by strong traditional gender roles, where the husband is expected to be the main breadwinner while his wife remains as the homemaker. A typical male in Japan will often work long hours as a salaryman, frequently remaining with the same company for his entire career. I read somewhere that if you ring a Japanese office at 10pm, it's very likely someone will be there to pick up. So I tried it. And lo and behold I was greeted by a weary-sounding male voice before I promptly hung up, Japanese small-talk not being my strong point. The pressures on salarymen are so great that some die from karōshi – basically death by working too much.

With such arduous working hours and often compulsory social activities, salarymen spend very little time with their wives. So, when retirement beckons, the problems begin, with both spouses often left with the feeling that they're living with a virtual stranger. The husband, who has spent his adult life introducing himself by his first name and the company he works for, may begin to resent his loss of social status and will not be used to contributing to home life. The wife, expected by society to attend to her husband's needs, can grow resentful and find it hard to deal with the sudden change in lifestyle. It's no surprise then that divorce rates among couples of retirement age in Japan have soared, rising 300 per cent between the late 1990s and early 2000s.

There's no threat of me being able to retire any time soon, but I can only imagine how my wife would feel if I was suddenly under her feet 24/7. There are, of course, a section of men around my age who are forced to retire – professional footballers. And Retired Husband Syndrome sounds exactly like what many of their wives go through.

A retired husband, wrote Ella Harris in *Chicken Soup for the Soul*, is often a wife's full-time job. A retired footballer can also mean plenty of overtime for their spouse.

The average marriage in the UK is expected to last 32 years. While divorce rates may be rising in Japan, a 2014 report from the Office for National Statistics revealed that the divorce rate in England and Wales was nearly 20 per cent lower than it was a decade earlier. In 2012, the divorce rate stood at 10.8 for every 1,000 married people, one fifth lower than its level ten years earlier and the lowest rate in the UK since the 1970s. One explanation is the growth of cohabitation before marriage, where any unhealthy relationships have ended long before wedding bells ring. People are getting married later in life, having often used cohabitation as a marriage trial. Another more practical reason is cost. Divorces are expensive and the most common reason for divorce in the UK is money. The recession has meant that many estranged couples simply can't afford to separate.

The most recent figures for the average age at which UK males get married is 30.8 years, according to the Office for National Statistics. Of course, footballers tend to get married much earlier. Clubs welcome a settled home life, with Sir Alex Ferguson renowned for encouraging his players to settle down at an early age. Brian Clough was another who liked his charges to marry young in an attempt to keep them away from other temptations.

Quite often a player will marry their childhood sweetheart, who he will have known since before he got his first big contract. This can lead to problems down the line, when the newly-moneyed player attracts admiring glances from other women. As we saw in the opening chapter, around one in three retired footballers will be divorced within 12 months of finishing their playing career. PFA figures suggest that a shocking 75 per cent will be divorced within three years of leaving the game.

James Hall of Anthony Collins Solicitors, who offers financial advice to many clients in the football world, doesn't believe that monetary reasons are the major factor behind the high divorce rates. 'It's very rare that divorces happen because the money's switched off, but it does happen,' he explains. 'It's more often because you have someone who is an active professional individual who is constantly occupied who suddenly finds they've got nothing to do. They've got no other plan, it's the classic scenario of when someone retires and they get under their other half's feet.'

Former Republic of Ireland international Matt Holland agrees, 'I can see how people struggle, definitely. It took me a long time to get my head around retirement. Not that I was depressed, but I missed football. For me, it was always what I wanted to do, so to actually do it for a living was perfect. You spend all that time away from home and all of a sudden you're at home, under your wife's feet. Obviously, financially you're not earning the money that you were earning as a footballer and it's difficult to get your head around that as well. You can't spend as you did before. You're almost in a bubble as a footballer, everything's done for you. You're almost like a kid at school really. They look after you to the nth degree. Everything's done for you, your food, even when you're going on an away trip they bring all your passports and hand them out at the airport. So, all of a sudden, that's gone and you're in the big, bad world and you've got it all to do yourself.'

Mark Ward, the former West Ham, Manchester City and Everton midfielder, concurs that the onset of retirement can cause a huge strain on marriages, 'I often go to reunions for my old clubs. I wasn't at Everton in 1985/86 but heard a stat that, out of that whole squad, there was only one of them still with their wife.'

Former Leeds United defender Jon Newsome went through a divorce shortly after he retired in 2000 and isn't surprised by XPRO's figures. 'I can see how that happens. You can't just blame the wife, which a lot of people will do, and say, "The money stopped coming in and all of a sudden people jump ship." I'm sure that does happen on occasion but some lads find it really difficult to get their heads around the fact that they're no longer playing. Some people get into gambling, maybe alcohol and drugs and have gone down that road.

'And it's not easy to come out of football and then try to start making a career in something else. I was 30 years of age, didn't really have any academic qualifications behind me because I'd gone straight into football from the age of 15 or 16. And, all of a sudden, it's a big wide world and, just because you've played 200, 300, 400 games, that doesn't pay your mortgage, that doesn't get you a job or earn you money. So it's difficult and I can see why that statistic is what it is.'

Sometimes the transition to a new career post-retirement can take its toll on a marriage. When former England and Tottenham defender Gary Stevens retired through injury he had set his sights on a career in coaching and management. 'I knew football and I had got my coaching qualifications,' he recalls. 'My then wife actually said, "Well, if you go into coaching and management we'll never see you." So, I decided to have a go at the media and it was about the time in the early 90s when franchises were being won and lost. I did okay at it but the truth was that I was suddenly away from home a lot working for GMTV and Capital Gold in London and we were living on the south coast so you can guess that the inevitable happened. My family did break up and we ended up getting divorced.

'I'm not sure why. It's difficult to put a finger on the reason. You obviously have a huge lifestyle change. Back then in the early to mid-90s, we weren't all retiring as multi-millionaires because there wasn't that sort of money in the game. So you had to get yourself a job. I wanted to go into coaching, my family didn't think that they would see very much of me. So I did something for the family, which meant that I maybe wasn't doing what I wanted to do. So that cranks up the pressure.'

James Hall has had to contend with all sorts of scenarios involving players who find themselves in trouble as they struggle with life post-career. 'When players retire, some don't know what to do with themselves and get into awful scrapes. One chap I acted for, who was an England international, within five years of retirement had a child with another lady and his wife had no idea about it. We were talking about what he was going to do to hide that but make sure some wealth could pass to that child after he died without his wife ever finding out.'

James reveals that although pre-nuptial agreements are not technically binding in English law, they shouldn't be disregarded. 'It doesn't mean one shouldn't be put in place because it's still very persuasive on a judge if it's done fairly. It's worth thinking about. Post-nuptial agreements are ones put in place after the marriage and are perfectly legally binding. It's at that point it's about persuading the spouse that this is a good idea. The main benefit is saving on huge legal bills in the event of a divorce.'

Kevin Harris-James is head of family law at Harrison Clark Rickerbys and has vast experience in dealing with professional footballers and their spouses upon relationship breakdowns and divorces. He is registered with the FA as an approved solicitor and can understand why people would be surprised at the divorce figures for retired footballers. As an aside, I thought I'd use this opportunity as a warning that's it not a great way to start your wedding anniversary by telling your wife you 'just have to call a divorce lawyer'.

'Several things, in my experience, arise at the end of a football career,' he explains. 'The first is obviously that the marriage or relationship suffers. Secondly, I see a lot of footballers really struggling to get to grips with what life looks like after football – they hit depression, they hit drink and, on certain occasions, they hit drugs. The one then does no more than compound the other. So, even if the marriage is strong at the point at which the player has ended his career, if he hasn't come to terms with the ending of his career and he goes off the rails, then that in itself can cause the marriage to end. So it becomes a self-fulfilling prophecy.'

While many outsiders would presume that financial reasons may contribute to these marital break-ups, it's becoming more apparent from everyone I spoke to that former footballers' difficulties in adjusting to their new life can play just as big a role. 'I've seen both,' says Kevin. 'I've seen the footballer's wife who has had the good life, the nice house and they've lived from day to day, spending most of their money and not really having prepared for life after football. So, when the financial reality hits home, it's the wife who leaves because she wants to go off in search of that same sort of lifestyle, which the player can't offer her any more. And I've also seen the other side where it's the player who struggles and goes off the rails and it's him who ultimately leaves his wife. It's 50/50, to be honest.'

As I'd already learned from several people with first-hand experience, many players are just not prepared for the vast change that retirement brings. 'They live in a bubble,' says Kevin. 'There are two sorts of footballers. There is the footballer who has had a career but never earned a great deal of money and there's the super-wealthy millionaire footballer. But, whichever type, from a very early age they live a life where they're famous, where they go in front of the crowd every Saturday and they're adored by their loving fans and they live their career where they're blessed to have a life like that. And then it's just taken away from them overnight. And that, in itself, perpetuates the problem. They're not ready for it; I see it so often.'

Kevin has just acted for a former footballer who played in the Premier League in its earlier days, so while his client didn't make millions he did enjoy a decent living. Perhaps too decent, Kevin explains. 'They had nice cars, nice houses and the truth is, even though they earned good money, they didn't live within their means. It's almost as if the more they earned the more they spent. And their whole married life, even though it was wonderful – the jewellery, clothing, cars and houses – it was built on this debt. His very good salary financed the debt. So, as long as he's got the salary to keep financing the debt, everything's all right and they have this great life.

'Of course, once the salary stops they can't meet the payments and then they have to start selling everything. And then the marriage collapses. And that's exactly what I've just seen with this player. And when you net it down, the total value of the wealth and take off all the debt they owe, they barely had half a million pounds left between them – the wife, husband and three kids. After a full career, after everything they'd been through – lovely house, holiday home abroad. Unless you are in the super-earning bracket, and not many players are, let's be honest, you are setting yourself up to fail.'

Kevin stresses that the game itself needs to do more to prepare players for life after a playing career and the relationship difficulties that can ensue. 'Nobody takes responsibility for what is going on during the playing career. Clubs say they do and they've got welfare officers, but only for as long as they've got a contract with that club. As soon as that contract is up they are no longer responsible for you so the buck is passed from club to club until there is no club. Most football players are caught in that bubble, that they're not living within their means, but they're able to get away with it because they've got the income, the cashflow, to keep the wolves at bay in terms of the finance arrangements, until the career comes to a sudden end and then the harsh reality of life after football sets in and the financial abyss.

'I think football as an industry should be taking more responsibility. So little of the money finds its way down the food chain to where it's really needed. Most of the money stays in the Premier League but it could be filtered down the system – given to the PFA, given to XPRO, it could do so much more to try and help players prepare for retirement. It's a failing in the system, in my opinion.'

Kevin gives a pertinent example of a player who needed assistance proactively, rather than the reactive help he eventually obtained. 'I acted for a player who had a very good career. His top salary was probably about £3,500 a week so he played in the Premier League in the early days before the super money started to come in. Like a lot of players, he ended up working his way down the leagues and eventually ended up playing non-league football at 40 years of age. But he had a terrible, terrible drink problem. His wife left him, he hit the bottle, lost his licence for drink-driving. It got so bad in the end that the court wouldn't let him see his kids until he sorted himself out. So he hit absolute rock bottom.

'And nobody stepped in when he really needed it. He had his PFA rep go to court with him and say he was a good guy, they helped him with a solicitor in the Criminal Court, but it was all too little too late. It was almost as if they were going through the motions to say, "Oh, we helped this player when he really needed it." Well, no you didn't. He really needed it when he came to you two years before to say he'd got a drink problem.'

Kevin reiterates James Hall's point that, while pre-nups aren't yet legally binding, the legal system will sometimes uphold them. This came after the 2010 Radmacher v Granatino case, which judged, 'The court should give effect to a nuptial agreement that is freely entered into by each party with a full appreciation of its implications unless in the circumstances prevailing it would not be fair to hold the parties to their agreement.'

'The Supreme Court, the highest court in the land, recently said, as long as certain conditions are met, that they will bend over backwards to uphold pre-nuptial agreements,' continues Kevin. 'Because the reality is the rest of the world acknowledges pre-nuptial agreements except us, so we're out of sync. So, pre-nuptial agreements do have judicial backing as long as certain conditions are met. In that sense, pre-nuptial agreements are being done and they're an integral part of wealth protection. I'm doing one at the moment for an England under-21 international who is getting married shortly, who obviously has a fantastic career ahead of him. Certainly with young footballers they're very, very important.'

I express some surprise that an under-21 player is planning to wed but, of course, footballers tend to marry younger. I ponder the reasons behind this and Kevin simply replies, 'Because they can.'

I wonder if pressure from clubs to settle down at a young age has any influence on these decisions, but Kevin doesn't agree. 'I don't know if that goes through the mind of a 21-year-old. In fact, I don't think a lot goes through the mind of a 21-year-old when his every footballing need is met by his club, his agent and his advisors generally. He is counselled in all aspects of his professional life but, in my experience, largely left to his own devices in his personal life and relationships.

'I don't think players marry young because of club pressure, I think they marry young because they can. In my experience, young footballers do tend to marry more so than cohabit – and that is possibly due to the financial security they are afforded compared to most. They've got the wealth, they usually attract, forgive me, very pretty, beautiful women that make them look good so I suppose it's a combination of all those sorts of things.'

He breaks down young footballers' marriages into three scenarios – marrying the childhood sweetheart, marrying the stunning beauty/minor celebrity and marrying the right person at the right time. The first tends to falter in later years as the couple grow apart and as the player becomes increasingly adored by his fans and other women. The second has a 50/50 chance of success and usually occurs when the player loves being in the limelight. Finally, marrying the soulmate usually stands the test of time.

He admits, though, that it is an uphill struggle to speak to young footballers about their future and the troubles that a potential divorce might bring. 'Last year I was invited by a Premier League club to go in and speak to the under-21s to show what divorce looks like and get them in to pre-nuptial agreements. They were on their mobile phones, busy doing whatever they do and I could see that it is a real struggle to try and get these young men to engage and realise what the real world looks like, and in particular the consequences of a failed relationship. They all seem to think they'll retire millionaires or become a media pundit, but everyone wants to be a media pundit – there aren't enough of those jobs out there.'

So, what can a footballer expect to lose in a divorce settlement? Well, it often depends on when his relationship began with his wife. As many players marry their childhood sweethearts or at a relatively young age, this can have even more devastating effects on their finances.

'If the wife is with the player from the beginning of his professional career then, in a nutshell, she can expect probably about half of the wealth,' explains Kevin. 'Plus maintenance, if he's still got a salary. If you look at some of the footballers' divorces, you can see that she's a fully entitled wife and she's fully entitled to half of his wealth. And the argument of "I'm brilliant, I'm the one who goes out and runs around the football pitch and makes all the money" doesn't wash, because the judge says, "Well, your wife is just as brilliant, because she's your wife and is the mother of your children and her contribution is just as important as yours."

'If on the other hand the player has an established career and then he marries his wife, well then you can argue that the pre-marital wealth should remain his and the post-marital wealth is what you then share.

'That's where a pre-nuptial agreement would take away the uncertainty. It would simply say the pre-marital wealth is not to be included.'

While maintenance is awarded, it will only be based on the husband's earning power. 'There are two sorts of maintenance,' concludes Kevin. 'Child maintenance, where the responsibility for the child continues until the child is 18. And spouse maintenance, where if it's not been possible to write a cheque and buy the wife off, if you like, then the maintenance liability continues indefinitely. But it's always proportionate to what the husband's earnings are, so it's reviewed and is not set in stone forever and a day.'

According to Kevin, the divorce court in England maintains absolute discretion when considering financial claims on divorce, and a judge is required to do what is 'fair' in line with some statutory considerations.

Of course divorce, whether it comes before or after retirement, can have huge financial ramifications for a footballer with a finite earning capacity. The landmark case when it comes to football divorces came in 2004 when the ex-wife of former England and Arsenal midfielder Ray Parlour was awarded one third of his future income. The pair's marriage had been dissolved two years earlier. Parlour married his childhood sweetheart Karen in 1998 but their marriage hit the rocks just three years later. Karen Parlour's divorce application cited her husband's 'loutish behaviour', substance abuse and gambling and his detached relationship with her and their children as the major factors in the breakdown of their marriage.

The Court of Appeal awarded her £440,000-a-year maintenance, increased from an initial £250,000 per annum, to be reviewed after four years. Parlour had offered her a sum of £120,000 per year. Karen had also been awarded two mortgage-free properties worth £1m and a £250,000 lump sum in the original settlement.

The player's lawyers, and critics of the ruling, argued that it was the footballer who played the game and dealt with all that comes with it, whereas his spouse did nothing to earn the money. However, the court felt that Karen had played a major role in her husband's career, not least her efforts in curbing her husband's addictions, and that the money earned by the latter could be seen as 'matrimonial property'.

This came after White v White in 2000, which changed everything in regards to payouts to divorcees. It ruled that in future 'there should be no bias in favour of the money-earner and against the homemaker and the child-carer'. The ruling opened the floodgates on future divorce cases that would have a detrimental impact on footballers' finances.

In the 2005 case, Q v Q, an England international's marital assets of £3.5m were equally split between him and his wife of ten years. In addition to this his wife was awarded 40 per cent of his future earnings for the remainder of his career. The player's annual basic wage at the time was just over £900,000 per annum, with various bonuses and incentives on top of that. The player was, however, allowed to retain his £15,000 toy collection.

However, it's not always cut-and-dried. One ex-wife of a retired Premier League and international player revealed to me that she's not receiving any maintenance at all after their divorce. 'I get not a penny from him now. Nobody would believe that, absolutely nobody. And two of my friends don't get anything from footballers. Everybody thinks it's something else – "it's easy for them".'

She is wary of 'tarring all footballers with the same brush' but believes, 'They have an arrogance about them but a lot of the time I think it's a front that they have to put on. And that arrogance normally comes across in the divorce. If they've made money, it's their money, they don't want the other person to have it. They've worked all their lives, they're not working any more. That's what I've found now.'

She agrees that replacing the buzz from playing can be a key factor in marriage breakdowns when a footballer retires. 'I think, the footballer himself, has been looked after, been in the limelight, had attention and I believe a lot of the time they don't want to admit it but they're afraid of losing all that as well.

'You've got so much time on your hands. So they might go and do things to keep their mind off that. And it's usually an addiction to something, whether it be gambling or sex. I do find that the pressure of something can cause that, especially if you've got more time on your hands because you're not playing as much or you're worried about something.

'I found that instead of discussing it and talking to you about it – because maybe they're a bit embarrassed or maybe they feel let down or maybe they feel low or depressed – they go and try and fulfil what they used to have with something or someone else.'

Even the imminence of retirement can put an enormous strain on a footballer's marriage. 'He was coming to the end of his career and you have to take what clubs you're given,' the former wife recalls. 'You've been used to earning all this amount of money and you can pick and choose your clubs, but eventually it comes to a point where there aren't three or four contracts on the table. And you have to look and make the best decision for your family financially. And that can cause a huge strain.'

The cracks started to appear in their marriage as the footballer neared retirement. 'Even some people now go, "Oh, you got married too soon." But over a decade in, it's not too soon, is it? We had a good marriage,' she continues. 'I think, within football, we had a decent marriage really, in terms of length. Our problems came before retirement really. I can imagine what he went through was very similar to the rest. He had such a high in his career and things started to end. I probably fought for my marriage a lot longer that I should have.'

She worked throughout her ex-husband's career – 'It kept me sane, it's such a lonely life' – and the couple often spoke about the effects retirement would have. 'I was prepared for it, we had two good houses, I worked, we had a chunk of money in the bank,' she reveals. 'It would have worked. Obviously you couldn't have lived the lifestyle that you did. Although we weren't big-time football people anyway, we didn't constantly flash cash about and things like that. Yeah, we would have been financially okay. He would have had to work and so would I. But, yeah, we'd spoken about retirement and how it would work. I'd been planning for that.'

However, she admits she was conscious of the problems facing footballers' marriages when they retired and did have some concerns about the future. 'I did worry. We'd had our problems, obviously, before the divorce. I think it was the pressure of, "What are you going to do after?" I worked and I earned quite a decent enough salary but you do try and plan.'

Nevertheless the inevitability of calling it a day on a playing career can still come as a shock. 'The pressure of knowing you're coming to the end of your career is huge. Because you never expect it, you don't plan for it. We were financially astute, I thought. Although there wasn't the money that's given now.'

The lack of support from the sport itself for those facing the transition to retirement is a common theme, and one she agrees with, but believes that players must also face up to the realities of their unavoidable departure from the game.

'In any company facing redundancies, the first thing you do is go home and speak to your partner, your family and discuss what you're going to do. You're normally prepared for that. With a footballer you either just ignore it or wait until it happens on that day. Every footballer that is still playing, and does not retire through injury, they sit waiting for a club. Until that one day when an offer doesn't come, that's the end of your career. And that, when you actually think about it, is nuts. Nobody else's work is like that. Other people go, "Well, they've had a great career, they must have millions in the bank."

'No one gets it, unless you're up playing at the highest level, it's not like that from what I've found and seen. Instead of talking about it to people or getting support – is it the footballer's fault about not going and looking for support about what is effectively losing their job forever?'

It's easy to look at the divorce statistics for players and put faces to them. Almost four in every starting 11 will divorce within a year of retirement, and over eight within three years. Quite often it's simple to neglect the other side of the story and the wives and children they've left behind. It rarely ends well. 'You're left as well. You've been looked after financially all your life, even though you've worked. And then all of a sudden, they've gone, football's gone, your future's gone, you're starting all over again, normally with children. Any of my friends who've been divorced have not had a good divorce,' says the player's former wife. Some, she adds, have 'gone through hell'.

While the wives are often left to pick up the pieces, the former footballer can be quick to put their marriage behind them. 'I've found the men move on very quickly because – the same again – they need something else,' she contends. 'I've never normally seen them leave their wives for others. I haven't actually. They don't really talk about it until afterwards. They move on to somebody else to fill that. A lot of the time I look back now and think [about other ex-wives], "She's taken a while to move on."'

Despite various court rulings, it seems that some former footballers are still adamant that any earnings from their career are theirs alone, regardless of the sacrifices made by their spouses. 'I divorced him and ended up staying in the house. I think I've been reasonable,' she says. 'Obviously everybody's devastated and hurt. But it's not amicable now and it never will be. And this is my point. This is my experience – he has such a strong arrogance about him – "I earned that money, that is my money, we shouldn't be in this position now, it's all my [her] fault."'

Her own career ambitions were curtailed due to the sometimes nomadic lifestyle of a footballer, men who are often left wanting for nothing. 'I looked after him, the clubs looked after him, he didn't have to do anything. He came off the pitch to me running around after him. Never did one thing. Because you felt you had to. But, actually, if you think about it, I'm working, he's working, it's just a job. We shouldn't have to put them up on a pedestal. It should have been joint. I put that down to my fault, but that's how it was.'

I had been intrigued as to whether the marital problems that face retired professional footballers in the UK are unique to the sport. Speaking to Dr Steven Ortiz, an associate professor in sociology at Oregon State University, that doesn't seem to be the case. Dr Ortiz has studied the marriages of elite sports stars in the US for over 25 years and discusses his findings in his forthcoming book about the sport marriage. He can certainly recognise the problems incurred by soccer players in Britain.

'I don't think it's specific to professional soccer,' he declares. 'There are domestic issues, there are financial issues, there are health issues. And I would agree with your findings in terms of some of the team sports here in America. Specifically, if we look at it sociologically, we're looking at retirement as a transitional process.

'If the professional athlete has prepared for the future financially or has post-career goals then retirement may be less traumatic. If he hasn't planned ahead, which is fairly common, then it may be difficult to let go of the identity and the role he has constructed as a professional athlete as he transitions into a different career and establishes different life goals.'

Dr Ortiz has also found that the change in the dynamic in US sports stars' marriages can lead to their downfall. 'One of the things I've found in my research — and I think it's really interesting — is that what holds these marriages together is a kind of teamwork that couples have developed over the years,' he explains. 'In some cases, if the teamwork is the only thing

*Toronto FC captain
Steven Caldwell, before
he was forced to retire
through injury.* Press
Association

*Former Tottenham and
England defender Gary
Stevens at the World
Cup in 1986. He's since
forged a managerial
career overseas.* Press
Association

Richie Sadlier celebrates scoring for Millwall with strike partner Neil Harris.
Press Association

David Busst suffering the horrific injury that led to his premature retirement.
Press Association

Jeff Astle scoring the winning goal in the 1968 FA Cup Final. Jeff was the first professional footballer confirmed to have died from chronic traumatic encephalopathy. Getty Images

West Brom fans holding up a 'Justice For Jeff' banner at Norwich City's Carrow Road. Getty Images

Mark Ward in action for West Ham. He later spent four years in prison for drugs offences. Press Association

Former Leicester City captain Steve Walsh celebrates scoring a goal at Wembley. He's admitted to suffering from many problems after retiring from the game. Getty Images

Espen Baardsen in goals for Tottenham. The Norwegian keeper hung up his gloves at the age of 25 after falling out of love with the game. Getty Images

David Bentley celebrating his hat-trick against Manchester United at Ewood Park. He retired early from football, claiming to have 'never felt like a footballer'. Press Association

'Britpop footballer' Paul McGregor singing with his former band, Merc.
Press Association

Lee Bowyer, right, in action for Leeds United against Manchester United.
He now owns and runs a fishing lake in France. Getty Images

From striker to vicar. Richard Leadbeater, who retired from football to pursue his faith. Press Association

Respected media pundit Pat Nevin during his playing days at Chelsea.
Press Association

Lance Armstrong, left, and former England football international Geoff Thomas, right behind, pedal during the charity ride 'Le Tour, One Day Ahead'.
Press Association

that kept the marriage together, when the husband's career is over, the marriage might also be over.'

The transitional process the ex-pro has to deal with can sometimes come as a shock to their spouse who has looked forward to spending more time with her husband. 'If they don't work on the marriage when the husband is home, particularly during the off-season, he may often be a stranger in his own home. During his career, the wife will frequently hope that, once his career is over, "We're going to have a normal family life."

'Wives, especially those who are tired of the unrelenting stress and pressures, may look forward to the day their husbands retire from the game so they can have a normal life, only to discover that they have to take on another burden in the marriage, which is to support the husband's transition into a different life after his career is over,' says Dr Ortiz.

'It's not uncommon for some husbands to delay the transition into a post-career occupation for many years after they leave the game because they are traumatised, or because they're going from being a "somebody" to being a "nobody". If their entire sense of self was invested in the role of professional athlete and they no longer have that role or identity, they're lost. When this happens, it's up to the wife to try and support her husband as he leaves the game, but if he's disoriented, confused, or depressed then it's going to be more difficult for her.'

This, of course, can be an unexpected burden on the retiree's wife, but her experiences during his career can often help her cope with this. Dr Ortiz has found, 'These women are highly intelligent. They are resilient and quite adaptable to changing situations. They have to keep the marriage and the family together during the husband's career. Because of the injuries, the constant moving around, the celebrity status, the fame, and many other pressures and demands, the wives necessarily develop coping skills that the men may not develop. As a result, the men learn to rely on their wives, especially when failures or setbacks occur unexpectedly during their careers.

'Unfortunately, many professional athletes are spoiled and they haven't had to develop coping skills, or certain life skills for that matter, during their careers, which makes it difficult for them to deal with failures and setbacks. But their wives have had to be extremely flexible in dealing with all the changing situations, so when a husband retires, a wife has a sense of how to adjust and how to move on. But this process is not without problems for wives, particularly when post-career issues emerge; for example, a financial crisis when the finances weren't properly managed, or infidelity, or health or disability issues, or just trying to reclaim those lost years.'

Dr Ortiz's experience is that the wives take on this support role in helping the husband deal with retirement. 'She may do this because she truly loves him or maybe because she wants to maintain a certain kind of lifestyle,' he continues. 'She may do it because she wants to include him in the family as a father to the children, and other related reasons. But there may be other factors involved. For instance, if she "married the man", she married him for who he is and not what he is — she would have married him regardless of his chosen career. But if she "married the professional athlete", she married the affluence, the fame, the celebrity, the glamour, and the spotlight. If she married the professional athlete rather than the man, after he retires she may be less understanding and supportive, and she may even divorce him and take the money.'

The former Leicester City defender Steve Walsh got divorced in the immediate aftermath of his retirement and suggests that this can be the case in certain marriages. 'I guess there's some women who just want the high life, they want to be one of these WAGs and as soon as it comes to an end, things change. That's the price we have to pay for not choosing the right woman!' jokes Steve.

Mark Hands is a divorce lawyer with Birmingham-based Irwin Mitchell and doesn't believe the reasons for retired footballers' divorces differ greatly from the general population, it's just they come at a different time. 'On the face of it, the actual factual reasons can be similar for the breakdown of the marriage. I do think, though, it's in a different context,' Mark contends. 'Typically, in normal day-to-day life, a lot of relationships end through one person being controlling, a breakdown in communication, arguments about money, a lack of sexual intimacy. When footballers retire, they're dragged into that normality.'

Mark himself recently retired from a semi-professional football career so has always affiliated himself to footballers. So when he got into divorce law and became a divorce lawyer, it was natural for him to seek out and source players as clients. 'You understand the industry and you probably have a better understanding of the difficulties footballers can face,' he reasons. 'And that might sound like a strange word, difficulties, but it's quite a harsh industry in many respects. If you take away the really top earners then you have a lot of people churning out a very good standard of living for eight or nine years and then it all comes to an abrupt end. That leads to various things and one of those is, unfortunately, divorce.'

He's acted for several former players and some ex-wives of footballers and all of those clients, bar one, have been footballers either coming towards the end of their career or already retired and believes there's a number of factors at play. 'One is that sometimes wives or partners will become accustomed to a standard of living,' says Mark. 'They will eat in nice restaurants, they will buy really nice clothes – even those players who are earning £3,000 or £4,000 a week, it's still a lot of money. And people become accustomed to a really high standard of living, they have children who go to private school.

'Then suddenly, when the contract ends and they realise they're not going to get another contract and they'll have to retire, the money's not there. And what can you place in your life to replace that type of money? It is often money-related. A lot of footballers just don't get the right financial advice at an early stage. Or, even worse, they get really bad advice and lose a lot of money, thinking they were investing money but they weren't.' Of course, we've already seen the effects of this in an earlier chapter.

This, coupled with the lack of earning power upon retirement, exacerbates the strains on the marriage. 'If a normal couple lost their jobs, they would be able to get another job. It might not pay as much as they were earning, but it would pay enough to keep their heads above water and for them to work through difficult times, as they've not generally enjoyed a luxurious standard of living,' continues Mark. 'When footballers end their career, there's nothing to replace that money. Sometimes, as well, the money conceals or papers over a lot of cracks in the marriage. Marriages are good when you've got loads of money, you can go on really nice holidays, send your wife on a spa break, you can go shopping – that makes people feel good and can paper over a lot of cracks. And, when it's not there, what's left is just the two of you and often a dwindling savings pot.'

Mark also believes that the law has become 'an ingredient in a toxic recipe' for divorce cases involving footballers, particularly since the aforementioned White v White landmark case. 'The law in this country facilitates divorce. It's become the divorce capital of the world. Prior to 2000 the wife's claims would be quite limited. We moved to an era where a husband could end up with less than half of the assets.

It's a toxic recipe for footballers because, firstly, the wives have the absolute ideal scenario,' he believes.

'They tick every box – because they've had children with the player, they've moved up and down the country from club to club with them, they've been told by the player not to go to work and all they have to say is, "I've sacrificed any prospects of a career, I moved around the country [or, sometimes, overseas] so he could develop his playing career, I looked after the children. Now we're divorced I haven't got a career because of him, he's got all the money because he earned it because of all the support I gave and now I want my chunk of it."

'Now, the footballer's faced with the prospect of giving a minimum of half his assets, half his pension, maintenance for the children, maintenance to her as she really can't earn that much. Secondly, it encourages people to get divorced because they know they're going to get a good share of the assets. Whereas, pre-2000, somebody might have thought, "I'm not going to get divorced as I'm not going to get much money out of it, I'll just stay with it." Now, the partners will be thinking, "I want to get married."' Mark believes it is important when representing a player in a divorce to anticipate these arguments and adopt an early and very clear strategy to dilute them.

Mark also lectures at clubs to players about protecting their assets in the future but concedes there are some players 'you cannot educate on this'. However, for those willing to listen, there are ways to limit the financial damage should a relationship break down. 'One of the best ways to protect your assets is not to have children,' says Mark. 'If you do have children, not getting married is a good way to protect your assets because the financial claims you can make on a divorce rather than a separation are much wider than if you weren't married. For example, if you marry and divorce, the wife will have the full range of financial claims open to her. If you're separated and weren't married, you won't have any claims unless you've got children. If you have children, your claims are limited to that child. So, for example, you could potentially get a football player to buy a property to live in with the child. In a divorce settlement, that would be the wife's property. If they weren't married then that property would be held on trust and would go back to the player when the child reaches 18.'

It all seems terribly unromantic and Mark agrees that some players adopt an 'easy come, easy go' attitude until they retire when their whole attitude quickly changes. He feels that the likes of XPRO and high-profile divorce cases involving footballers are raising the awareness, though. 'In many respects, at the top end, many players don't live a normal life. The level of spending is uncontrollable. It requires a complete adjustment in every aspect of life to what they've been used to. The minute you retire is a huge comedown from where you've been. And if the relationship isn't a solid one, this can be the cause of many difficulties.' He agrees with the ex-wife I spoke to that it's almost always the wife who ends the marriage, and that 'some of the players don't like to accept the marriage is over, or were not aware of the problems'.

Another problem he's seen is a lack of understanding among the legal profession towards the career of a footballer, which often leads to unrealistic expectations from the ex-wife. 'The wife sometimes tries to make claims on the retired footballer as if they were still playing and they're struggling to accept that they're not earning the same type of money that they were during the marriage,' he says. 'They almost want to have their cake and eat it sometimes – they want the divorce and to continue with a high standard of living.'

Mark admits his own retirement from the semi-professional game has 'left a void in my life now' so can empathise with the impact retirement can have on mental health and, consequently, a marriage. 'I think about my own situation and I was involved at a modest standard of non-league football for over a decade. If it does that to me, imagine what it does to a professional footballer at the top end of the sport; imagine the gap that would be left in your life after that. I spoke to a client and asked, "Do you miss it?" and he said, "Desperately, I just desperately miss everything about it."

'People underestimate significantly the mental health issues within football. It really frustrates me. We have a society that has no sympathy for footballers whatsoever. They think they're overpaid, arrogant, egotistical and will have no sympathy whatsoever were they to have mental health problems. People think that because you've got loads of money and the glitz and the glamour that there's no reason why you should have mental health issues.

'But actually it can be quite an isolating industry. Not just that, you have to remember that some of these players have had 50,000 people chanting their name or have had "that feeling" after scoring a goal. I think that can manifest into mental health problems. You've lived your life not only though the fans and the excitement and the money, but also, you've probably developed a lot of your social circles through your football club for a number of years and it's quite difficult then to be kicked out of the tent, effectively.

'The mental health issues are not only unrecognised by society and professionals but by footballers themselves. The first step is footballers themselves recognising they've got mental health issues because, in this industry, there's a stigma attached to saying you're ill or that you've got mental health issues. Because you're in an environment where you cannot show any weakness, all of this bravado could actually conceal some quite difficult mental health issues. The footballers aren't identifying the mental health issues.'

This lack of awareness can then lead to detrimental effects on the newly-retired player's marriage, believes Mark. 'So, let's take that into a divorce scenario. They've finished their career, they have a huge void in their life, perhaps they've struggled with their mental health through that period of playing without realising it. Now they're in a home environment where it's them and their wife and children. It's normality and they're struggling to deal with that.

'They haven't identified their mental health problems and now that's impacting on everyday life and everyone around you. You might be distant, you'll be down at times, you will struggle to communicate with your partner. And, over a period of time, that will grind away to the point where the wife says, "I'm no longer happy in this relationship," and that leads to a breakdown in the marriage. I've had players say, "I didn't even expect her to say that she didn't want to be with me any more, it just came out of the blue." But, in reality, it's come over a period of time.'

Of course, every divorce, like every marriage, is different. Sometimes a spouse can be left to wonder where it all went wrong, with a reason difficult to pinpoint. Another ex-pro I spoke to, who played for two clubs in the Premier League, had been with his wife for '20-odd years, three kids, everything was good. I'd never cheated on her'.

He'd just finished his playing career when his wife dropped the bombshell that she'd had an affair, was moving out and taking the kids with her. 'It was a bolt from the blue, I didn't think it would ever happen,' he reveals. 'I couldn't tell you why. It wasn't like I was depressed because I'd finished playing or anything like that. I wasn't earning as much but I don't think it was about money.'

The former player's divorce left him fiscally devastated. 'Financially, it's killed me,' he admits. 'When I finished playing, I had a little nest egg, but that's all gone now. I had to sell my house, she got her half of everything and I got my half. I had all the debts and that sort of stuff that had started building up.'

When she left him he stopped working to concentrate on looking after his kids, a decision that heavily impacted on his savings. 'That killed me financially as the money I had put away slowly dwindled away over that year. She wasn't paying anything towards the kids. Now I'm working, I've got child maintenance to pay – it crucifies you financially. No matter what I earn in the future, she's still going to take money off me because obviously there's kids involved.

'She cheated on me, I never did anything to hurt her at any time. The hardest thing from my point of view is I speak to everybody who I've known for years and every single one of them says that you couldn't ask for a better husband than the one I was. And then she still did what she did.'

The divorce has also impacted on his football ambitions, with plans to go into coaching put on hold. 'You just have to move on from it but it's not helped me further my football career either.

'Obviously, as I took a year out to look after my kids, I didn't have that coaching role to walk into straight after playing. And now I'm out of the game and trying to get back into it, which is probably the hardest thing to do.'

He has been coaching a youth team and playing non-league football as he 'still loves the game' but is eager to return to a full-time coaching or managerial position. 'I'm just desperate to get back into football, but it's got to be the right job. You know what it's like now – one job and if it doesn't go well, you're knackered for the rest of your career. So I'm trying to bide my time and do my apprenticeship again.'

He still speaks to his ex-wife for the sake of their children but has moved on with his life. 'I've found somebody else; I've got a beautiful new partner who the kids get on well with. I look at it from that point of view and I'm probably happier now than I was,' he says.

I realise that it may have been quite naïve of me when I started writing this book to view the problems encountered by footballers upon retirement as standalone issues. They're clearly all interlinked. A premature injury can lead to financial problems. Financial problems can lead to divorce. Divorce can lead to financial problems. One thing can lead to another. After 20 years as a professional footballer, quickly followed by a costly divorce, he is left – as he puts it – 'without a pot to piss in'.

6

Mental Health

'AS a working environment, sitting in a therapist's chair in a room with a client is as far away as I can imagine from standing on the pitch at The Den playing football for Millwall.'

Richie Sadlier has come a long way since his premature retirement from football. The Dubliner, 37, balances a punditry role with RTÉ with a new career as a counsellor. His move into psychotherapy is in no small part down to his own experiences in coming to terms with the end of his playing days aged just 24.

He first went to counselling in his early 20s in London when he was still playing, after his mother suggested it might help with his emotional state at the time. 'I've never been diagnosed with depression. At the time I just felt kind of overwhelmed, whether it was expectations with family, or homesickness, or pressures of the job, the media or fans. I don't know what it was, a whole load of things that I couldn't put a name on,' he recalls.

'My head was fried and I wasn't enjoying football but I didn't want to leave football. I just felt a little bit lost – "I'm not enjoying this. I'm not enjoying the life that comes with it. Do I have the option to leave it? No, not really, because I haven't trained myself in anything else." And then all the managers and coaches and teachers and my family that put so much into it, I can't let them down. I came out of it quickly enough, but when you're in it, it's a bit daunting.'

After his premature retirement through injury, he took a Sports Science degree and a question in one of the modules seemed specifically written about his own experience – 'How, as a psychologist, would you work with an elite sportsperson who is facing early career transition?'

'Basically, it was me written on the page in the case study,' he says. 'Within a few months of retirement things got fairly bad fairly quickly in my head about the whole thing. This was the first time I thought there were actually people out there who could help as I identified with everything on the page.' He approached the sports psychologist after class and saw her once or twice a week for several months.

'There was a lot of self-pity and "poor me" around the whole thing. Just angry for ages. Crying was the constant, I was just constantly crying on my own. And then, when I went to counselling, I could talk openly about what was going on. It was the loss of identity, that was a massive thing. I was "Richie the footballer" since I was eight, that's how everyone interacted with me and it was how I saw myself. Now the footballer bit was gone, what was left? I really struggled with that,' he admits.

'And, just total loss of self-esteem. I just thought that I could bring nothing to the table in any situation. I was just heartbroken, I was crying all the time. It was grieving. But, at the time, I felt it was inappropriate to be grieving because I'd an insurance payout coming. I'd seven years of living the dream. How dare I complain about my lot? I didn't really feel as if it was appropriate for me to open up and say how upset and heartbroken I was to non-footballers because I thought most non-footballers would look at me and go, "You've had seven years being a footballer, what have you to moan about?" So it was this self-imposed kind of isolation, even though I was physically around people.'

He had always considered that retirement meant 'getting a job, earning something' so kept himself busy with his studies and a role as a football agent, but he had underestimated the emotional impact of the transition away from the game. 'A lot of people are of the view that if you've enough money in the bank, you're fine. I never thought the money in the bank wouldn't be enough to override things like feeling useless, or missing out, or low self-worth, or feeling lost or isolated – all the things that come from finishing. I was completely floored by it, even though it came a year and a half after day one of getting the injury.

'So it wasn't sudden like break a leg on a Monday, retire on a Tuesday kind of thing. I was totally floored. I remember at the time I didn't know how to handle that because – and I've spoken to other lads who've done the same – I felt awkward around footballers and I assumed they felt awkward around me,' he says. 'The conversation among footballers will be like, "Was training shit this morning? Is the ref any good that's coming up at the weekend? What is the crowd like? What's been written about me in the paper?" All stuff which would sound fairly trivial and a bit self-indulgent if you're sitting next to someone who's just been told they'll never play again. So, I just figured out that no one was really comfortable with me being there. I kind of isolated myself a little bit from being around footballers.'

While he believes that research on the psychological impact of retirement from football has improved, the environment within the game makes it difficult for people to admit to having problems. 'It's a culture which is predominantly alpha males;

it's a hyper-competitive environment where any weakness or perception of weakness is pounced on or honed in on by your own supporters, opposition supporters, opposition players or your team-mates, certainly by your coaches if they think the other fella is better off in your position than you are,' he says.

'It's a self-preservation thing, if you have a sore knee you play down the extent of it because you don't want to risk your place in the team. So if you've got something going on in your head, which you mightn't even understand as fitting into the box of anxiety for depression or any of the other numerous things it can be, your instinctive response is, "Don't let anyone in."

'In every training ground in England, there's probably a leaflet or poster from the PFA about the essential number to ring if you want counselling and the courses to prepare for a life outside football. But if people are really struggling, they won't even admit to themselves that that poster might apply to them. The culture of professional football isn't really conducive to that. It takes a big, big step, certainly, to allow other people to know where you're at. In the simplest terms, it can cost you your place in the team. The broader concern is what if it gets out, the newspapers write about it, what if fans or the internet and Twitter find out, then you're *that* guy.

'Things have changed though. It is nearly 20 years since I made that journey to England. And I assume the world of mental health or emotional support and well-being is a different world from what it was then. That said, a lot of the issues are still there today that were there ten years ago. Whether it's a male thing, or a football thing or a culture of professional football thing, it can be difficult to come forward. But there are people that can help you. There are psychologists, there are therapists, there are former footballers who will share their experiences. There's more awareness of it out there. Which doesn't mean that people will still access or avail of the help that's out there.'

It was his own treatment upon retirement that led to his new role in the therapist's chair. 'I remember the last session I had with my therapist in 2004. We had a final session and we kind of just had a chat about comparing the first session to the final one and the difference was like night and day,' Richie recalls. 'And I remember at the time thinking, "Her job satisfaction right now must be pretty sweet." And, that was it, I didn't go anywhere with the thought but it kind of planted a seed. It was always something I thought I'd be interested in doing or comfortable in doing.

'In 2009, the media stuff was going well but it doesn't take up much time. I wanted to do something. I did a Counselling & Psychotherapy H Dip for two years and a Masters for another two years. I loved it. I do that in a couple of different places, general psychotherapy, it's not sports specific, general counselling.'

Not many players can say they've played for Serie A's Juventus and Havant & Waterlooville of the Conference South. Not any, you'd think. But Vincent Pericard can. Early in his career, the striker was the subject of a French documentary entitled *The Man Who Could Be Worth Billions*, but ended up playing in front of hundreds in the sixth tier of English football. His potential unfulfilled, he retired from the game at just 29 years of age. In between, he played for eight other clubs and the constant moves to new countries, cities and towns had taken their toll on the French-Cameroonian. Many players hang up their boots after struggling with injuries, Pericard did so following years of battling depression.

Upon retirement, Pericard set about establishing a company called Elite Welfare Management, aimed at helping foreign players adjust to a new country and preventing them from suffering the stress, loneliness and depression that he went through when he moved to the Premier League at the age of 20. He set up the firm with John Duncan, a psychological coach whom he credits with helping him get out of 'the dark period' he was in while at Stoke City.

Duncan has gone on to found Coach 24/7, a technology-led service backed up and supported by a team of psychological coaches who work with elite sports professionals. As well as Premier League stars, he has worked a great deal with Olympians and reveals that difficulties with the transition to retired life aren't exclusive to footballers.

'No matter what sport you deal with, whether it's cricket, rugby, judo, the sport doesn't really look after the player at the end of their career,' says John. 'What's fascinating me is that I also work with Olympians, and some of the issues that I'm dealing with now involve the fear that they know this is their last Olympics. The fear is consuming them – "What if I get injured, what if I don't make this Games? Because there won't be another one after this." I had an Olympian who had a breakdown the day after the London Games finished, thought it was their last Games, and the sport was nowhere to support them.'

He also believes that it's often a loss of identity that proves most difficult to deal with. 'For the many, many sportspeople I've spoken to and many, many footballers it's the loss of identity and status,' he continues. 'There are people around footballers who are only there because of their status and fame. They very quickly lose that network of friends, it becomes very small very quickly, when they finish the game. It's like a soldier, they've been conditioned to perform. To eat, sleep, perform, win, be competitive and then – nothing. Gary Neville said retirement was like falling into a black hole.'

John has dealt with newly-retired players for whom even simple things like being able to do the school run can come as a shock to the system. 'That was a role which one ex-player's wife had always done and he's infringing on that role, all those boundaries. He's at home a lot more, he's quite bored. How does he now get back?' John asks. 'While he's playing the game, the highs and lows are extreme. Now he's out of the game, where does he go for that emotional hit? A lot of people fall into low-mood depression and will turn to recreational drugs, turn to food, turn to relationships, turn to gambling to get that hit to replace what's missing.'

Duncan is another who believes that the world of football doesn't do enough to help players prepare for life after the game. 'My biggest criticism of the game is that everything's reactive,' he says. 'The PFA have put a helpline of counsellors together for when you are depressed, when you are stressed. For me, and the way we work, we use behavioural psychology. We use Skinner's ABC – Antecedent, Behaviour, Consequence. We're always looking to engage at A, the Antecedent, to prevent anything from happening. Or to give people skills to put the right Behaviour in place to ensure the Consequences are good.'

Due to the taboo around mental health, Geoff Scott of XPRO had revealed to me that some former players are often too proud to seek help, 'Much of the time it's not direct. It tends to be a wife or daughter who comes to us first.' Geoff concedes that his hardest job is often getting players to admit that there is a problem.

Based on his experiences, John echoes this common scenario, using one well-known former player as an example. 'I've had the same thing. As they were finishing the game, they were having certain problems but it was a friend of the player who contacted us. We got this person into rehab and all sorts of things. If somebody else does it on their behalf, they aren't showing that they've got any weakness. It's a case of, "I didn't really want this help, I didn't think there was anything wrong with me, but I'll accept it now it's here."'

He has just finished filming a documentary on mental health in football, which will be aired in 2016, but admits it's difficult to determine the true numbers of footballers suffering from mental health issues. 'How many players are walking around with depression? It's impossible to say as there's no place in a competitive environment where you can put your hand up and say, "I'm struggling."'

Current footballers may still find it difficult to admit to mental health problems, quite often due to the fear of not having their contract renewed. The reactions of fans can also prove a barrier to baring any issues. After the press revealed in the 1990s that former Scotland and Glasgow Rangers goalkeeper Andy Goram was suffering with a mild form of schizophrenia, supporters bombarded him with chants of 'there's only two Andy Gorams, two Andy Gorams'. However, research is growing into the prevalence of mental health issues among retired players.

Research in 2015 from FIFPro, the worldwide representative organisation for professional footballers, suggests that retired players are more susceptible to mental health problems than members of the general public. Furthermore, it is a universal problem. Retired players from a wide range of countries including Belgium, Chile, Sweden, Paraguay, France, Finland, Japan, Norway, Peru, Spain and Switzerland were questioned to assess both the stressors and symptoms related to mental disorders.

The study, titled 'Prevalence and determinants of symptoms related to mental disorders in retired male professional footballers', reveals that over one third of former professionals, the majority of whom played at the highest level in their country for the bulk of their career, reported suffering from symptoms of depression and/or anxiety. Furthermore, 25 per cent reported adverse behaviour in relation to alcohol use. The research also revealed relationships between the symptoms of mental disorders and severe injuries, recent life events and dissatisfaction with playing careers. Other symptoms related to mental disorders established by the study included 11 per cent of retired players with adverse smoking behaviour and 65 per cent with adverse nutritional behaviour.

Another 2014 FIFPro study, 'Mortality in international professional football', looked at mortality rates from 2007 to 2013 in professional footballers. It found that suicide accounted for a staggering 11 per cent.

The 2015 findings concurred with an earlier preliminary FIFPro study, which also established that the symptoms related to common mental disorders were more prevalent among retired footballers than for those who were still playing. The 2015 report concluded by recommending, 'Supportive measures such as an exit-career examination should be developed and implemented in order to promote and empower the sustainable mental health and functioning of professional footballers in their post-sport life.'

Dr Vincent Gouttebarge, chief medical officer of FIFPro, helped author the study and is under no illusions that the transition to retirement can be detrimental to a former player's mental health. 'The period around retirement from professional football is a very difficult period for most players,' he explains. 'Transitioning out of football is something that should be prepared carefully over several years and should be included in a proper "career planning". Several reasons can be acknowledged, among others: the social support around a player, such as team-mates and coaches, stops once retired, and the structure in life implied by a football career such as training and competing stops as well. If not prepared, then it remains difficult to figure out what to do in the near and longer future; a player has to find his new challenge in life. In addition to that, most players have a particular attention from the media and public during their career but this stops once retired. That might lead to a decrease in self-esteem and subsequently lead to mental health problems.'

The Frenchman, who was a player himself for the likes of Auxerre before retiring to concentrate on his academic career, believes preparation is the key to reducing the rates of depression and anxiety upon retirement from the game.

'A proper "career planning" that includes not only football-related matters but also long-term perspectives in life such as education and a second occupational career is needed,' he continues. 'Being thoroughly informed about the potential hazards when transitioning out of football – mental health problems but also osteoarthritis, for example – should also be a minimum standard. Learning proper coping skills might prove favourable to avoiding mental health problems after a career, and in cases of more severe problems, daring to seek help is necessary.'

The mean age of the retired players who participated in FIFPro's study was 36. But what of those who are forced from the game at a younger age? We've already learned that 98 per cent of players at clubs aged 16 will no longer be playing football by their 21st birthday. It transpires that the psychological impact on this demographic can be even greater than those who retire in their 30s.

David Blakelock was a promising attacking midfielder at Newcastle United and Nottingham Forest before being released by the latter in his late teens. 'When I signed for four years at 14, I thought I had a good future at the club [Forest]. However, after a series of staff changes, I had the sense that my face didn't quite fit with some of the new staff and I wasn't enjoying playing as much as I had been.

'I wouldn't say I experienced any significant psychological distress such as depression following release. The news was slightly unexpected though as I had been given some positive comments from some staff members in the weeks and months leading up to decisions being made. I think what helped me adjust was that I maintained other development such as my education and I think that acted as a buffer against more serious psychological consequences.

'However I did notice a change in my identity over time. I mean, for a long time everyone knew me for playing football and that's what my identity was based around. By exploring and developing other aspects of myself that I had either neglected or not invested in, I was able to widen my identity. It also felt good to be recognised for achievements outside of football.'

At 18, he was offered a place at Durham University. 'I thought I'd give it a go and that if I really wanted to get back into football I could give it a push during or after uni, but I never really got that desire back.' Now Dr David Blakelock, he eventually revisited the world of football as part of his Doctorate in Clinical Psychology. His study, 'Psychological Distress in Elite Adolescent Soccer Players Following Deselection', was published in the *Journal Of Clinical Sport Psychology* in early 2016 and aimed to examine the proportion of elite adolescent players who experienced clinical levels of psychological distress following release from their clubs. There is also an intention to publish additional findings relating to coping strategies and personality traits associated with such distress.

The study found that, within a week of being released by their clubs, 35.7 per cent of players experienced clinical levels of psychological distress. By three weeks, this figure had risen to 54.5 per cent, which suggests that the harsh realities of rejection take a while to sink in. Many players have described to me a sort of honeymoon period upon retirement, which ends quickly when they realise the full implications of their career ending so young. Not surprisingly, these released youngsters had significantly higher levels of psychological distress than players who had been retained by their clubs. Almost 100 players between the ages of 15 and 18 from

English and Scottish professional clubs were studied, using the 12-item General Health Questionnaire – a common screening tool for depression, anxiety, loss of confidence and impaired daily functioning.

The research recommended that clubs and organisations such as the PFA consider offering more support to footballers who are discarded in their mid-to-late teens. It suggests that a 'therapeutic, problem-oriented service could be developed for players experiencing psychological problems following release, along with a preventative, developmental, solution-focused approach so that "at risk" players can develop transition resources and a state of readiness to meet the task demands of release'.

Research undertaken on behalf of the Professional Players Federation (PPF) in 2013 revealed that 34 per cent of those questioned didn't feel in control of their lives two years after finishing their playing careers, with problems around depression and anxiety rife in the first 12 months of retirement. The study, called 'Life After Sport', examined the lives of more than 1,000 professional sportsmen from football, rugby union, rugby league, cricket and horse racing and how they transitioned in what was found to be the important two years after they stopped performing.

The PPF, in conjunction with the Sport + Recreation Alliance, launched a Mental Health Charter for Sport and Recreation in 2015, which sets out 'how sport can use its collective power to tackle mental health and the stigma that surrounds it'.

Simon Taylor, the PPF's chief executive, explains, 'The objectives and long-term aims of the Charter are to encourage professional sportspeople to be more open to talk about mental health and to remove the stigma around this issue. We also want to use professional sportspeople talking about their feelings and mental health as a way of improving society's attitudes to mental health. There is a view that getting players to front up campaigns for the general public is good for players as well as the wider population.'

The PPF are not specifically focused on football, but work with professional player associations from a wide range of sports. As such, Simon has also found that the mental health issues and other problems athletes are faced with on retirement are not unique to football. 'What's interesting is that the issues are remarkably similar in every sport,' he explains. 'We did some research with jockeys, which is very much a solo sport, and the results were similar to the cricketers and footballers. So it's not just a team sport thing and there's no reason why it should be. Jockeys will talk about the camaraderie of the weighing room and I imagine it's a bit similar with the golf, snooker and darts players.'

In Ireland, the term 'fail to prepare, prepare to fail' is synonymous with Roy Keane following an interview he gave after leaving the Irish football squad during the 2002 World Cup. It can easily be applied to the success, or otherwise, of the transition to retirement, says Simon, when he discusses the PPF's 2013 research. 'The major drivers to happiness were how you prepare for life after sport. Whether that's making the most of your time in sport – if you enjoy your time playing sport you're more likely to have no regrets afterwards. If you feel you've not fulfilled yourself within your sport you might have more regrets, which can cause a bit more of a difficult transition.

'It's also a question of having control over the time to retire. Some people have a long, bright career and reach the end and choose to retire themselves; others break their leg and have no choice. Others still don't make the grade, whether it's at 18, 21 or 25 and find themselves slipping down the leagues. So that can be a key driver of how well you cope with the transition.'

While problems with retirement are not unique to football, Simon explains that they're not even unique to sport. It's just that they come at a different stage in the life cycle to most people. 'I think it's interesting to compare sportspeople with other people who retire. There are huge issues around people, particularly men, who retire from their work at 65, or whatever age. There's a loss of identity, there's a loss of perhaps being the breadwinner, there's a loss of routine, there's a loss of camaraderie with the workforce,' he continues.

'And I think one of the problems with a sportsman is that this happens in their thirties rather than at 65. At 35, traditionally, it's peak expenditure time – you've got a mortgage, you've got kids and you've got a lot of outgoings and a whole life in front of you. You've then got to re-assess, re-train and, perhaps, start at the bottom of another career. As a 65-year-old, there are similar issues but, in a way, there's less pressure to earn and to decide what you want to do with your life. Your income will be lower but your expenditure will be lower as well.

'Having said that, there's a real issue of professional sportsmen, perhaps more so than in most other careers, in that they will often define themselves and be defined as professional sportsmen. And when that gets taken away it can be emotional and you've got to re-assess who you are and what you want to do in this world. And that is very tricky for most of us.'

Although he admits there is a stigma around mental health issues in sport, Simon believes things are 'getting better' and that players' associations such as the PFA have 'led the way in the support available for elite athletes'.

'I would always say the glass is half-full rather than half-empty. On the wider mental health preventative side they are doing some great work. They invest significant money in dual career education and training – preparing players for life after sport,' he says. 'Education can be a huge driver in being prepared for your life after your sport, so the transition is very much easier. There are also counselling services and 24/7 telephone helplines, you can speak to someone, be assessed, and be put in touch with free local counselling. There is also the residential addiction treatment centre, Sporting Chance Clinic, set up by Tony Adams and funded by the PFA. It's worth paying great tribute to the work Tony Adams has played on this one. The Sporting Chance Clinic has literally been a life-saver for many people, who have had problems with gambling addiction or alcohol or prescription drugs.'

Dr Philip Hopley is a consultant psychiatrist and managing director of Cognacity, the UK's leading provider of confidential counselling in elite professional sport. He heads up Cognacity's Sports Division, which currently looks after 14 sports in the UK – a mixture of team sports and individual sports including football, rugby, cricket, rowing, swimming, hockey, tennis and golf. Established for almost eight years, 'We have a good data set and extensive experience of looking after players who run into a range of difficulties.'

Philip, who played semi-professional rugby for London Wasps, believes mental health issues are not always immediately apparent after retirement. 'A lot of the people I see have dealt well with the immediate post-retirement period, enjoying the excitement that goes with thinking about what they might get involved in,' he says. 'And then the reality sinks in, so that three, six, nine months down the line they find themselves having slipped slowly into a depressive state as they struggle with the adjustment. Depression doesn't come on all of a sudden, it's often an insidious process, and before they know it they're really struggling.'

Even though 'it wasn't Premier League football intensity level', his rugby career helps him empathise with that loss of identity upon retirement that can often lead to mental health issues. 'Once you've retired, you can find yourself feeling uncomfortable back in the company of your former team-mates who are still playing,' he explains, echoing Richie Sadlier's earlier sentiments. 'It can also be difficult around people who would have been watching you as fans for a number of years. In the past the conversation was about performance and how the team was doing, whereas once retired there is no clear common ground other than the past. As a result when you're no longer part of the team or squad you feel very much an outsider, as irrational as that is. So a common theme when players retire and move into a new era is the loss of their peer group and their core identity as a sportsman or woman. Overcoming this sense of loss is critically important.'

The high-profile suicides of Wales manager Gary Speed and German international goalkeeper Robert Enke in recent years have thankfully led to a gradual move away from attitudes that used to permeate the sport. In 1999 Aston Villa striker Stan Collymore confessed to his manager John Gregory that he was suffering from clinical depression. Gregory responded by asking what someone on £20,000 a week had to be depressed about. However, there certainly still seems to be a stigma surrounding mental health in football. While many players were willing to discuss with me their marriage problems, financial difficulties and prison spells, several were reluctant to discuss their battles with mental health issues. The majority of sportspeople Cognacity see come to them through a confidential helpline, which they run of behalf of players' associations.

'The emphasis on confidential support is critical because there is still definitely a massive stigma surrounding mental health in all sports, particularly in football,' says Philip. However, he believes it's not just football's problem. 'We still have an issue with stigma in all sports and in society as a whole so this is not just specific to sport. If you think about the general level of banter around sporting clubs, and the way in which the competitive edge drives the culture, you can see how difficult it would be for someone to say, "Oh and by the way, I'm feeling a bit anxious this week. My mood's been a bit on the down side, lads." As the culture in these environments doesn't lend itself naturally to people opening up, it is therefore essential to have access to a range of trusted people who they can open up to.

'Whether it's an advisor, an agent, a representative from the players' association, a confidential helpline – as long as there is someone there who can listen. We often get referrals from team support staff such as medics, physios, strength and conditioning coaches etc., because quite often the medical room is the place where these things first come out. These staff have developed a professional relationship, they come from the caring professions and they are usually working in a discreet area one-on-one with an established level of confidentiality afforded. Under these circumstances the barriers seem to come down more naturally than they would in a group environment with their peers.'

Philip believes that the PFA 'has been great; there's been a sea change over the last five or ten years with an acceptance on their part that this is a significant issue and needs to be one of their main focuses for funding'. He's in no doubt that this is due, in no small part, to the several widely-publicised cases involving people in the football community. 'High-profile sportspeople speaking openly about their own experiences or tragedies like a suicide very much sharpen the collective attention to this as a real, live issue,' he says.

'I deeply respect and take my hat off to people like ex-footballer Clarke Carlisle and Martin Ling, the football manager, and others who have spoken very bravely and openly about what's gone on. That sort of exposure is brilliant for two reasons. It's great for the players themselves but beyond that, sport is in a wonderful position to influence public opinion. So the public health benefits of someone like Clarke leading a campaign to try and raise the profile on mental health has a really positive knock-on effect.'

In most cases, it's often a third party who'll encourage those affected to reach out for help. 'Roughly two-thirds of those we see come to us because they've spoken to somebody who works with the player association or to a player who has used our services. And then about one third of them pick up a phone and ring our 24/7 helpline number,' reveals Philip. 'When they call they are assessed by myself or a colleague to get a very good handle on exactly what the problems are. We then link them up with one of our nationwide team local to where they live.'

Cognacity act as backup to the PFA, who have their own nationwide network of counsellors. 'The PFA use us for people with more significant psychological health problems, who might need psychiatric input or admission to hospital. The PFA, just like the rugby and cricket players' associations, have representatives that cover the various clubs. They're in there on a relatively regular basis; they'd be in dialogue with the players and keeping an eye on them. There are awareness-raising posters and business cards around the team rooms, there's a newsletter which goes out with advice. They're regularly messaging out to their members, highlighting preventative approaches to keeping well but also letting them know if they do have problems to get in touch.'

There does seem to be a growing level of support available to players approaching retirement across all sports, according to Philip. 'The players' associations do a lot of preparatory work to help players with the transition from being active in sport to their next chapter in life,' he says. 'And that covers a range of areas. It might be financial advice, it might be legal advice, it might be training and further education, it might be looking at career opportunities. Increasingly, there's an awareness of the need to help players to be prepped ahead of time so that not only do they know what sources of support are available but, also, they can do some thinking ahead of time about what this might be like.

'Any current player who gets injured or gets dropped, goes through a mini-grieving process. They're missing out on the thing that they love doing, they're missing out on the opportunity to get the adulation or the opportunity to do things well and be appreciated and to get that positive feedback. But when you retire, then it's removed from you completely. And, of course, those that are forced into retirement through injury – particularly those for whom it happens at a younger age – they often have significant difficulties in coming to terms with it. However, the important take-away point is that help is only a phone call away.'

Research in the United States suggests a link between retired NFL players with a history of concussion during their career and symptoms of depression during their retirement. The study, 'Depressive symptoms and concussions in ageing retired NFL players', found a 'significant correlation between the number of lifetime concussions and depressive symptom severity' among retired NFL athletes. Unfortunately, there seems to be no similar studies in relation to football, although mental health problems are just one manifestation of the causes of neuro-degeneration we looked at in an earlier chapter.

We also saw earlier that up to 80 per cent of former footballers suffer from osteoarthritis, which has itself been linked in scientific studies to depression. A 2010 study, 'Prevalence of anxiety and depression in osteoarthritis', found a strong interrelationship between mental health, pain and disability.

And it's not just the pain from the joint disease that affects the mood; the opposite is also true. A 2011 study published in *The Journal of Bone and Joint Surgery* revealed that depression can have just as strong an effect on knee pain as physical damage for those suffering from osteoarthritis. The researchers admit the reasons for this is not clear but several hypotheses have been advanced. For example, those suffering from depression may partake less in physical activity and have less sleep quality. Furthermore, high levels of depression can limit someone's ability to cope with the pain involved in osteoarthritis.

The former England and Tottenham defender Gary Stevens admitted it took him a decade to come to terms with his premature retirement. He acknowledges that it's difficult for someone in any profession to lose their job, but that the transition to retirement for a footballer can definitely affect one's mental health. 'Footballers aren't any different to, for example, a bank manager or a factory worker who gets made redundant. It's a tough situation for anyone to find themselves in. But from a very privileged lifestyle, you could argue that it becomes more difficult or the differences are greater. I think the contrast for somebody who has played and had such adulation, to lose their career or have to retire from that great career, it's a very difficult transition. And, who knows, some of these high-profile situations where players have actually committed suicide – whether that's because of the change in their situations I don't know but that's how bad it can be for a lot of us.'

Stevens' experience is common among athletes for whom retirement is often compared to the process of dying. According to the Kübler-Ross model, there are five stages to the grieving process – denial, anger, bargaining, depression and acceptance. It's not much of a stretch to suggest a similar model could be applied to retirement from elite sport, particularly for those who retire prematurely. Indeed, Kübler-Ross later expanded her model to incorporate any form of personal loss, including that of a job, career or income. The initial reaction may be denial, perhaps that an injury incurred will heal just as they have before or that a club will surely offer a contract soon. When neither come to pass, frustration and anger set in.

A player may become bitter as an injury takes longer to recover from than in the past or when his club do not offer him a new contract. A period of bargaining follows, where a player may attempt to get through 'just one more season' or go on trial at 'just one more club'. They may be prepared to take a drastic cut in salary or drop down to a league that they'd never previously considered. Depression often follows when the inevitability of retirement sets in. Finally a footballer accepts his fate although, as we have seen, it can take years for this acceptance to manifest itself. It may even come about because they recognise that they are able to remain involved in the sport, whether that be in a management, coaching or a media role.

The PFA's Nationwide Network of counsellors was accessed by 197 professionals in 2014, 70 per cent of whom were former players. Michael Bennett, the PFA's head of player welfare, believes the higher proportion of retired players is down to their difficulties in transitioning from the sport.

'It's a kind of bereavement for the life they once had and trying to chase that buzz they had while playing football,' he explains. 'We've found that a lot of former players were encountering mental health or well-being issues because of that. It's something we're aiming to address with the Player Welfare department.'

It was his own experiences as a player that prompted Michael to pursue his current career. He had just made the

England under-20 squad in 1991, but injured his anterior cruciate ligament playing for Charlton and struggled mentally with the aftermath of this blow. 'I remember at the time I was in the gym on my own and really wanted to talk to somebody about how I felt, but there was nothing in place. I spoke to my parents and then girlfriend, now wife, about it but they didn't really understand football. So you had to have that mentality where you rolled your sleeves up and got on with it,' he recalls.

'Everybody deals with things differently, some players may well have gone out and drank, or taken drugs or gambled to deal with their issues. That's the way some may have dealt with it then when help wasn't available. It's available now so we want players to come forward to discuss how they're feeling, so we can avoid addiction issues, suicidal issues and mental health issues.'

Later on in his career he had several players ask him for football and life advice and was advised by a careers officer at his local college to consider a career in counselling. He qualified in 2004 as a counsellor and has spent much of his time since focusing on mental health and well-being issues in sport. 'I wanted to work with sportspeople because I think there's pressure on them as there's an attitude that, "There is a perception that footballers shouldn't have any problems because they supposedly earn large amounts of money,"' he explains.

'Well, no, they were a person before they were a footballer and they'll be a person after they leave football. I work with the person rather than the high-profile footballer, which helps brings the barriers down. They're often asked how football is, but not how they are.'

He believes that a smooth transition to retirement can help allay mental health problems. 'From my own experience of playing the game, people say to you, "Get yourself ready for retirement," but you always think you've got loads of time to go before that happens,' says Michael. 'I think there's a bit of putting your head in the sand and not wanting to face reality, until reality is forced upon you. That's an issue that we've encountered in the past and are still encountering but the PFA is constantly trying to get players to look at the importance of transitioning from the game. Again, it's getting the players to buy in to the importance of transitioning, and that's what we're working on right now.'

Michael admits that there's still a stigma and taboo surrounding mental health and well-being issues in the game as, in many cases, footballers don't identify that they might be suffering themselves. 'When I've spoken to some players about it before they sometimes had an image of a padded cell or a strait-jacket,' he reveals. 'The PFA are trying to break down these taboos as there are many mental health issues that players can encounter. For example, they could encounter mental health issues if they move from a foreign country without their family or friends, or if they suffer a long-term injury, are not in the team and have fallen out of favour as well as marital and financial issues. The players weren't looking at it like that but when you've broken it down like that they were able to recognise it. When you have former players that are sharing their mental health and well-being experiences I believe it will become easier for other players to feel comfortable about talking about it and accessing the PFA welfare services.'

The figures who accessed the PFA's services have grown since 2014, with the organisation working closely with former players' associations and directly with the clubs themselves. 'Each Premier League club now employs a designated mental health first-aider, we plan to extend this programme to all Football League clubs,' says Michael. 'We also plan to roll out a PFA mental health workshop – we believe the key is to educate our members about what mental health and well-being looks like. The aim is to enable our members to better understand mental health and well-being, so as to identify it when they encounter this experience. On recognising it, they can come forward and seek the relevant support. We're trying to encourage more players to come forward and talk about their experiences, and feel comfortable to talk and know that there's now something in place at the PFA where they can come and talk about their issues in a confidential setting.'

Those who have shared their experiences hope that their openness will lead to a sea change in attitudes within the game, where younger players will realise that it's okay to ask for help.

The former Middlesbrough and Hull City striker Dean Windass admitted that he cried every day for two years after retirement and subsequently tried to take his own life. He believes that there are hundreds of footballers similarly affected, who feel they have nothing to get up for in the morning.

Leon McKenzie played for Crystal Palace and Norwich City in the Premier League before going on to forge a career in professional boxing post-retirement. In October 2015, McKenzie stopped John McCallum in six rounds to edge closer to a shot at the British super-middleweight title. His fight with depression, however, proved a more difficult opponent. In 2009 he attempted suicide and has spoken about how he felt lost when he finished playing.

Neither Windass nor McKenzie would have been considered shrinking violets on the pitch. And neither would Steve Walsh. The former Leicester City captain cultivated a hardman image during a career in which he amassed 13 red cards – a joint Football League record. His no-nonsense approach made him a cult hero with Leicester fans, who nicknamed him 'Captain Fantastic'.

I'd originally wanted to speak to Steve about the football academy he now runs with former Foxes team-mate Muzzy

Izzet. However, when he heard I was writing a book about what happens to footballers when they finish playing he pointed me towards his autobiography, *50 Shades of Blue*.

I was soon captivated and, after reading it in one sitting, it was clear to me that Walsh had endured almost every problem a footballer can encounter upon retirement. He wrote, 'Divorce, alcohol abuse, depression, anxiety, bankruptcy and near total breakdown followed when I could no longer rely in "real life" on that feeling of "nobody is going to beat me" I had on the pitch.'

He believes his acrimonious departure from Leicester City, where he spent almost 15 years, marked the beginning of his problems. When Martin O'Neill left the club to manage Celtic in 2000, Walsh and his team-mate Tony Cottee applied for the vacant managerial role. It was, instead, given to Peter Taylor who quickly showed Walsh the door.

'When you've been that long at a club and familiar with everything, things change. And it's the change that does it,' says Steve. 'The way I left Leicester left a bitter taste and I felt aggrieved with that. Peter Taylor did what he wanted to do, which was to get the old school out. To his cost really, because he had some good, first-hand help from pros who had been there and done it.'

His playing career never really recovered and, after short spells at Norwich City and Coventry City, he retired in 2003. He admits he had little preparation for retirement which, allied to personal problems, combined to take their toll. 'There wasn't much preparation for retirement from the game, but it was starting. The PFA were doing surveys to look at these issues, to try and help all its members and push them in to the right thing when they finish football. When things don't go right for you as well off the field, then that creates a lot of other issues, which mentally you have to deal with and be strong. I guess that although I was very strong on the pitch, off it things that were happening and imploding were taking their effect. All these problems are interlinked and they all have this effect on you that sometimes you don't realise is happening until further down the line.

'You don't like to admit it but I guess retirement made it worse. Everybody wanted me to stay at Leicester. I should have probably sat tight and not left but the way I was pushed out was wrong. It might have been an easier progression towards finishing, a natural thing – taking my coaching badges at Leicester and learning my trade in management.'

He saw a counsellor and was on anti-depressants for six months but recognised that he needed to deal with his problems himself. A return to the game, through his academy and working back at Leicester on matchdays, has helped but time has been the greatest healer.

'You try to be more positive. I must admit, I've started to get into that frame of mind. It's never been me, I've never been negative about anything. Getting over the football side of it, I think now I've gone back into football with Muzzy has helped,' says Steve. 'Also, the new owners at Leicester have been very good to me. They've certainly made me feel more than welcome and have brought me back into the picture. They're really good people. I've accepted things now and moved on. I think it's just a time period that's needed for acceptance. You have to look at change, look at what you're doing and focus on your new life.'

I ask him if it was the loss of identity as a footballer that was the most pertinent contributor to his depression and anxiety. 'I guess it was. Sometimes you don't like to say it but, deep down, I think the deep-rooted problem is that the life you lived as a footballer is totally different to now. You can't get it back, can you?' he concludes.

You can't. But, sometimes, having another passion to pursue can make that transition a whole lot easier.

7

A Fresh Start

SHANE Supple readily admits his story is a strange one. Like many talented young Irish footballers, he left his homeland for England at an early age – he was just 15 when he joined Ipswich Town in 2002. He and his contemporary Darren Randolph, born eight days apart, were both tipped as future successors to Irish goalkeeping legends Pat Bonner and Shay Given. While West Ham's Randolph earned plaudits in the Republic of Ireland's shock Euro 2016 qualifiers win over Germany in October 2015, Supple watched the game in Dublin with his father and friends with an air of 'that could have been Shane' hanging over them. However, he insists he has no regrets about his unusual decision.

'I have never really spoken about it in detail, but there were a number of factors which made me come to the decision to retire from professional football at 22,' admits the Dubliner. 'The first time I started to think football wasn't what I thought it would be was when I was brought into the first-team squad around 17 and I saw the way lads were carrying on and talking about the game and how the club didn't mean anything to them.

'Now I know I was very naïve, but I came from a different place and background. At the time I was on the bench for the Ipswich first team and we were going well in the league, second at the time, but we eventually finished third and lost to West Ham in the play-off semi-final. The lads weren't happy because obviously the play-offs would eat into their holidays, some lads wouldn't be kept on if we got promoted and this annoyed me coming from lads who I looked up to and had played at the highest level.

'Another reason was the people involved in the game didn't have any principles and were yes men that would do anything to keep themselves in a job,' he continues. 'Basically I felt I couldn't trust anyone within the club.'

With depression in football becoming more of an issue, Supple admits his own welfare was a factor.

'There wasn't one thing that triggered it, I don't think, and it's not a story you hear every day, but I felt that for the sake of my own well-being I had to get out at 22, while I was still young. I suppose now with all the stuff around mental health it makes me think about what I was going through back then in Ipswich. I did nearly pack it in a few years before, but because of not wanting to let my dad down I stayed a bit longer and, I suppose, when you put so much effort into becoming a footballer, it was hard to take that this wasn't for me any more. However, I have never once regretted my decision.'

Shane had planned to go back to school and get the grades he needed to apply to join the Irish police force – An Garda Síochána – but the deep recession in Ireland scuppered his plans.

'At the time, when I returned home, things were starting to go really bad in the economy and Garda recruitment was frozen and wasn't re-opened for five years so I went to work in a hospital for a couple of years before joining a sports management company, where I am now.'

He now works alongside Dublin Gaelic football stars Bernard and James Brogan in Legacy Consultants, providing talent representation, sponsorship consultancy, digital, PR and event management services to clients in the sports and entertainment industries.

If you're going to drop a bombshell that you wish to retire from professional football at an early age, there must be easier people to break the news to than Roy Keane. But Supple reveals that his then Ipswich Town manager was sympathetic, 'Keano was the manager when I left and was brilliant the way he dealt with it. He was shocked but understood my reasons.'

Matt Holland, at Ipswich around the same time, was surprised but felt it was a brave decision. 'I take my hat off to him. If you're not enjoying it, you have to do what's right for you as an individual,' he said.

Supple admits that playing Gaelic football with pals he grew up with – as a goalkeeper, of course – when he returned home, helped ease the effects of retirement from professional soccer.

'I play for St Brigid's in Dublin, where I'd played growing up, and the club has been great,' he remarks. 'I captained the team to a county title in 2011 and that was a massive relief and an unreal feeling to win something that is really difficult to win with your friends, which was the icing on the cake.'

Roy Keane's office may be an unusual setting in which to retire, but a Tesco in Sheffield is an even more unlikely location unless, of course, you work in a Tesco in Sheffield.

Only a few miles from the Dublin offices of Legacy Consultants lives another former player with a lot more in common with Supple than mere geographic location. Former Norwegian international goalkeeper Espen Baardsen is 38 now, but he looks like he could still command a penalty box. He's younger than several current Premier League keepers and could very well still be playing if he hadn't made the huge decision to hang up his gloves at the age of 25.

We met in a coffee shop near Dublin's Misery Hill but he says he is happier now than he ever was as a player. Like Supple, he harbours no regrets about leaving the sport so young and claims not to miss football at all, although he does look out for Tottenham's results now and then.

Baardsen grew up in the East Bay area of San Francisco, where he was spotted by Spurs at the age of 14. He signed his first professional three-year contract at 17 but remained in the States for a further year to complete his high school education. Ian Walker, whom he replaced for his debut against Liverpool at Anfield, was his competition for the number one spot at the club. However, the actual reality of being a pro wasn't as exciting as he'd envisaged and he quickly became disillusioned with the game.

'I didn't enjoy the total lack of flexibility within your time schedule,' he admits. 'In almost every other profession, you can take a summer holiday when you like or an extra day on a Bank Holiday weekend. But these things are impossible. People talk about footballers having free time, but who cares about having Monday afternoons off from two to five? You also couldn't plan anything. You didn't know if you'd be training until the day before a lot of the time.'

He also felt the need to be stimulated more intellectually, something he felt that the sport couldn't give him. The typical dressing room banter didn't bother him but it clearly didn't excite him either. 'It just wasn't fulfilling. So all those factors met together and I didn't have the hunger or the enthusiasm that I would have had when I was in my late teens,' he recalls. 'The problem is, without that, you're really fighting at a big disadvantage. You can't play football just going through the motions. There may be some players who are incredibly gifted who can do that. But I wasn't one of them.'

Like with Shane Supple, it wasn't an overnight decision, with doubts already forming at 20 or 21. Baardsen says, 'When I lost my place to Ian Walker under George Graham I was pretty bummed. I tried to pick myself up after moving to Watford and had a good pre-season, but a combination of events and poor performance from the team contributed to it all.'

Baardsen had several interests outside football and found a hard taskmaster at Watford in the form of Gianluca Vialli. 'His summary was that he thought about football 23 hours a day, leaving one hour for sex. He distinctly disliked anything less than a full-on focus on football.' Vialli, therefore, wasn't overly impressed with his goalkeeper studying finance and for an Open University degree in Social Sciences in his spare time. After an acrimonious departure from the Hornets, Baardsen thought, 'That is pretty much it.' However, there was to be a short stint at Everton under David Moyes, where he admits to being out of shape as he 'hated' what he was doing. He spent his time with the club cooped up in a Liverpool hotel and drinking beer in the afternoon. By this stage, though, he was more interested in his junk bond portfolio than playing football.

He met Neil Warnock at Sheffield United and was offered a contract as backup goalkeeper with a 90 per cent drop in salary or, as he recalls thinking, 'half the salary of a Tube driver in London'. He laughs at the memory of Warnock stressing that there'd be an appearance bonus on top of that before mentioning that he never included a goalkeeper among his five substitutes. Baardsen had checked in to a Sheffield hotel earlier that day but quickly checked out of it – and his career in football. 'I went to Tesco in Sheffield for a sandwich or something and I think that took me over the edge. I thought to myself, "Right, what am I doing?" So I got in my car and drove home.' His last act as a professional footballer was calling his agent and telling him not to contact him again.

He immediately set about fulfilling his ambition of travelling the world, taking a gap year before beginning to make some contacts in the world of finance. He'd visited many outposts during his football career but regretted only seeing the insides of hotels and football grounds on his travels. While playing, he had enjoyed investing his own money in stocks and derivatives and he set about forging a new career as a financial trader and property investor, and now juggles his time between Dublin, London and France.

Baardsen does miss the adrenaline rushes that football gave him, including a place in Norway's 1998 World Cup squad, but they came all too infrequently. 'If football was just about that, it would be the greatest thing imaginable. A lot of supporters somehow think that that's what most of it is. And that's why they might sit there and scratch their heads and wonder why would you quit early, especially when it's all that? But it isn't all that.'

Voluntary retirements at an early age are incredibly uncommon in professional football. Probably the most recent, high-profile example is that of David Bentley, who retired at just 29 claiming he 'never felt like a footballer'. The midfielder, who once cost Tottenham £15m, is now running a chain of restaurants after becoming disillusioned with 'all the bullshit that goes with football'.

'Yeah, I never really felt like a footballer,' he admits as he takes a break from planning marketing for one of the restaurants he co-owns and runs in Marbella. 'I'm still discovering myself and discovering why and what, and answering the questions I've had in my head. For me, it definitely felt like I just didn't fit into the mould psychologically. Life's about playing a game and it's all a game. Some people play it better than others. For me, it felt like the game that needed playing, I wasn't good at or willing to do. To be in the structure and being owned like a piece of meat, that never sat well with me and I always wanted to break free of that. It just felt very controlling.'

Like the others I spoke to, Bentley's doubts about the game first manifested themselves years earlier, in his case over a decade before he finally made his career-ending decision.

'I first had thoughts when I was 18 or 19,' he recalls. 'I got to the point where the further I got in my career, the less interested I became. It was a strange one; it was an upside-down thing, because normally you'd say you'd get more interested. Which was a shame. You're playing with friends, your family are all loving it. But the more involved, the more serious it became, the more pressure there was on me, the more pressure there was on my family. It just became less interesting. It took the fun, the artistry out of it. The love of the game became boring. To the point of my contract ending, I had a decision to make. I had twins on the way; my daughter was just starting full-time school; I wasn't going to take a two- or three-year contract somewhere or move abroad or something like that. I wanted to go and live my life the way I wanted to live it.'

The advent of social media and the intense pressures surrounding the game became too much for the player who was often touted as 'the next David Beckham'.

'No matter where you were, playing golf or sat in a restaurant having a couple of glasses of wine, it'd be on social media that you were drinking. Everything was so focused, the bullshit, the money, the agents, the people, the crap that's around it, the opinions. To be honest, it all just became a bit boring,' he reveals. 'The actual playing, crossing the white line and playing football, I still love it. But you can't do that without taking on board all that other stuff that comes with it.'

Even those closest to Bentley found it difficult to understand the decision of a player who once scored a Premier

League hat-trick against Manchester United and won seven England caps.

'They didn't get it. Some people don't get it,' he continues. 'There are people who judge their life on financial reward, it's the way the world's set up. Set up to be driven to succeed financially. For me, it wasn't about that. They were understanding of my decision; they backed my decision but they found it strange that I retired. Some people don't get it even when I speak to them now.'

Bentley is grateful to the team that have been a consistent part of his life since he started in the game for ensuring he had the financial security to come to his decision. 'I was looked after by my agent Robert [Segal] since I was 15 years old. All the financial team, and all the people that were around him, it was my decision to stay with the same ones. I've had the same bank manager, same accountant. They looked after me really, whereas a lot of players don't get looked after.

'That's the thing: you can make a creative decision but I've got children, I've got a life. I had financial freedom to make my own creative decision, that's how I look at it. It's all good saying, "I don't want to do this, I don't want to do that," but if I had to play I would still be playing, if it were a case of having to pay bills and stuff. But I was in a lucky position where I did have the choice. I don't regret it. I still follow the game, watch it, and still love it. I don't regret not playing it though, no.'

We spoke as he sat outside La Sala, basking in the Andalusian sun, and it certainly seems like an enviable lifestyle. 'It keeps us all very busy,' he says. 'It's a great family environment, we're all friends; some of us have got kids the same age. Stephen Carr [a former Tottenham team-mate] is involved. We're all really good friends; it's a great thing. Socially, we're all together; business side of things, we're together. I've got my twins and my six-year-old daughter, so they take up a lot of my time, which is what I love. I love being a part of their lives, bringing them to school and picking them up every day, which I wouldn't have been able to do before. I'm in a good place, to be honest. Mentally, I'm in a much better place now than I was when I used to play.'

Bentley appeared in a 2015 documentary on Irish television called *The Toughest Trade*, where sports stars swapped disciplines and tried their hand at a new sport. In it, he played Gaelic football for Crossmaglen Rangers and seemed to embrace the togetherness of those involved in the sport. He agrees that it reminded him of the qualities that made him first fall in love with football. 'It was a great experience for me, I loved it. Because of the fundamental values that Gaelic football has, and what the Irish in general have, that sense of community. That was what I fell in love with when I first started playing. Now, it's gone to a different place.'

In the past couple of years, the restaurant business has been rolled out to the UK, but David sees his future firmly in Spain. 'I'll never go back to England,' he says. 'My six-year-old goes to a Spanish school and is fluent in the language. I like the culture and the environment. I like the ease of life, their approach to it.'

He admits he enjoys the management and coaching side of the game but is happy with his lot right now, 'Maybe I'll re-address that – maybe in 20 years or something, but not now, not now.'

He may not be in a rush to get back to football, but it's still with him. After we chat he sends me a video he's filmed to help promote his restaurants. In it, he delivers a trademark cross straight to a colleague from 30 or 40 yards, reminding me of a talent who Arsène Wenger once pleaded with not to leave Arsenal.

I found myself empathising with all three early retirees. Football fans are often bewildered when a player retires early, wondering how they can throw away so abruptly a career they've pursued since childhood. But it's often a slow build-up, with doubts creeping in years before a final decision is made.

Growing up, all I watched on television, apart from football, was comedy. I wondered what it would be like to write jokes, go on stage and make rooms full of strangers laugh. In August 2004, I found out. Living in Australia for a year, I noticed an advertisement in the *Sydney Morning Herald* for the Sydney Comedy Store. Within a week I was on its stage. It went okay and I gigged more and more during my spell Down Under, reaching the finals of several comedy competitions. Upon my return to Ireland, comedy became my major focus although the rise was gradual. After a few years I'd gigged with some comedy heroes, had written for TV and radio and ran a number of successful comedy clubs. Now, I was never going to be getting a call from Michael McIntyre to appear on his next roadshow, but I was happy with my lot in the lower leagues of comedy.

However, after a few years, doubts started creeping in. When people are sitting at home watching *Live at the Apollo* they're seeing the comedy equivalent of one of Espen Baardsen's implausible saves or a David Bentley volley into the top corner. However, most of a comedian's life is spent networking, writing jokes that will never see the light of day and spending hours travelling to and from gigs for a few minutes' stage time. With a young family and other commitments, increasingly in recent years I've been distancing myself from stand-up. I guess I'd seen behind the curtain and, to quote Bentley, 'didn't like the bullshit that went along with it'. So, albeit on a much smaller scale, I can understand how a footballer can make a decision to draw a line under something that they once loved but isn't for them any more.

Supple, Baardsen and Bentley, though, are outliers, rare examples of those who retired because they'd fallen out of love with the game. For most, they hang up their boots as the game has fallen out of love with them. With age, injuries or fading talent catching up with them, most footballers have the decision to retire taken for them. Gary Neville said in the BBC documentary *Class of 92: Out of Their League*, 'If you've had something that's so good, like standing in that tunnel, walking out in front of 75,000 people, it's like you've got to fill that with something. And it better be good. 'Cause that was good.'

Like Neville, who has balanced punditry, coaching with Valencia and England as well as co-owning a non-league club during retirement, many will strive to remain in the game that is all they've known. However, there are only so many clubs to manage, only so many seats on the *Match of the Day* panel to fill. Others follow more unusual paths. The lucky ones are those who have other passions or talents to pursue.

Eric Cantona once said, 'Football is the most beautiful of the arts; because it is an art. Art is about spontaneity. Every artist tries to find spontaneity in what they do.' According to Cantona's logic, then, all footballers are potentially artists. Whether you agree with this or not, you can't argue with certain cases. Like that of Jody Craddock.

Craddock played as a central defender for Sunderland and Wolverhampton Wanderers in the Premier League before retiring from the game in 2013 and pursuing a rather unusual new career.

'I didn't set out to be an artist,' he admits. 'It just sort of happened. I always wanted to be a footballer, whether I was going to be one was a different story. I did A Level Art, so it was something that was always there, but it never crossed my mind to make a living from it, to be an artist. I didn't think I was at that level, so it's something I never really thought about.'

Art was merely a hobby during the former Wolves captain's playing days. 'It was just something I enjoyed doing.

The more I did it, the better I got. Somebody spotted work in my house and said, "You should do something with this." So I started showing some people. It's quite easy being in the Premier League to get it on to TV or whatever I wanted to do with it. It got a bit of interest and I started selling to the lads really.'

He began a nice little sideline selling paintings of their kids or goal celebrations to team-mates. 'It's not a common hobby among footballers but it was just something I enjoyed doing, drawing and painting. I am self-taught, I've got something in me where if I like something I'll keep going until I've done it, so to speak. With football, I had the free time in the afternoon. The more I did the better I seemed to get.'

Jody certainly agrees that having another passion in life negated the downsides of retiring from football. 'When I was at Sunderland, I did my coaching badges, my B Licence, so the aim was to be a coach. As a footballer, it's a pretty short-lived career so you need something to fall back on. I did a couple of courses, too, one in Fitness & Nutrition, the other in Sports Psychology so the thought was I'd stay in football and go into something along those lines. I never really even considered the art, but it just seemed like a natural progression. I'd done it for ten to 12 years alongside the football. The question was, "Do I go with my head or go with my heart?"'

Jody's heart triumphed, as it was the painting that he 'really wanted to do'. He sees himself now as an artist. 'I was a footballer who used to do a bit of painting. Now I'd like to be seen as an artist who used to play football. I will continue to do it; if I can't sell them, I'll just have to stack them up in the studio!'

He doesn't really miss football but goes to watch Wolves' home games. 'I felt like I'd done my fair share. I'd done 20 years so that's a good stretch in anyone's football career. It felt like the right time to retire. I was at the point in my career, at 37 or 38, where if I couldn't get through a whole season without getting injured then I'd quit. And I didn't think I would. It was a quite comfortable decision, the right time and it wasn't a problem to retire.'

Jody's son had just been diagnosed with leukaemia at exactly the same time, which solidified his decision. He was 'match fit' but Wolves' new manager Ståle Solbakken wasn't prepared to offer him a new contract. 'I didn't have the opportunity to even show him what I could do, and I was thinking, "My son's got leukaemia, do I want to be going to other clubs on trial just for a one-year contract?" The answer was no. It seemed like the right thing to do was retire and concentrate on what my son was going through.'

Thankfully, his son is now in remission after a three-year course of treatment and has been given the all-clear. A typical day for Jody now involves splitting the school runs with his wife and sitting in his studio and concentrating on his art.

His work has clearly evolved over the years, from portraits of fellow players and their families to a trademark style he's comfortable in calling his own. 'My latest collection is my identity. I've been searching for that and working on that over the past year. As an artist, you want to be taken seriously and for someone to see one of your paintings in another part of the country and be able to recognise your work without looking at the name. That's what having an identity is about. I'm really pleased with it.'

When I spoke to Jody he had just successfully finished his first exhibition – 'La Bellezza Della Fusione', which translates as 'The Beauty of Fusion', symbolising his bringing together of two artistic styles in one painting. However, he hadn't totally forgotten his football roots. The exhibition kicked off at 3pm on a Saturday, and ended just in time for the full-time results.

I read somewhere once that the music you love when you're aged 18 is the music that will stay with you for life.

Not entirely true in my case, as when I left school the Britpop craze was in full swing. I must admit, however, that I did fall under its spell. While some of its legacy has stood the test of time, I won't be searching for the likes of Menswe@r on Spotify any time soon. The era also spawned many other things, including the first 'Britpop footballer'. It wasn't a tag that the then Nottingham Forest striker Paul McGregor felt comfortable with but he concedes he 'went along with it'.

'I thought it was very silly at the time,' he admits. 'I remember getting very bored with the Britpop thing very quickly the second everybody started to look identical; Oasis started to become a parody of themselves and The Verve started making silly music. I was looking around and that old quote came to me about not wanting to be part of a group or society that would have me. We started going to techno clubs and it was just how I imagined going to see The Stooges would be – physically grabbing you and pulsating you and just being absolutely incredible and really powerful. That became a really big influence as well, combining really hard techno with The Jesus & Mary Chain's thrilling, thrashing guitars and the sloganeering of the Manic Street Preachers.

'Both music and football were genuine loves. I was one of the first footballers to actually do both properly. I'd do interviews and I'd be sat there in an obscure Velvet Underground t-shirt and stuff and then the people from the *Mirror*, for example, would turn up and say, "Oh, this kid means it. He's not just trying to be an Ocean Colour Scene or something ridiculous. There's no bandwagon jumping here, this is what he's done his whole life." It just so happened that football paid first.'

Paul's passion for both was formed growing up, where his earliest memories include being thrown out of shops for kicking around his ball. 'I always had this thing at my feet,' he remembers. Music also was an enormous backdrop to his childhood. Born in Liverpool, The Beatles were a constant presence and he recalls, '[I was] climbing into bed with my mum and dad, and they used to get woken up by the radio, and hearing things like "Wuthering Heights" by Kate Bush or "Vienna". Just hearing these sounds! Even to this day I'm still thrilled by sounds and bands that are really dissonant and creepy and scare me almost. I can remember lying in bed, feeling safe with my mum and dad, but shaking. Not knowing then that these guys were using certain chord structures and all this to create this really odd atmosphere. And that's what I really love now.'

Football became Paul's first obsession with music coming later, as he explains: 'I guess there are more options as a six-, seven-, eight-year-old kid to be playing football regularly than to be playing in a band. So kids don't go on the playground and get their guitars out, the ball's out constantly.'

After signing for Forest on schoolboy forms – 'I was playing for the county, scoring for fun, playing really well and getting all the plaudits' – he was becoming increasingly intrigued by, as he puts it in ironic air quotes, 'the alternative scene'.

'I had a friend in my class whose brother was the coolest kid around. He had this really long fringe, used to skateboard in winklepickers, listened to Velvet Underground and all these great anorak bands from the late 80s like The Pooh Sticks and The Stupids and all your kind of original indie bands. Really early The Jesus & Mary Chain, really early Primal Scream,' he recalls. 'I had this really bizarre clash of worlds, of wanting to look like Richey from the Manics or David Bowie and being quite androgynous, and wearing eyeliner and winklepickers and then slamming into this rather masculine world of football and doing well in it.'

Paul formed his first band at school at 14, but when he signed on professional terms with Brian Clough's Forest a year later, music took a back seat. 'When I was first at Forest, it was a case of, "This is your first job, knuckle down." Football became very serious, very quickly, and you start realising that a lot of big dreams that you had can come true very quickly if you work hard at this.' However, while team-mates went clubbing, he was back in his village hall with his band 'doing Small Faces and Manics cover versions and getting into the Stone Roses and things like that. It was a very odd little world but I kind of kept it to myself for a while and then all the lads started catching on, "Oh, he's in a band. Are you doing gigs?" and that kind of stuff.'

Paul found a kindred spirit in Frank Clark, who took over from Brian Clough just as Britpop was taking hold on the public consciousness and his school band, Merc, were being 'thrust into the limelight'.

'I was very lucky with Frank Clark being a manager at that time,' he explains. 'I can remember that great year we were in Europe and being at one of the airports and all the press were around, just as we were about to leave and go and play Bayern Munich. I was stood next to the gaffer and I looked down and his bag was open and inside was the Danny Sugerman book about The Doors – *No One Here Gets Out Alive*. So I went, "Oh, gaffer, do you like The Doors?" as I had Jim Morrison posters on my wall from a very young age. He said, "Yeah, yeah, yeah, I'm really into them." And he used to play guitar at Christmas do's and stuff like that. We had a good chat, so he could understand to some degree those two passions. So I was very lucky with that. But they never clashed and I was always very keen for people to know it was all about football. But I can't underplay the role the times were playing – when football and laddism and all that really smashed together, and everybody wanted a rock star footballer.'

Paul admits that the attention came way too soon for Merc. 'We were nowhere near ready for it, not even close.

We had about six or seven songs, we had a manager on board. All of a sudden I had an agent for that side of things who had me out modelling, going to gigs, making public appearances, all this rubbish. And it all happened too quickly. We had a cracking guitarist but we were a bunch of misfits.

'At school, it's total pot luck. You don't have time to evolve as a band. It's like, "Oh, who can play drums? He can play drums." Sometimes it works but it's very, very rare. I felt I was doing the two to the best of my ability. But I knew, and particularly the guitarist knew as well, that this wasn't going to be the band that was going to do anything.'

The band were informed that the then Oasis manager and head of Creations Records, Alan McGee, was coming to watch one of their London gigs. 'I'm so very glad he didn't make it,' says Paul. 'We started getting a little bit embarrassed about some of the tours we were being offered. We just thought, "We can't do this, this isn't the right band," so we ended it.'

Clark had assured him that he'd start the season on the right wing with the then England winger Steve Stone to be moved inside to accommodate him, but an injury setback scuppered his progress. 'The last game of pre-season I snapped my cruciate ligament and my lateral ligament ruptured, which was soul-destroying. By the time I came back, six months later to the day, we'd had three managers. You go from being on absolute fire to not being recognised in the corridor by the coaching staff. It was tough, it was really, really hard.'

Ron Atkinson had been appointed as the new manager and McGregor was aware that he'd touted him a few months previously alongside the likes of Robbie Fowler as some of the best young talent in England. The striker fought his way back to fitness and was enthusiastic about the new regime. That is, until Atkinson met the first-team squad on his first day. Paul recalls, 'He walks on the training ground and says, "Let's see what we've got here lads," and points to me out of all the squad, and says, "Because I don't want any fucking rock stars in my team." You know that feeling when life drains from you and you go white? I just felt like that staring at him. I just felt, "Well this is me done at Forest.'"

Paul enjoyed spells at Carlisle United, where he was first name on the team sheet every week, and Preston North End where he spent afternoons training with David Moyes. A stint at Plymouth Argyle followed, where he was top scorer and Player of the Year. His housemate in Plymouth worked in a local studio, where McGregor spent his spare time with his new band, Ulterior, recording and learning the technical side of production.

However, an unhappy spell at Northampton Town 'knocked the love for football out of me completely'. He says, 'It's a dreadful club, it's just run so poorly. Not getting paid your wages, bad coaches. It was just not a good time.'

He'd been spending time on the London scene with his brother. 'Before we knew it we had a great band. People were talking about us, and it was all on that dark underground warehouse scene that bands like The Horrors were coming out of.' Then came a contract offer from 'Grimsby or Hull' and he had a big decision to make.

'I thought, "Why the hell do I want to go and live in Grimsby or Hull?" And I just saw this career in front of me that was playing in front of 4,000 every week for all right money,' continues Paul. 'I genuinely didn't care about the money, I loved playing football. But the money wasn't worth some guy, who's never done anything in football, screaming and shouting at you on a Tuesday morning. I just thought, "I've had enough of this, this is not me." It just so happened the week before I decided to retire that the front page of the *NME* featured the new dark wave of London and our band was named as part of it. I was 28 and I thought, "Well, I've got a decision to make." So I made it and I walked away from football and we hit the London scene hard. It was great; there was no looking back.'

Paul spent the first three years after leaving the game in his bedroom reading and writing and living off his savings from football. 'I did the old chestnut of not looking at my bank account until I got the feeling that I needed to look at my bank account. And then I looked at it and there was about £400 in it. You'd be surprised at how many footballers do that when they finish,' he reveals. 'I just got a little bit scared, so then came a few little jobs.'

Meanwhile, Ulterior became his main motivation, recording a debut album, working with people they respected and touring Europe with the likes of Sisters of Mercy. 'We played sold-out shows all over the place. We became quite a big underground band. We toured South Africa, Japan twice, Europe extensively. We turned down two contracts with majors because the money was dreadful. And I'm still making music now,' says Paul.

'The UK didn't like us because we use drum machines and we're not an indie band. The Europeans like us because they grew up with Kraftwerk and heavy metal, we grew up with The Beatles. It's ingrained in them really, if you're loud and noisy and have got drum machines, you're laughing over there. We just wanted to be the electronic Stooges. We were just always thrilled with bands who were electronic but could provide that level of ferocity that The Stooges did. Bands like Suicide were a really big influence for us. That was the making of the band, that's what we wanted to do.'

Paul still pops to his local pub to watch Premier League games as he doesn't have a TV at home and keeps track of some of his former clubs. He admits there are some aspects of a footballer's life he misses but, like Espen Baardsen, the dressing room atmosphere certainly isn't one of them. 'I miss the Saturdays, I miss the playing, I miss the build-up, I miss the nerves, I miss the pain. It's a hard thing to say but I miss being physical, I miss my shins hurting, I miss a slight hamstring pull, I miss the hustle and bustle of it – especially when you come away from it – because it makes you feel alive,' he continues.

'I don't particularly miss the "banter". When I look back it's a load of one-upmanship and there's so much in the way of bullying. I've known quite a few players that have suffered on various levels with mental health issues. You've got a dressing room with 30 alpha males. Times are changing, you're going to get people like me in a dressing room. I'd be coming in with skinny white jeans, an enormous Stone Island puffa jacket with mental hair and they'd be, "You're gay, you're gay." And then they'd all be there in the gym an hour later with their tops off pumping weights and going, "Oh yeah, your muscles look big." And I'd be like, "Lads, have you ever been to a gay club? They all look like you. They're not all in there trying to look like Lou Reed." It's so weird and overly-masculine, it's a really odd place to be. The levels of bullying if you slightly don't fit in can be really hard to take.'

The highlight of his football career, he says, was the week he scored for Forest against Lyon in the UEFA Cup – 'My picture was on the back of every national newspaper the next morning and I heard my mum screaming because she'd been to get the papers and couldn't believe it' – which was followed three days later with a goal on his home debut against Manchester United, made even sweeter by the fact he grew up supporting Liverpool. 'That was a pretty special week. I look back at that and think, "Wow, that was a quite cool thing to do."'

However, it's clear from our conversation which passion takes precedence – he's more animated discussing Irish band Sultans of Ping FC than Northampton Town FC, for example. On Thursdays he writes and rehearses some solo material, in a little room in a converted warehouse near his home. 'I get as much joy from that as any Saturday playing football,' he concludes.

Carp fishing in France with Lee Bowyer sounds like a programme idea an increasingly desperate Alan Partridge might pitch when faced with an unimpressed television commissioner. I have to admit I'd watch it, though. But book a lodge at Etang De Bows – which roughly translates as 'Bows' Pond' – in the Champagne-Ardenne region of France, and you can do just that. Bowyer retired in 2012 after a successful career and is probably best remembered as part of David O'Leary's Leeds United side that reached the Champions League semi-finals in 2001, as well as for some well-documented off-the-field controversies.

As a player, the Londoner spent a week every June fishing in France to unwind from the football season. When he retired he decided to take a break from the game and his thoughts drifted back to France. To paraphrase Victor Kiam's famous slogan, Bowyer liked a lake so much, he bought the company. Anyone who watched Bowyer as a player may find it hard to reconcile the combative midfielder with such a tranquil profession. But he seems to have found peace in this north-eastern region of France famous for its sparkling white wine.

'I started fishing as a kid on the canal behind where I used to live. As I got older I got into bigger fish,' explains Lee, whose amiable personality belies the public image often portrayed during his playing days. 'I always liked carp fishing and I used to go out to France every summer and fish for a week as a little getaway to recharge the batteries. It's something that I really like and enjoy.'

He'd spent some time after retirement at home but, when the lake he'd been to several years before came on the market, he quickly snapped it up. 'When I was playing, I wanted to get a lake but obviously I just didn't have the time,' he says. 'It happened once I retired. I was lucky that a lake that I fished at years ago came up for sale. I thought that it would be something to keep me occupied. It's an interest of mine, so that's why I went and got it. After three years of sitting at home and doing hardly anything, doing school runs and stuff I thought, "Well, yeah, this is the right time now," and then that just fell into my lap. It was a good lake so I thought, "It's perfect."'

Lee agrees that having another passion away from the sport is crucial in making the transition to a post-playing career smoother. 'It's definitely helped me,' he acknowledges. 'Like I said, for the first three years I wasn't really doing anything. I did a couple of coaching badges. Even then, when you've been in the game that long, as long as I was, for me football wasn't the thing I wanted to do straight away. It was just perfect. It's not too highly strenuous, I can get away, pop back and forth to France. It's something to keep me occupied and it's a lot better than sitting around the house.'

It's seasonal work and when we spoke, in late January, the lake was closed but it is still Lee's 'busiest time of the year'.

'I have to go out there and cut trees back, tidy the place up around the lake, remove stuff that's fallen in during the year – just doing maintenance work really,' he says. He does all the work himself, joking that his wife Gemma 'lets me use the chainsaw'.

'I'm back and forth quite a bit doing that at the moment,' he continues. 'And then in the summer it just runs itself. Week by week we have different groups coming out. I go out there through the year; this year I tried to go out there every two or three weeks and meet as many groups as I could. It's a social thing; obviously I like fishing so it's good to see people coming, catching, going home happy, me meeting them, so it's good.'

Lee says he found retirement 'quite easy' as he knew instinctively when it was time to call it a day. 'Again, because

I played for so long, it was my body that said I couldn't do this any more. It wasn't injury or anything like that. I was fortunate enough to play until I couldn't play any more. Don't get me wrong, I could have still played and dropped down the divisions but it just wouldn't have been enjoyable. I played because I loved the game, so if I'm not enjoying it any more, waking up stiff every day, then it's just not enjoyable. So I just stopped and it was the right time for me.

'I had two young kids then so I was able to do stuff with them before they started school, go on holidays, go away for Christmas, which I'd never been able to do before, because obviously in the football season it's the busiest time. The first couple of years we did that quite a bit and spent nice time together which took my mind off football, really.'

Lee recently enjoyed a spell coaching at Watford, where he assisted his friend and former Leeds team-mate Harry Kewell. While he still holds ambitions to get back into the game, it's not something he is in a rush to return to. 'I went with Harry and helped out for a bit. The time I was there with him was enjoyable, it was good to see him again and we worked well together, which I'd no doubt we would. It was good to see you were making a difference to the kids,' he says. 'We had the under-21s, so they can play, so you're just passing on your knowledge, which is all I wanted to do anyway. You can't replace the atmosphere in the game, being around the football every day. So, I will go back into it, maybe in a year or two.

'Did I miss it? Not really. Yes and no. I missed the everyday banter, the atmosphere running on to the pitch, scoring goals. But it was time to finish so I just accepted it and moved on.'

Bowyer's Premier League career included clashes with Liverpool's Vegard Heggem and, instead of swapping shirts at the final whistle, they may have regaled each other with fishing tales. Heggem was well respected at Anfield and earned 20 caps for his country before his career was cut short, the full-back retiring through injury at just 28. He returned to the remote Norwegian farm on which he was raised and set about developing a salmon fishing lodge, where you can even sleep in a cabin called Anfield.

Every side will produce its fair share of coaches and pundits from its players when they retire, but not everyone can stay in the game. A dip into a box of loose Panini stickers from the late 1980s and early 90s, which I must have had as spares, reveals plenty of interesting stories. Nigel Spink, a European Cup winner with Aston Villa, now runs his own courier company in Sutton Coldfield called S&M Couriers.

The back of a *Football 90* sticker informs me that Luton Town's Darron McDonough was a 'very quick, determined ball-winner'. Google tells me the former defender, who was Kevin Keegan's first signing at Newcastle United, now runs his own joinery business and lives in a house he built himself.

Greg Downs, an FA Cup winner with Coventry City in 1987, became a policeman after retiring from the professional game. Downs's Sky Blues team-mate Micky Gynn became a postman when he hung up his boots but he certainly didn't distance himself from the club, with City's training ground part of his daily round.

Lee Crooks, a defensive midfielder with Manchester City in the 1990s, is now a gunner in the RAF Regiment, and was deployed to Afghanistan in 2012. Alan Dickens, a stylish midfielder with West Ham and Chelsea, is now a black cab driver in Barking.

Many other players may not have had a passion to fall back on but still pursue a diverse range of careers away from the game. Arjan de Zeeuw, Forensic Detective, sounds like a gritty Dutch crime series but that's exactly what the former Wigan Athletic and Portsmouth defender is up to these days. De Zeeuw had planned to study for a medical degree when he retired but the lengthy studies involved put him off. Instead he took up an opportunity to be fast-tracked as a detective in the Dutch police force, an apt move for someone once nicknamed 'The Peacemaker'.

Diego Maradona once claimed, 'Football isn't a game, nor a sport, it's a religion.' So, it's no surprise to learn that many former players have followed their faith after retiring from football. Peter Knowles starred for Wolverhampton Wanderers in the 1960s and scored over 100 goals for the club but, after a spell in the United States, he retired from the game at just 24 to become a Jehovah's Witness. The club retained his registration for 12 years in the hope he'd return to football but it never transpired.

Former Northern Irish international Phil Mulryne played for Manchester United in the mid-90s before spending most of his career with Norwich City. During his playing days, Mulryne dated model Nicola Chapman and was once sent home from the Northern Ireland squad for a breach of discipline after breaking a curfew to go drinking with Jeff Whitley. Upon retirement in 2009, he surprised former team-mates by beginning training to become a Roman Catholic priest.

Gavin Peacock is another former footballer who turned to God when his playing days ended. He played for Chelsea alongside the likes of Ruud Gullit and scored the winner twice in one season against Manchester United. While he was still playing he became a preacher at his local church and even hosted the BBC's *Songs of Praise* in 2008 before moving to Canada where he is now an elder and pastor at Calvary Grace Church.

Richard Leadbeater also made the move from, as he puts it, pitch to pulpit. He began at Wolves before spending most of his career playing in the lower leagues and the Conference. A Christian since the age of 16, Leadbeater began studying for a Theology degree while still playing. He is now a pastor at King's Church in Guildford, which he helped establish in 2014. He agrees wholeheartedly with Maradona's comparison between football and religion. 'I think football is probably more of a religion than Christianity is! I think Christianity is much more about the relationship than a religion. There are massive similarities. People gather at a sports stadium, they gather at a church building. People sing songs about those they adore, people sing hymns about Jesus. People give money in both settings, people sacrifice things. You feel good, you feel bad, you go with your mates, there's a community element to both. It's where people find happiness, meaning, purpose. If you're going to use the word religion for both of them, though, I think Christianity is a much better religion than football.'

Richard left school at 16 to join Wolves on a full-time contract. Around the same time his sister became a Christian through a friend at work. 'I used to think Christians were nutcases because the only Christians I knew or had seen on TV were just weird. But my sister wasn't weird so I couldn't work out how you could be a Christian and not be weird,' he recalls. He was soon visiting a local church with his sister and was surprised at what he found. 'I suppose the big thing that happened was that I thought I knew what Christianity was about until I actually heard somebody telling me what the Bible said it was about.'

At first Richard was uncomfortable with disclosing his newly-found faith among his team-mates. 'Initially, I kept a low profile for a number of reasons. Firstly, I was embarrassed and I didn't want anyone to find out. Also, I didn't understand that Christianity affected the whole of your life. I thought it was just for a Sunday morning, where I'd be a Christian between the hours of 11 and 12 at church and then go to training on a Monday morning and be exactly the same as I was before, as if Christianity was a sort of hobby I did on a

Sunday. Some people played golf, some people went shopping, I went to church. Initially, I didn't understand that following Jesus meant following Jesus with everything all the time.'

His hesitancy in revealing his faith changed when an older colleague, a well-respected Welsh international and fellow Christian, approached him on the training ground. 'Brian Law came up to me one day and said, "You're a Christian, aren't you?" And Brian Law was a scary centre-back and I was a very weak centre-forward. Him saying it shocked me into admitting it in public for the first time.'

There was a bit of teasing at first but he became more confident in his faith among his fellow players. He began to focus more on his religion rather than football and was soon playing part-time for Stevenage, where he was earning more money than when he had been playing full-time. 'Having had football as my dream, the longer I was a Christian the less I wanted to play football and the more I wanted to serve in a church.'

The end of Richard's football career came at 26. He wasn't enjoying it any more and struggled with football as a business rather than a sport he had loved. 'It had always been something I'd done for fun. I was having a wrestle with it. Is this what I want to do with my life? Is this worth it? Is this a good thing to do with one's time and money? I had grown to see and believe that Christianity is life-changing, true and it matters. I know we think it does but it doesn't *ultimately* matter if Manchester City or Chelsea win the league, if Agüero scores four, if England win the World Cup. It's nice but it is a sport. I started to see things from a slightly different perspective. Because if Christianity is true – and I know not everyone thinks it is – it has claims about life and death, and meaning and purpose and life beyond the grave and all those kind of things. I grew up in the football world where the most important thing is three points on a Saturday away at

Morecambe and you kind of think, "Hang on a minute, is that of real importance and value?"'

It wasn't long before Richard had completed his degree in Theology and started working for a church in Birmingham. At 30 he went off to 'vicar school' to get ordained by the Church of England. He now spends his days preparing for Bible studies, out meeting people and building up his new church.

He still keeps an eye on the football results and watches *Match of the Day* but isn't entirely comfortable with the way the game has gone. 'Football can be an influence for good, and it can be a massive influence for bad. I think the amount of money that, for example, people earn in football is not good at all, when you think of the kind of things you could do with money like that around the world. In the grand scheme of things, I believe what I'm doing now is much more valuable and worthwhile.'

Liverpool's Kolo Touré once pretended to be a used-car salesman called Francois, while having an affair with a student. However, it's a route that many former players have actually travelled. Phil Mulryne's partner-in-crime Jeff Whitley, the former Manchester City midfielder, is a salesman for Stockport Car Supermarket. Whitley has admitted he has suffered from alcohol and drug addictions, which left him 'praying' he would die. He now balances his time selling cars with visits to the academies of professional clubs to share his experiences with young players.

Malcolm Christie is another who's made the transform-ation from the football pitch to sales pitch, selling Aston Martins in a Stockton-on-Tees dealership. Christie played for Derby County and Middlesbrough in the Premier League but was forced to retire with a spinal injury, having already lost his appetite for the game.

Jon Newsome played in the Premier League for Sheffield Wednesday, Leeds United and Norwich City and is still living life in the fast lane. Newsome won the league title with Leeds before becoming, in 1994, the Canaries' first £1m signing and now owns Sheffield-based motor dealership AutoMarques. He admits he fell into his new career after retiring in 2000.

'My next-door neighbour was a motor dealer and asked me to do something with him. I was living in my parents' house and needed to earn a living as I knew I'd got a divorce on the horizon. And, as a man, you're not going to walk out of that with pockets full of money. I started working with him for six to 12 months. He showed me the ropes and I shadowed him for a while. We set up a company called AutoMarques which, after a couple of years, I bought him out of and, ten years later, I'm still doing it.'

Jon enjoys the motor trade but has found it's no replacement for his previous career. 'It's not playing football. It'll never replace the love of football and the joy of walking out and playing a game. But it's something that's allowed a lot of flexibility for me, which, with having young kids, is an important part for me. Every day is a different day. Some days I'm out trying to buy cars, others I'm dealing with customers. I do it all by myself and it keeps me busy and it has been a fabulous career for the past ten years.'

His past as a footballer hasn't really helped or hindered him but, occasionally, a customer may have unrealistic expectations. 'People sometimes come in and realise you were a footballer and expect a massive discount because they think you're rolling in money, which is a bit far-fetched really. But I think most of my customers have dealt with me because of the product I've had rather than the fact I used to kick a ball about.'

He still watches Wednesday's home games and keeps an eye on the results of his old clubs, but doesn't feel he'll ever return to the game. 'A couple of times people have asked me whether I'd consider going back into football and it's difficult, really, because when you're out of football you get your life back in your own hands. It's enjoyable to have the weekend off or go away mid-season, but if you're involved in the game, that's not an option. I do different things now, I play golf and I cycle. That's where I find myself these days. But football's something that never leaves you. I still love the game but your life moves on.'

It is evident that a passion for something outside the game can be critical when navigating a path into retirement. But as Jon said, 'Football's something that never leaves you.' And many find it difficult to leave it.

For those who don't have another passion, they often strive to remain in a game that's all they know or have known. Fierce competition exists, though, for managerial, coaching and media roles; but for many – who may not have their equivalent of a fishing lake, paintbrush, pulpit or band to turn to – staying in the game is their only option.

8

Staying In
The Game

WHILE I have often wondered why some players don't pursue a career in management after retiring, probably a more pertinent question is why any bother at all. For those 'lucky' enough to get a break into management, it's not exactly a stable profession – I probably have food in my fridge with a longer shelf life than the current Leeds United manager, for example. The average 'life expectancy' of a Premier League manager at the time of writing is 2.13 years, although one incumbent skews those statistics dramatically. Take Arsène Wenger, who has been in charge at Arsenal since 1996, out of the equation and the figure drops significantly to just over one year.

Ironically, as I typed the above sentence I heard the news that Garry Monk had been relieved of his duties as Swansea City manager. He lasted 22 months at the helm, having previously played for the Swans for almost ten years, captaining the club in English football's top four divisions.

He became the 21st manager to leave his position since the beginning of the season until the start of December across the main four divisions. In other words, 23 per cent of managers who'd started the season with such high hopes just four months earlier were no longer in their jobs as the first strains of 'Fairytale of New York' made their annual appearance on the festive airwaves.

Highlighting the precarious nature of the profession, Monk had been nominated for the Premier League Manager of the Month award just three months prior to his dismissal after masterminding a victory over Manchester United and had been talked of in some quarters as a future England manager. He led Swansea to their best Premier League finish of eighth the previous season and had been generally perceived as a bright young managerial talent. So, why had a club generally considered to be one of the better-run in the top flight taken such a hasty decision?

Upon hearing the news I took to Twitter and conducted a simple straw poll among football fans – 'Did Garry Monk deserve the sack from Swansea City?' A few hours later 237 people had replied, 75 per cent of whom felt the club had made the wrong decision.

However, a quick perusal online of Swansea fans' opinions told a different story. They pointed to the club going backwards during Monk's tenure with the quick, passing style of play honed under Roberto Martínez, Paulo Sousa, Brendan Rodgers and Michael Laudrup jettisoned for a more defensive approach. Many took the view that the club was facing inevitable relegation under Monk. To casual onlookers, Monk's sacking looked harsh, but to those who followed the club it was sadly unavoidable. After a 12-year association, a run of one win in 12 games finally did for Monk. Unfortunately for him he may find it difficult to fill another managerial vacancy.

'Look at the numbers who – and the percentage is phenomenally high – after their first managerial job, never get another job anywhere in football, let alone as a manager,' says Professor Chris Brady, who teaches on the FA's Pro Licence course. Indeed, such is the competitiveness in the profession that Brady reckons, 'About 50 per cent of the League 2 managers are not getting paid. They just need a way back in [to the game].'

In the Championship the environment is even more precarious with the average managerial reign lasting 0.86 years, as at the end of the 2014/15 season. Across the 92 league clubs, there were 47 managerial dismissals and 17 resignations during 2014/15, the most since 2001/02. Seventeen of those sackings were first-time managers, who may find it difficult to find a managerial role again. Allied to this, over 150 coaches lost their jobs as a result of managerial changes.

The average tenure of dismissed managers is also decreasing and stood at 1.04 years in 2014/15, compared to 1.84 years just two seasons prior to that. A retired player could conceivably spend 20 years playing, several years earning the requisite coaching badges, land his dream managerial role and see it end after just 12 months. As we read earlier with the case of Mark Ward, a sacking in your first managerial role can set alarm bells ringing among club chairmen and may mean never getting the chance to manage again.

As of November 2015 there were just four black, Asian and minority ethnic (BAME) managers out of 92 in the league – Chris Hughton at Brighton & Hove Albion, Jimmy Floyd Hasselbaink at Queens Park Rangers, Ricardo Moniz at Notts County and Keith Curle at Carlisle United. This 4.35 per cent representation compares unfavourably with the level of BAME footballers currently playing, with PFA figures suggesting that approximately 25 per cent of professional footballers are BAME individuals.

Figures from the League Managers Association (LMA) suggest that 18 per cent of those studying football management and coaching qualifications and 16 per cent of all students of the association's Diploma in Football Management are from a BAME background. There have been just 50 BAME managers since 1960, with 64 per cent failing to secure a second managerial post. Chris Kiwomya and Terry Connor are just two examples of BAME managers who have struggled to find a second managerial role in recent years.

The figures clearly suggest there are barriers to the appointment of BAME managers, but what are they and how can they be addressed?

Research carried out for the LMA hints at institutional racism and a perceived old boys' network at play in the English game. A lack of transparency in the recruitment process has also been cited as a frustration among BAME candidates.

Hasselbaink had impressed in his first managerial role at Burton Albion before earning his move to QPR. However, he could have moved a lot sooner were it not for racial issues. Port Vale had been linked with appointing the Dutchman but their owner, Norman Smurthwaite, admitted he feared it would lead to racist abuse from the club's fans. The Valiants had previously been investigated by the FA for racist chanting in 2013.

There has though been some progress made with the Football League's introduction of its version of American football's 'Rooney Rule'. From August 2016 clubs across its three divisions will interview at least one BAME candidate for every managerial or head coach role, should there be relevant applications. While it doesn't guarantee BAME appointments, it at least gives candidates a chance at jobs they may have been overlooked for up to this point. However, there are no plans for the Premier League to follow suit.

The 'Rooney Rule' has been a relative success in the NFL. Prior to its introduction in 2003, minorities filled just seven of the previous 92 head coach vacancies – less than eight per cent. From 2003, this rose to 17 of the following 87 vacancies – or almost 20 per cent.

The FA plans to spend £1.4m over the next five seasons to assist more coaches from BAME backgrounds into the licensed coaching system. It also appointed Dr Wayne Allison, who made over 750 appearances over a 22-year playing career, as its new BAME project manager in October 2015 to help improve these figures.

The influx of managers and coaches who haven't played professionally has created another barrier for retired players striving to break into management. The likes of André Villas-Boas, Avram Grant and Gérard Houllier have all landed Premier League jobs in recent years despite never playing the game professionally.

Houllier was a schoolteacher, while completing his degree in English, until the age of 26 when he became player-manager of amateur side Le Touquet. He worked his way up the divisions in France before landing his first big job as manager of Paris Saint-Germain. There, he won the league before taking over firstly as national team boss then technical director.

Furthermore, the likes of Arsène Wenger, José Mourinho and Brendan Rodgers only enjoyed relatively modest playing careers. For example, as a youngster Wenger played for a number of French amateur sides, which he took upon himself to manage due to a lack of resources. He continued his studies in medicine, politics and economics before joining Ligue 2 club AS Cannes as assistant manager as a 34-year-old. Such was his impression at Cannes that Michel Platini's father recommended him as manager to Nancy just a year later. He then joined Monaco, where he won the league in his debut season with the likes of Englishmen Glenn Hoddle and Mark Hateley in his side.

At one stage he was wanted as manager of Bayern Munich but stayed with Monaco, who sacked him in 1994. He then spent 18 months managing in Japan before joining Arsenal to questions of 'Arsène who?' The rest, of course, is history.

The influx of foreign managers and coaches into the English game has also limited the number of opportunities for British ex-players. Some, however, have turned the tables and sought opportunities abroad. Gary Stevens, the former England and Tottenham defender, spent several years in the media and running his own business before getting an urge to return to the game. However, he felt his chances were best served away from the UK, after a spell with Charlton Athletic's academy.

Stevens says, 'I'd gone from the precarious media business into the precarious business of coaching and management. The way I view it is, invariably, if one door shuts another will open for you if you're any good. For example, it went very well at Charlton. But instead of the under-21 league coming in in the early 2000s, which is where my job was going to be, the chairman decided that the side was surplus to requirements so I was basically made redundant.

'My feeling was that there were more and more imports coming into England in a coaching capacity. So I thought, "Well, let's have a look the other way and see what else is out there." British coaches have been accused of being a little bit insular in the past so I thought, "Open up a little bit and see what I can come up with." I've been in and out of work but I've generally been in work as opposed to out of work.'

The first port of call on his adventure was as assistant manager to Tony Adams at Azerbaijani side Gabala SC. It quickly became apparent that a career in management overseas was just as precarious as it was back home. 'When Tony left I was in charge for a few games and then they appointed another coach who brought his own team in and that was me gone,' recalls Gary.

Undeterred, he joined Ian Baraclough at Sligo Rovers, who had just won the League of Ireland. The duo had worked together on their Pro Licence course and proceeded to win the FAI Cup in their first season together, followed by a League Cup success the following campaign. However, it wasn't enough for Sligo's demanding board. 'We won the FAI Cup and then the League Cup and, off the back of that, we got sacked. It's absolutely nuts,' laments Gary.

While Baraclough was appointed as manager of Motherwell, Stevens's wanderlust found him conscripted as boss of Thailand's Army United. Again, his spell in charge would be a battle.

Despite lifting his troops to fourth in the Thai Premier League, he was fired before winding up at Port FC, the most successful club in Thai football history. Despite a further dismissal – by text message – Stevens intends to remain in south-east Asia, where his stock remains high. 'I've probably got a better chance of getting a good coaching position out here than back home in the UK at the moment,' admits Gary, who hasn't even had the courtesy of a reply from some positions he's applied for in England.

As of January 2016, only four of the 20 Premier League managers were English, something Gary alludes to when discussing the dearth of opportunities in England. 'You only have to look at the Premier League and go through each club and you see the number of non-British coaches and managers. It's quite a high percentage at the moment and that obviously pushes some really quite high-profile, good British coaches and managers further down the pyramid. However, there are lots of other opportunities in academies and so on. But if you want to be the head coach at a club I think it is very difficult now to secure a job in England.'

Of course, demand far outweighs the supply of managerial roles in the English game. As Professor Chris Brady puts it succinctly, 'Let's imagine there's 30 players at a club. One hundred professional clubs. Three thousand players. There are only 100 jobs for 3,000 people.'

Stevens still has ambitions as a manager and hopes his managerial legacy can surpass his playing one. 'As the years go by, I'll hopefully be remembered more as a coach and a manager and I'll have a positive impact on players and teams. And let's be honest, I left Spurs in 1990 so unless somebody is into their 40s they probably won't remember me playing.'

The constant reminders of his playing days are welcome but he prefers to look towards the future. 'People say stuff like, "You shouldn't look back, the past is gone, the future's yet to come so it's all about today." But whenever I've gone to work or even now on social media, people say to me, "What about that game in 1984 when you won the UEFA Cup? What about in 1983 when you scored that goal for Brighton against Man United in the FA Cup Final? What was it like to play for England in the World Cup in Mexico 86?" It's all well-meaning stuff and I like the fact that people want to talk about it but all it does is drag up an amazing time in your life. And I'm not saying my life isn't great now, because a lot of people would love my life and I'm very lucky and privileged to have it, but I'm forever being dragged back to the past.'

Over 70 per cent of PFA members indicate a desire to remain in the game upon retirement so, taking the 60,000 ex-pros figure from earlier, in theory there are 42,000 former footballers across Britain and Ireland who'd like to be a football manager or coach – and only 92 league clubs. It's immediately clear that not everyone is going to land their plum job after they retire.

Furthermore, a highly decorated playing career is no guarantee of success in management and coaching, as

Professor Chris Brady attests, 'There is zero correlation between having a top playing career and a top coaching career. A top player can be a top coach or a poor coach. A poor player can be a top coach or a poor coach. You can have a Johan Cruyff who was brilliant at both or you can have a Bobby Charlton who was only a brilliant player.

'The key issue is that when people are hiring managers, are they thinking carefully about his managerial skill set or are they just going for Fred Bloggs because he used to play there? Real Madrid, for example, hired Rafa Benitez primarily on the basis of a reasonable managerial career; but he had been a player at the club and they may have felt there'd be a cultural fit. But it doesn't necessarily mean there's a cultural fit. You're looking for the managerial skill set to be a cultural fit with the place, not the person.'

Chris points to something Gordon Strachan has said, that a successful player turned manager will get accepted because of their playing career, but it doesn't last very long. Although you get accepted for your name, from day one the players are judging you. In some cases, you don't even have to have played professionally at all to gain respect in the dressing room. He recently interviewed a lot of elite managers for a book he's written with Carlo Ancelotti and has found a common trend. 'They all say that, when transitioning from a player to a manager, you are given a very short honeymoon period by the players, who are very selfish. So they will judge you very quickly.

'If you're Zinedine Zidane, you've been better than anyone in that club now other than Ronaldo, but players will decide very quickly whether you can add any value to them personally. And if the answer to that is "no" then they don't care who you've played for. And if the answer to that is "yes" they don't care if you never played at all.

'So when the Chelsea players got Mourinho not one of them cared about the fact he'd never played. Why? Because he can add value to us. Talented people are naturally very, very selfish. So when a new manager comes in they ask what is it that he can do for me? The story goes that Mourinho's first team-talk first time around at Chelsea was, "I've won the Champions League, none of you have won the Champions League. Follow me and I'll take you there." And they're like, "Right, okay, I've not won the Champions League, we'll follow this guy until he shows us he can't do it."' Mourinho, of course, didn't win a Champions League in either spell at Stamford Bridge but brought enough success to validate the players' belief in him.

Former players don't always recognise this, believing that, because they've played the game at a high level, management should be straightforward. Steve Claridge, who made over 800 professional appearances in England, reportedly once said that sending him on a coaching course was like asking Gordon Ramsay to make beans on toast. His reign as player-manager at Portsmouth subsequently lasted just 25 games. To be fair, Claridge has carved out a successful career in the media and, at the time of writing, has guided Salisbury to the top of the Wessex Football League table.

Conversely, when asked about his credentials as a football manager having never played professionally, legendary Italian manager Arrigo Sacchi retorted that he 'never realised that in order to become a jockey you have to have been a horse first'. His managerial honours include two European Cups and leading Italy to the final of the 1994 World Cup.

Brady has authored several books on management and, in his role as a presenter on the FA's Pro Licence course, he can assess the ex-players who may make a successful manager. 'Again, it comes back to looking for what would be good managerial skills in any sector. Are they prepared to learn? You get the guys who are very opinionated and strong and people think, "Oh great." But how long are they going to last?

And then you find the ones who are maybe too timid and so on. There are managerial skill sets that will be natural in any sector that seem to come through. So, when I'm looking at people on the Pro Licence, I'm looking at them and thinking to myself, "Yeah, these guys are really engaging in the learning process so they've probably got a better chance than the ones who think they know it all." Because when that goes against you, you've got a problem.

'The one thing that really strikes me about these guys is that they are a bizarre mix of arrogance and insecurity. So if you can get someone who's fairly level-headed throughout all of this, that's a real bonus.'

With the perilous nature of the industry and the high turnover involved, why so many former players put all their hopes into securing a management role is somewhat puzzling. For Chris, it's simple, 'They've nothing else to do. You've basically been in the game since maybe the age of nine, almost certainly uneducated, you've lived in this bubble. How do you test managerial skills? When a player stops playing, how do they test that? And they don't. The clubs just take a gamble, and the ex-player just wants to do it and he won't say no as he wants to stay in the game.'

The instability of the profession is apparent even among those on his Pro Licence course where, 'Because the turnaround or cycle in management is so short, during a two-year course people can get a job, lose it and get another job. Or they could come in as a top manager and by the time they leave they're out of work, or vice-versa. On a two-year course, statistically you're going to have people who get fired.'

The PFA's Coaching Department helps its members to prepare for a secondary career in the game. Jim Hicks has been the organisation's head of coaching for 12 years and ensures that newly-retired players are aware of the competitive nature of the industry. 'We always make sure that people have a reality check about how tough and competitive it is. And that's a big driver for us,' says Hicks. 'If I've got 25 people on a course, one of the things we do at the start is say, "The best people in this room will probably go on to find work within a club if they apply themselves. But, unless you're very, very well-connected, getting through the door with your name and prestige is only going to get you so far. If you're not good, you're going to get sacked. What's going to keep you there is the quality of your work." We have to really convince people of that. Being well-known alone won't sustain you, it's just a door-opener initially.'

Despite the competition, the majority of players want to remain in the game in some capacity when they retire. Hicks feels this is down to a number of factors. 'I can make a few guesses. People love the idea of being outside, they love the rapport, they love the idea of having to offer something back to the game that has served them well. It might be hard to re-train and do something else. Football is really where your skills are going to be and where you feel most comfortable.'

The PFA is in constant dialogue with members and is increasingly focused on assisting younger players who may not make it professionally. 'One of the things we're working really hard on at the moment is to try and find out how we can better influence the players when they're scholars,' says Hicks. 'The vast majority of lads do not get a career in football. When they become a scholar at 16 they realise that, unless they've got a professional contract pre-arranged with the club, the next two years become very important.

'It can be important to display, as a player, what you can do, and to find out what you're going to do if it doesn't lead to a contract. Your PFA delegate becomes very important. "What are you going to do? Are you going to do an NVQ? Are you going to do A Levels?" That's what we're getting much better at now. There's still a fall-out. People still focus most of their attention on being a player, and they have to. They have to, otherwise they'd never get there.'

The PFA works hard at preparing players for retirement, espousing the benefits to players of getting qualifications as early as possible in their playing careers. 'The PFA's got a huge educational sway within clubs. If any player approaching the end of his career wants to prepare for a secondary career, it'll come through the PFA,' continues Hicks. 'Every club has got a nominated PFA staff member who will have that club as their responsibility, and that person works in delegate liaison. They'll go and link in with the PFA delegate in the club, who is a nominated current player.

'When the PFA meet up with this delegate they'll say, "Who's in your club at the moment? What are they thinking about doing? Would any of the lads like to get involved in coaching or management? Re-train and go into business? What are they going to do?"

'And then they'll sit and discuss what the needs are of all the players. That's the theory behind it. In some cases, players leave it until the last minute so they'll be trying to get qualified as they retire and go into their new career. We are continuously working to change that type of mindset.'

Hicks is adamant that the PFA offers as much assistance as possible to ensure that anyone who wants to complete a course can do so. 'The PFA will help get you on to courses, which are well-funded. It's about your own personal enthusiasm and application,' he says. 'On the coaching side of things, everything is subsidised. We're really trying to pare it down so that there cannot be an excuse for somebody to say, "I don't have the resources to get on this course." In hardship cases, we'll even give it to them for free. But a lot of times, if you've a free course, it almost devalues it. If you've got something invested you'll take some responsibility for being there and giving it your best go.'

While the PFA 'can't create employment for people', the organisation's close links with clubs can help land successful participants a post in the professional game. 'There's nothing formal but a lot of networking goes on,' reveals Hicks. 'A lot of clubs will come to us at the end of a course and say, "The course you just finished there, Jim, who was really good on that?" I am happy to offer those people up. We use that as an incentive on the courses and say, "We are well-connected with the clubs so if you show good application here, we will refer you on to a club."'

The PFA also assists retired players, considering a career in management, in acquiring the requisite skills to pursue a managerial role. Hicks explains, 'We say to them, "You need to start thinking about things that will help you get employment long-term." That includes having some business experience, how they write down and record what their philosophy is and principles are, how they present to a board. You're trying to build some material for them so they can walk into a room, have some presence and have an idea of some of the questions which might come their way. And, also, what are they going to present? They often don't think about the practicalities of getting a job, which is really important.'

While the lifespan of a football manager can be notoriously short, Hicks believes that there are more opportunities than ever for those who wish to remain in the sport. 'It depends on what you want to do. If you choose to go into management, you have to have a very realistic plan about what's going to happen if that doesn't work out and what your alternative is going to be,' he says. 'If you go to some of the academies now, some of them might have 25 or 30 coaches. These are big enterprises. You're not going to be very, very well-paid but you could have a sustainable career as a player developer.

'There are lots of other parallel careers in football. If you have the inclination to go to university to study and get a degree in Sports Science, Strength Training, Nutrition or Sports Psychology, clubs are looking for these sorts of people all the time. You've obviously got the physiotherapy and doctor side of things too. There is a huge field now in performance analysis and, at the top level, clubs use these people.'

Even if a former player is able to navigate the barriers to landing – and keeping – a managerial position, the stresses involved in the job can take their toll. Dr Dorian Dugmore is a world leader in cardiovascular health, preventative medicine and wellness. In the past he has worked with the FA as a county coaching representative and senior coach, as well as coaching at the World Student Games. He has also tested over 100 football managers and created the Fit to Manage and Fit to Perform programmes for the League Managers Association, so has seen at first hand the effects of a move from the playing staff to football management.

'There's a lot of stress and pressures on the managers, most of whom are previous players. In the past, they could go from being a player to then changing their lifestyle in a short period of time,' says Dr Dugmore. 'Instead of them performing for somebody else and focusing on their own health and well-being, now they find themselves in a completely different situation where they're looking after everybody else. Often, the last person that gets looked after is themselves. There can be a huge lifestyle change. Often they're not exercising enough, not eating well, they're working long hours, doing everything from managing the first team to overseeing recruitment of other players and managing the business of the club. All of a sudden there's a major, major change in their approach. Is it any wonder that some of them develop challenges to their health and well-being?'

Football management can be a mentally and physically demanding profession so the programme aims to assist managers to look after their own well-being due to the stresses of their job. 'Basically, what it does is to assess the cardio and respiratory health of managers together with their lifestyle,' continues Dr Dugmore. 'It looks at the function of their heart, their response to exercise from the heart's point of view, their nutrition and their musculoskeletal health. They use a device that identifies the quality of their sleep and their heart rate variability, which also can be a stress indicator.

'And then we put all that together and, at the end of their assessment, they're counselled and guided on managing their exercise, nutrition and lifestyle, together with trying to take care of any health-related risks. The big message is that an ounce of prevention is worth a tonne of treatment.'

The programme's constant monitoring of participants' health is crucial, insists Dr Dugmore. 'The big value is in the serial testing – ongoing, annual testing. A lot of people in leadership roles, whether it's business or football management, they'll look at the profit or loss of their business or, in the manager's case, of their performance, if you like. Many people when they're having health assessments will go to specialist clinics, have themselves tested and not bother for the next five years. That's often too late. A chief executive or manager wouldn't dream of looking at the results of one particular season and not bothering for the next five, would they?

'These guys handle multi-million pound budgets and they've really got to look after themselves. The whole idea is to do it in an ongoing, interventional way. We've managed to head off many problems in the past and get them sorted out before they've become very serious health issues. Which is great really. It's very, very innovatory.'

Football management only seems suited to a certain type of individual. Arsène Wenger has said in the past that he can quickly spot players that are apposite for a career in coaching and management. However, he concedes that it is not necessarily for everyone, with many players feeling they've sacrificed enough of their lives to the game and unwilling to dedicate a large portion of their post-playing career to the constant travel and hotel stays. A career in the media can present the same issues.

* * *

When I moved my TV package to Sky last year it took a pleasant Polish engineer about an hour to install the necessary equipment and give me a quick demo. When Gary Neville moved to Sky in 2011 the installation took considerably longer. Their new pundit insisted on having a Sky Sports interactive touchscreen fitted in his home in order to practise before his punditry debut. Unfortunately for Neville, he discovered the station had updated its technology by the time he started his new role. It was an early setback in the former England and Manchester United star's fledgling career, but one he took in his stride.

Almost everyone I spoke to cited Neville as football's best pundit and, personally, I was disappointed when he moved into management with Valencia – a move which left a gaping hole on Sky Sports's *Monday Night Football*. His success was such that there was no obvious successor to join Jamie Carragher on the show, with the station resorting to a rotating panel of guests. So, what made Neville so special? What makes a good pundit? And does it take a certain type of former player to make it a success?

'Football punditry is an art form and I'm not sure people give it enough credit.' These are the views of Barney Francis, managing director of Sky Sports, and while many may disagree, it is clearly a vocation that does not suit all former footballers.

Former Scotland and Chelsea player Pat Nevin is one of the UK's most respected pundits, but he admits it's not a career he'd meticulously planned for. He started writing for various music and arts magazines at the age of 20, using a pen name as he 'wanted to be accepted for my ability as opposed to my name'.

He explained, 'So I kind of learned a bit of a trade as I was going along. The idea was that writing and journalism was where I would go. When I got into my 30s I was asked to do some radio for Radio 5 live and I went, "Yeah, okay, that sounds like a bit of fun."

'It was planned, yes, but it was not planned the way it has gone. I didn't expect to do as much TV as I do now, or as much radio as I do now. I do write quite a lot, every week I write two or three articles so part of the plan did work. But you need to be adaptable. Which brings you back to playing football, those skills are not that adaptable, so you need to have other ones in the background.'

I query as to what makes the perfect pundit but Pat admits he's the 'wrong person' to ask. 'The reason being, what I think is a good pundit is absolutely not what the media thinks is a good pundit,' he states. 'I don't know what makes a good one. You can sometimes see what will make a successful one, which is a very different thing from a good one. In the past it was something different from what it is now. Now, unless you have your own niche – which I fortunately have – it seems to be: speak very loud, be terribly controversial and tweet a lot. I'd kind of hoped journalism was more than that, but there you go.'

Since his retirement, former Republic of Ireland midfielder Matt Holland has worked for various media outlets including Sky Sports, the BBC, ESPN, RTÉ and talkSPORT. He hadn't planned to quit in 2009 but had already set the foundations for a new career in the media.

'I didn't know my last-ever game for Charlton would be my last as a professional. I knew my contract was up and that the manager, Phil Parkinson, wanted me to stay. Money wasn't the issue, so for whatever reason a new contract didn't materialise,' he says. However, he didn't regret not knowing it was to be his last game. 'When your time's up, your time's up. I wasn't worried about a big fanfare and them waving me off and all that sort of stuff. I was lucky. I played until I was 35. If someone had said to me at 18 that I'd play until 35 I'd have snapped their hand off.'

He admits that he was prepared for the media side of things when he hung up his boots. 'I honestly thought I'd still be playing. I wasn't intending to retire the year I did. Charlton had gone down to League 1, my contract was up but I expected to carry on playing. I went and trained at my local team Colchester for a couple of weeks just to try and keep fit and I had a couple of offers to carry on playing. But it would have meant me moving away from home, a year's contract in the lower leagues, which I didn't really want to do at that age.

'I had another offer in September, which if it had come about six weeks earlier I probably would have carried on. It was more local and I wouldn't have had to move. But I actually had a few irons in the fire with the media stuff. I got asked to present a show on BBC local television called *Late Kick Off*. I started doing more and more bits and pieces, commentary here and there and I found myself really busy, so I decided not to take the offer.'

Holland enjoys his media work but, for him, it's no substitute for being involved on the pitch. 'I missed football when I retired. Even now when I go to a game, I wish I had my boots on, I wish I was playing. Punditry is a good second best though. You're still involved, still meeting people, still talking to people that you played with. I really enjoy it.

213

'Management is something I would have considered and I do wonder what might have been had I gone down that route. I did my UEFA B Licence, really enjoyed the course and if I'd had an offer just after I'd retired I might have taken it. Now, I'd never say never. When the kids grow up, it's a different life. You try and leave as many doors open as possible.

'I was actually offered the Charlton reserve team manager's job when Iain Dowie was manager. I was only 32 at the time and, to be honest, I still saw myself as a player, I didn't see myself going down the management route at that age. I jokingly said to Iain Dowie, "What are you trying to do, pension me off?" I wasn't ready to be part of it.'

Holland did a few commentary jobs in his late 20s to ensure he had that option available when retirement inevitably arrived. 'I think the key for me was trying to leave as many doors open as possible for when I finished playing. I remember Alvin Martin at West Ham, he was 35 and I was a young lad. He warned, "Enjoy your career, because it goes like that." And as a kid you laugh and you joke, "Yeah, course it does, that's 20 years away!" And then it's me, at 34 or 35, saying to younger players, "Listen, enjoy your career because it's gonna be over like that."

'In terms of planning for afterwards, you never know when it's going to finish but I suppose from my late 20s I was thinking, "What am I going to do?" I almost fell into the media side of things but I was prepared and ready to go into that side of it.'

I wonder if there is a certain personality of player who is destined for the media, but it seems that a player's career path can even surprise their team-mates. 'You look around a dressing room and you have an idea of who'll go into management and who'll go into the media,' says Matt. 'People always felt I'd be a manager because I'd been captain at a lot of clubs. And there are players about whom

I'd have said, "No chance will they ever go into it," and there they are now coaching at academies and things like that. It's really difficult to judge people actually. You think you know, but there's players you thought would have gone into management and haven't and those that have gone into management who I'd have thought there was no chance of that happening to.'

Former Sheffield Wednesday striker Gordon Watson feels big-name punditry appointments are sometimes not warranted and believes lower-profile former players can often do a better job. 'I think it's wrong. I'd stand up and have my view against absolutely anyone who has played a million times for their country. But I didn't play for Liverpool or Manchester United. It's such lazy recruitment on behalf of the TV companies. They're thinking, "Oh, he played for Liverpool, so he'll have a big viewership following." But the stuff that comes out of their mouths, I could have got someone at a bus stop to say the same.'

We spoke the day Gary Neville left Sky Sports to manage Valencia. Watson agrees that Neville has been an exception to the rule. 'He's the governor, he's scarily good. And you've got the five boys on Sky's *Soccer Saturday*. That's a proper team, it's got everything in it, hats off to them.'

Watson is hoping to get a break in the media, using his experience in scouting to offer a different angle to read a game.

It's clear that a highly successful career at the top of the game does not guarantee that a player will become a good pundit. So what does make one? 'Not to be worried about calling it as it is, when it is,' suggests Gordon. 'Because it's our national game, people already have a massive understanding. Don't be repeating exactly what everyone has already seen at home. My skill used to be I could look at two line-ups and see holes, where there's match-ups that are obviously going to go the wrong way.

'I find that a lot of the pundits don't want to step on anyone's toes and call it as it is, because they might be having a drink with them in a few weeks. It's just not right – they're paid to give an opinion. You get more respect if you call it as it is.'

It's clearly a highly competitive industry with many ex-players citing difficulties in breaking into the media world. The advent of the Premier League increased media opportunities but also led to increased competition for roles. Gary Stevens moved into the media world after retiring from Portsmouth in 1992. He worked for many organisations such as the BBC, ITV, Sky Sports, ESPN and talkSPORT and has noticed the industry gradually becoming more cut-throat.

'There probably weren't as many media outlets at that stage but it was starting to grow,' he recalls. 'And, likewise, there weren't as many people chasing the media outlets because a lot of ex-players didn't see it as being an option. As the media outlets grew, more and more people got involved in it. I did okay, I made a living for ten years at it. I worked for a lot of organisations although most of it was not contracted. You got a phone call and you went and did it, and if you didn't do it you might not get another phone call again. So you do your damnedest to be there because if you didn't do it somebody else would and that might be you out of it.'

Many former players lament the fact that media work is quite often part-time and done mainly to supplement alternative income streams. So, what do broadcasters look for in a pundit?

Growing up in Ireland, I'd always been taken with the football coverage from RTÉ, the Irish national broadcaster. Many of the matches it covered would also have been shown on UK channels but I'd find myself drawn to my indigenous station despite its lack of resources in relation to its British counterparts. While UK coverage would often feature pundits who were household names as players, RTÉ tended to rely on an iconic panel featuring a voice of reason in former Leeds United midfielder Johnny Giles, the maverick Eamon Dunphy and former Arsenal and Juventus star Liam Brady, all wonderfully chaired by the late Bill O'Herlihy.

Ryle Nugent, head of RTÉ Sport, agrees that the broadcaster made a conscious decision in the 1980s to differentiate itself from the UK offering. Due to its position on the edge of Europe and the influence and significant impact of UK broadcasters, RTÉ's sports coverage needed to offer something distinctive to its audience.

'The then head of sport in the 1980s, Tim O'Connor, made a very clear decision on what RTÉ could bring to the party that others possibly couldn't or definitively weren't at the time,' explains Ryle. 'And I think that was that RTÉ was never going to be able to match the production budgets or the scale of the productions that the UK broadcasters could. So, what were we going to do that was going to engage Irish audiences? Bear in mind that, really, in Ireland, there's no such thing as an exclusive sports right any more.

'Yes, you have exclusivity from Irish broadcasters but, frankly, of the top 20 sports programmes watched in 2014, 19 of them were available on two or more channels. So you have to distinguish yourself in a different way. The BBC and ITV both did the World Cup Final, and we did as well. Champions League finals, Six Nations, even our own GAA Championships finals are now available on Sky. It was foreseen that we were going to have to identify ourselves without having those massive programme budgets. So the panels were something that the then head of sport decided were going to differentiate us, and I think that still holds true today.'

They say 'honesty is the best policy' and that certainly seems to be the case if you want to be a pundit with the Irish national broadcaster. It seems a refreshing approach when compared to the sometimes anodyne punditry on offer across the Irish Sea. 'That differentiation was that we were going to get a group of people together and put them in a position to actually reflect what the Irish audience was thinking, saying and talking about themselves,' continues Ryle. 'We were going to allow people to be provocative, once they were in a position to back that provocation up with a sense that it was a genuinely held view from someone who is in a position to offer and to propagate that view, rather than having it for the sake of having it.

'At no time have we ever encouraged people to be extremist in what they say. What we've said to them is, "We're employing you for an honest opinion. And if you feel like you can't give us an honest opinion, an honest appraisal and an honest analysis of the game, the sport, where we are, then this isn't for you." And we don't tend to carry people like that on our panels.

'What happened in the 80s was that the then head of sport and production teams went in search of the right people for those panels. And those panels, by and large, developed over a three- to five-year period and were in place predominantly as the same panels up until about five to six years ago. There's been substantial change and there'll continue to be substantial change but the essence of what we're trying to do I think still holds firm. Which is – put a group of people in who we know are not necessarily going to be collegiate all the time in what they think and what they say. Offer as many and diverse opinions from qualified people as you can to reflect what people are thinking and saying at home.'

Retired footballers should be well used to teamwork from their playing days but the synergy on an analysis panel is often overlooked, argues Ryle. 'I think you then need to recognise that there is a required chemistry. And that comes from the anchor and the two or three that are on the panel. And you can't force that, that's something that takes time to come. You can have somebody who you feel has a forthright opinion, is qualified to offer that opinion, is respected in some, if not all, quarters, and yet they may just not fit into that matrix because of the other personalities that are there. And I think that is not necessarily recognised by everybody, it takes time. You can't flick a switch.

'We had to give the people that were coming in time to understand the roles that they were there to fulfil, to get used to and accept the sterile environment that TV studios can be. To give them that experience, to tinker a little bit and try and come up with a formula and a group of people that, when we migrated totally, weren't raw and weren't raw to the audience.

'I think the audience struggles, subconsciously, with fundamental change overnight. They get used to people, they get used to anchors, they get used to panels. They're like an old pair of slippers that they like to put on when a major event comes and that makes them feel comfortable. Conversely, if you don't get that right, consciously the audience step away from it and they look for what they want somewhere else. And clearly there are lots of other places to go to.'

A lot of criticism around media work I've heard from ex-players is the reliance on big-name pundits from the likes of Liverpool and Manchester United. It's a fair point when you switch on some British coverage but, just like with a football club, Ryle doesn't agree that just pooling the biggest stars together will work.

'It isn't simply, "Get the three biggest names, pay them the largest amounts of money, put a stereotypical anchor into it and off you go and that will work." We are firm believers that there's got to be a lot more to it. There is a psychology, or some sort of social science to it, in terms of providing a panel that is engaging, educating, analytical and, ultimately, entertaining the audience when they sit down to watch a sports event. The UK and Ireland markets are very, very different and need to be approached differently. It's not a one-size-fits-all and they've got a different level and set of criteria that they need to deal with that people don't necessarily care to see or choose to see.

'It would be fair to say that some of the broadcasters have attempted to "big-name buy" their way into a situation where the panel engages with the audience. In some cases it hasn't worked; in a couple of cases it's worked okay.'

Ryle is another who cites Gary Neville's emergence on the scene as a watershed moment. 'The arrival of Neville to Sky showed that there's a level of work and commitment required that maybe the UK audience hadn't seen to that point, with the honourable exception of the Hansen engagement with *Match of the Day*. There was a comfort with that and an easiness with it that the audience clearly liked. I think Neville showed that a) you need to be passionate about it and b) it's hard work. It's not just a matter of rocking up, throwing out a couple of clichés and hoping it will stick, because the audience will find that out real quick. I think you can trade on your name and on your success for a short period of time, but after that you have to back it up with something that people actually want to engage with.'

Nevertheless, RTÉ is renowned for appointing former footballers who've enjoyed more modest playing careers, often very successfully. 'There's a role for people to come in from slightly left of field,' agrees Ryle. 'People who come in with different experiences, a different view on the world. I think Eamon [Dunphy] would be the first to say he wasn't a world-class footballer, but he came in with a journalistic background, a real desire to make an impact, to engage with the audience and did so in a different way. In recent times, there's someone like Richie Sadlier whose playing career was cut short.'

As we saw earlier, Sadlier played for Millwall and represented the Republic of Ireland before being forced to retire through injury at just 24 years of age. In recent years, he's become a well-known and respected face on RTÉ's football panels, but Ryle believes that he almost certainly wouldn't have got a break in the UK media.

'What does he bring? He doesn't bring the £150,000-plus a week, pampered, one-dimensional view of Premier League or European football. He comes with a view of a guy who was there, looked at the big, bright lights, had it cut short and is now looking at the world through a different lens but fundamentally understands top-class football. And I think that brings a different dimension to a conversation about football when he's in the room. Because he doesn't see it through the bright lights and the dollar signs that others would.'

Sadlier himself agrees he probably wouldn't have got a TV break in the UK, although he did do some radio work in London when he retired. For him, a career in the media 'sort of fell in my lap in a way'. He explains, 'It wasn't an aspiration. I wasn't looking at any pundit on TV saying, 'That's the job I want.' I did make a decision though to try any opportunities that came my way.'

It began with a weekly column in the *Sunday Independent*, which led to some punditry work with Setanta Sports. Initially, Richie tried to steer clear of voicing his opinions. 'Looking back, I was quite bashful,' he says. 'I was kind of reluctant to criticise anyone. I thought, "Well, they're all better than me anyway." I don't want to be sitting there slagging Ronaldo and Duff and Robben, who were playing at the time.'

With a huge number of retired players in search of media work, opportunities to break into the industry can be difficult. Ryle explains that it is sometimes only during major tournaments that they get the opportunity to trial new talent. 'We are always looking over the horizon to see who's there or who might be available. Generally, the opportunities come around things like European Championships or World Cups where you've got 30, 40, 50 games and you're not going to put the same guys out for every game. They tend to be the places where we have the opportunity to look at people on a guest appearance basis.'

However, it can be difficult to determine just how serious some recently-retired players are about pursuing a new career in front of the cameras. 'The trouble, and I think it is an issue in the UK as well, is that the guys at the very, very top of their game are coming off the back of a career where they were making 150, 200, 300 grand a week and now they're finished. What's their motivation? Because no broadcaster, even those with the deepest pockets, are going to be able to make an indent on that kind of salary level expectation, if it's there. Are players at that level going to show up for a fee of three grand, five grand, two grand, whatever it might be? In the UK maybe it's ten grand or 15 grand an appearance? And, if they are, are they going to put in the level of work that's required to be successful at it?

'The first question is, "Does he want it?" And then, "Is he going to be any good at it?" And there are some significant contracts that have been leaked into the media in the UK at the moment that are mind-bendingly high for people who, for me, haven't delivered anything. You have to know what their motivation is. Is it that they want to eke out a career and they want to do something that's going to engage them, something that's going to keep them involved in the game, albeit on the periphery? But something that they recognise is a different career, with a different pay scale and a different set of demands. And, my gut feeling is, the very, very top guys don't really need it.'

So, what else do broadcasters look for when selecting retired footballers as pundits? Former players and their agents are in constant contact with the station looking for work. However, there are a number of boxes that must be ticked and not everyone will be able to tick them just because they were adept at kicking a ball around, according to Ryle. 'Our production team are regularly approached with "X" is available or "Y" is available. There is definitely a regular connection with the world of agents. There are some requirements if you are going to go into the business. A strong command of the English language, an ability to communicate, an ability to understand the role and that working in a team isn't just about that individual. And a sense of what it is that the audience expect from you – in a sense of entertaining, educating, analysing and engaging.'

Ryle also wholeheartedly concurs with Barney Francis's assertion that punditry is like art. 'Sports broadcasting itself is an art form,' he agrees. 'Whether it's in the commentary box or in the presentation box. They are disciplines and require a level of ability that not everybody has. You need people who have the basic tools and are prepared to work at it.'

I muse as to what makes the perfect pundit, but Ryle doesn't believe they exist, with the audience being the number one consideration. 'It depends on your blend. In my estimation, in our estimation, covering off as many of the requirements as you can in your panel for your audience is the starting point. Your audience is aged between eight and 80. Your audience is both fanatical and passing in interest. Your audience is engaged absolutely in the nuances of the game or has a passing interest in the game. Your audience's benchmark is the 1960s, 70s, 80s, 90s or 00s. In terms of the individual requirements, it is an ability, again, to understand that this is about educating, engaging, entertaining and informing the audience.'

Ryle considers putting together a panel similar to that of a manager choosing his starting 11. There's no point throwing your 11 best players in and hoping for the best, it needs to be the best starting selection for the team. 'For me, it's no different. There's a job to do and nobody can do it alone. Let's take Liam Brady. He ticks the following – played at the highest level for Arsenal and Juventus, one of the first players to go abroad, a European superstar, played at the highest level internationally and has had a very significant role in the development of academy players at the present time. He ticks a whole load of boxes.

'You bring in someone like Didi Hamann beside him and he's played in a World Cup Final, played in a Champions League Final, brings a continental view of football, having also played in the UK. And then you have a guy like Richie who's played in the League of Ireland, played in the UK and played for his country but is potentially coming at things from a different perspective. You put those ingredients together, now you're ticking all the boxes.

'There isn't an analyst that ticks every box. Because if you put someone up with all those things, they'll say, "He's too old, he's too peripheral, he's too inexperienced, he didn't play for a top four club, he hasn't played in Europe." There's always going to be a criticism. But if you can mould your panel to tick all those boxes, then you're on to something. For us, it is about securing quality rather than just a name. And you can see very quickly whether the quality or potential of quality is there or not.'

Ryle is, however, quick to highlight the importance of an often forgotten role in the TV studio. 'I think an awful lot of the importance and the success of the pundits depends on how good the anchor is. How good is the anchor at drawing these experiences, opinions and information out of the people he or she has in front of him or her? When does he or she know that a point being made at that time has a wider agenda? How does he or she pull that out, bring the other people on the panel into that discussion and facilitate that? The ability of an anchor to do that is, arguably, the singularly most important role of the three or four that are sitting in the studio. The most successful panellists and analysts will tell you that a good anchor was key to them being able to do their jobs the way they needed to do them.'

Gary Stevens concurs with Ryle, and is speaking from experience, 'I was learning a new trade in the media when I retired. I tried to get on the other side of the microphone, rather than be the pundit. I wanted to try to be the presenter but that is a very difficult skill in its own right and, in the end, I came to the conclusion I wasn't good enough to do it. So the punditry was what I ended up doing more of.'

Pat Nevin works extensively in a wide range of media outlets in the UK and Ireland but believes that the standard is higher in the latter. 'I prefer the sports journalism in Ireland to that in the UK,' he admits. 'The great thing is I cannot be half-hearted in Ireland. If I turn up for one of those Irish shows, I better be prepped, I better have something to say, it better be good. Because if it's not any good, you'll get done, they'll be waiting for you, and rightly so. Whereas in the UK, there are places where you could just turn up and blather on if you wanted – not that I would personally.'

Since its launch in 2013, BT Sport has certainly taken a different approach from RTÉ. In a short space of time it has acquired the sole UK rights to Champions League and Europa League football as well as around 40 Premier League games per season. It has put its faith in big-name ex-pros in punditry and co-commentary positions, including the likes of Rio Ferdinand, Michael Owen and Paul Scholes. This is something that the director of BT Sport, Simon Green, reveals was deliberate.

'The main quality is that they have to have a credible record as a footballer,' concedes Simon. 'It takes a long time to build television talent to the point that they have that credibility as a television pundit. Our team is relatively young, they're fresh out of the game so they're still on the road to building that credibility. Our ambition was to be as young as we could in terms of our presentation talent, and we've managed that mostly, but it has meant that we have hired some inexperienced ex-pros. We still feel that this is the right thing to do, because over a period of time we will build them into being better at what they were hired to do.'

With the advent of social media, Simon admits the one thing those in the role must have is thick skin. A quick perusal of Twitter during a live UK match can reveal just how people can react to pundits and commentators. 'Pundits must become a little bit humble in themselves, because they will find that they will get severe criticism from all angles,' warns Simon. As a broadcaster he pays attention to it 'but if you've one person telling you that they're really entertained by Robbie Savage and another person telling you that Robbie Savage is the worst thing since Hitler, which is how serious social media can get sometimes, then you have to take it all and try and make sense of it over a period of time'.

Simon does echo Ryle Nugent's assertion that team-work and communication skills in a media position are just as important as in any sport. 'Often, it's putting them into a team in a similar way to how they've been put into a team on a football pitch. There are different roles that they can sometimes develop into that are not entirely clear when they first get into the world of broadcasting and media. They must be willing to become part of a team that you are prepared to work in and support. They need to be able to communicate with our viewers and their fellow pundits in an entertaining and constructive way. But there is no golden skill that any television executive is looking for when hiring a personality.'

He reveals that it is rare for former players to approach the organisation directly regarding media work, relying instead on their agents to source employment in their newly chosen profession. However, broadcasters are already talent-spotting footballers during their playing careers. 'You can normally spot them as they've done television interviews in their time, so you've an idea what their personality is and an expectation as to how they will fit into a team and how well they can communicate,' says Simon.

BT Sport has also introduced a number of football experts who didn't enjoy the privilege of a playing career. Most notable is its *Champions League Goals Show* chaired by James Richardson, which features a number of football journalists and ex-referee Howard Webb. Some former players may question the credentials of those involved but Simon is clear that it doesn't signify a trend away from using ex-pros. 'There is a role [for those who haven't played]. That *Goals Show*, for example, is only on air at the same time as we're showing other matches live, where we're using ex-pros as pundits in a different capacity. Raphael Honigstein, for example, who is on that show, is used regularly on *Fletch & Sav* on a Saturday morning. He's brilliant at what he does with regards to German football. And I think sometimes viewers do appreciate that. However, there will be viewers that will look at him and say, "He's never kicked a ball, he's never crossed that line, what does he know?" So, therefore, you have to have that balance. It becomes a team, you have to have roles.'

Mark Demuth, controller of sport production at ITV, is another who agrees with that comparison of punditry and art. 'It's harder than most people think,' he believes. 'In ITV when we have a half-time chat, half-time is 15 minutes but you have commercial breaks so you're limited to six or seven minutes of chat. In that time you need to distil the key points from the game and add some insights that the viewer hasn't been able to see themselves. You have to do that in a very short space of time – you could be one of three pundits, so you don't have all that time for yourself. The presenter could come to you third in line, so you have to have something fresh to say that hasn't been said already.

'We want someone to be succinct, to the point, make a contribution that the audience is going to be interested in and do it in about 30 seconds. While at the same time, they might have talkback on so they might be hearing chatter in the gallery from the director and the editor about when we're going to go to the break.

'You're trying to recreate a relaxed environment where you're having a chat about football, you're in the studio with ten to 15 studio technicians and personnel crawling around on their hands and knees plugging things in, and you're supposed to be relaxed, comfortable, erudite and make your point in 30 seconds and move on to the next point. It can be quite hard for those that come in thinking it's going to be easy. They think it's easy because the good ones make it look easy. You're trying to recreate a natural conversation between people talking about football in a very unnatural environment. People who come to it for the first time, they always say, "That went quickly," "It was so swift," "I didn't make that point, I wish I'd said this." It's a tricky profession.'

Mark doesn't believe that a pundit needs 'to have won five Champions Leagues and 15 Premier League titles' but he feels that experience in the upper echelons of the game is essential. 'A good pundit in our eyes would be someone who offers opinion, is engaging with the audience, gives a view but is not there just to wield the axe for their own purposes,' says Mark. 'Someone who has played the game at the top level – international football and the Premier League – is articulate, has an opinion and reads the game well. We don't want people who are going to be there simply to make a headline, because the audience will see through that.

'You can't just have someone criticise players and games the whole time, it needs to be structured. The main thing is that their personality comes through at home so that the audience responds to them. We're realistic enough to realise that not every football fan watching will be a fan of a pundit, possibly because of the associations with clubs they played for. You want them to be a lively presence.'

Mark says the station looks at players as potential pundits while they're still playing but it's often difficult for current footballers to shine. 'Sometimes it's good to have current players, when their schedule permits. You want to have someone who's free enough to offer an opinion. It's very hard with current players, because they're going to be loath to criticise their own team, obviously. But equally they'll be loath to criticise opponents, who they might be coming up against in a few weeks' time. The interesting thing now is that players are so well paid that the option to go on TV may not be that compelling as perhaps was the case 20 or 30 years ago.'

Brian Barwick enjoyed a long and distinguished career in sports broadcasting before becoming chief executive of the Football Association in 2005. He rose through the ranks in the BBC, producing *Football Focus* in the 1980s before becoming editor on *Match of the Day* for several years as well as senior editor for two World Cup tournaments. He was eventually appointed head of BBC Sport in 1995, but moved to ITV three years later as controller of sport, overseeing the channel's highest-ever audience of almost 24 million viewers for the 1998 World Cup match between England and Argentina.

He believes that successful pundits need to be developed and that they don't just emerge fully formed from the game. This includes two household names he gave television breaks to – Alan Hansen and Gary Lineker.

Brian was already acquainted with the former when the defender was forced to retire through injury and knew that 'he spoke very intelligently about football' and 'looked good, was telegenic'. Brian had kept an eye on Hansen throughout his career – 'If you're a television professional, you've always got your eye out for the next important voice and face' – and took him to the BBC, where 'he was very quickly able to establish himself'.

Brian continues, 'Alan had been around the game for 14 or 15 years, playing in big games for Liverpool and Scotland. Like everybody else he needed to be helped along. I said to him for the job on *Match of the Day*, "For the first three months, why don't you watch the same game as me in the afternoon? And the trick is that you'll see something in the game that I don't. Because I've watched a thousand games, but you've played a thousand games. So the trick is for you, at ten o'clock tonight, to show something to the viewer that isn't necessarily something you would see as a fan or a supporter but as a seasoned professional and international you would."

'In that way, you try and illuminate the programme, and add credible analysis to a set of action highlights. Alan very quickly picked it up. I think for the first two or three programmes he wanted my support, but very quickly he wanted to fly solo and he had the confidence and intelligence to be able do it. He made a massive second career for himself. His career in football was probably matched by about the same length of time in broadcasting.'

Brian reveals that Lineker and his agent had always felt the former England striker had a future career in broadcasting. Again, a period of training was required before he began presenting on air. 'He came into the BBC when he was playing for Tottenham,' says Brian. 'There used to be a programme called *Friday Sports Time*. We would hold the studio back and let him present a dummy version of the show where he would write his own links and deliver them. Occasionally we'd create a breakdown in the broadcast – albeit it wasn't being broadcast – and I would slot in as the studio guest that had been in the actual programme. And, over a number of weeks, he worked very hard. He did some radio, which helped his vocal delivery. And, slowly but surely, we were able to put him across from an analyst position into a presentation position because we thought he had the ability to carry that. And, of course, he was able to.'

Despite maintaining that a pundit must have an accomplished record as a player, Barwick believes that even the best players need help in developing a second career in the media. 'There is a misconception that a great footballer can be a great broadcaster overnight. It just doesn't happen. They need help and sometimes that assistance is criticism, albeit constructive criticism,' he says.

'They need to be told when they say a certain word too often or that they end every sentence with a certain phrase. Things they're not aware of, and why would they be? And sometimes you need good advice from the people who are directing and producing the programmes. Sometimes an ex-footballer's fame makes it difficult for broadcasters to criticise and opine in a way that's not positive. If you bring them along, though, they become very good broadcasters as well as having been very good footballers. That's the art and the craft of the producer and director of the shows. Gradually, you're able to iron out some of those idiosyncrasies. Week on week, month on month, year on year, they become stronger, their opinions are given more credibility and they become an integral part of the show.'

While the competition for punditry positions is increasingly fierce, Barwick believes that there has never been as many openings for retired players. 'It's changing all the time because there's so many outlets, different ways you can get involved in broadcasting. When I started out there were two outlets – BBC and ITV – where you could make your mark,' he continues.

'Nowadays there are lots of broadcast outlets, there's a necessity to fill the airtime. And football pundits are part of the rhythm of a broadcast. There are good ones and bad ones like there are good footballers and bad footballers. If you want to make a career out of it, and that's what people are able to do these days, you have to put some thought into it, some work into it and understand your role.

'It is a significant career for people, it keeps them in the football family, it takes them to some of the biggest games in the world, it gives them a profile from which they can earn. So it is a legitimate and very serious second career.

'Also, with the amount of money that broadcasters are paying for television rights for football, they need to be able to present it in a way that's different and better than somebody else. And one of the traditional and established ingredients in any football programme on television is the analyst and pundit.'

Barwick, who has literally written the book on the history of football on television – titled *Are You Watching The Match Tonight?* – recommends that anyone trying to break into punditry must devour the media from as many viewpoints as they can. 'Read as many newspapers as possible so that you read a football report or story from the perspective of *The Times*, the *Mirror*, the *Mail*. Listen to as many radio programmes as possible, and go on as many radio programmes as possible to try and create and develop your voice,' he advises. 'And to think about how a viewer would watch a game and what they would want to take from the enjoyment of a game. And not to try and knock the skittles over every time you bowl a ball down the alley.'

As well as a respected playing career, Brian insists a good pundit must be, 'Somebody who shows the ability to have an opinion, is able to analyse what he sees in non-technical football speak. In other words, is able to bring the viewer along with him. And someone who is not a shock jock, somebody who is saying sensible things in a coherent way and is not jumping from one controversy to the next. There are those who do that, but they won't be doing it overly long.'

Brian adds that the selection of pundits is very important for broadcasters. 'In truth, if you think about a football broadcast, you're actually in the company of the commentator and the co-commentator much longer than with the studio pundits who make the headlines. They have the ability to take something and show it from a different angle or a different perspective,' he stresses. 'And when you're actually watching the game you tend to be engrossed in the game. Although the co-commentary is very important to it, you tend to be carried along with the action. When it comes back to a studio, the art and the craft is to come up with something different and to come up with something strong and be able to articulate it in an eloquent way.'

It is clear that there is a growth in media opportunities available to former players, but it's still not enough to offer full-time employment for everyone. For this, particularly in the UK, it seems that a high-profile playing career is essential.

Pat Nevin concludes, 'There's a lot of media out there. It might not be *Match of the Day* and those sort of things. A lot more clubs are going to have their own television stations, a lot more clubs will have their own media outlets within the club through online, etc. There are other media opportunities for ex-players but you only notice them because they're there in front of your face. It's still only one in 500 that are going to get to make a living out of that. It's not a sensible idea to go in and say, "Well, I'm going to concentrate on a media career." Not unless you're incredibly, incredibly famous. And then you can probably walk into it.'

We have seen that second careers in the competitive media and management landscapes can be a lot shorter and more fragile than a playing one. It is clear that the transition from a footballing career to 'the real world' can be a difficult one to navigate. According to the PFA, the average age of retirement for a player is 35 years old, while the life expectancy for males in the United Kingdom is 79. So, how do footballers fill their time for 44 years, or over 16,000 days? Not easily, it seems.

9

The End

IN his 1956 autobiography, *The Clown Prince of Soccer*, Sunderland legend Len Shackleton famously titled one chapter 'The Average Director's Knowledge of Football'. It simply consisted of one blank page. This chapter could quite easily have just replicated that. It is quite apparent that nothing can really fill the void left from no longer playing football professionally if a player doesn't have another passion to pursue. Which is a major problem, considering the relatively early stage of life at which retirement from the game is necessitated. There is only so much golf one can play, only so many after-dinner speeches one can make.

One retired professional, who starred for Manchester City in the top flight, told me that it's 'impossible' to fill the days after retirement. He tried several options, from business ventures to coaching, but for one reason or another they all failed.

He found it difficult to gain employment as most employers were sceptical as to why a former footballer would need a job. He enjoyed playing golf for a while but knee, ankle and pelvic injuries incurred during his career put paid to that. The only job that came close to replacing being a player for him was coaching in the non-league, but that was on a voluntary basis. This came after a spell with the youth system at a professional club, where the internal politics made the job 'more or less impossible', and he resigned on principle.

His most financially rewarding job was on a zero-hours contract and, despite not being part of the bankruptcy figures, his home was repossessed not long after his playing career ended. This led to marriage and health problems, culminating in him seeking help from the Sporting Chance Clinic for depression and anxiety. The only thing that gives him the same return as playing is spending time with his grandchildren.

Former England and Arsenal captain Tony Adams battled some well-documented demons during his playing career and co-founded the clinic in 2000. It has since helped former players such as Paul Gascoigne, Matthew Etherington, Alex Rae and Noel Whelan with addictive illnesses.

Gordon Watson, the former Sheffield Wednesday and Southampton striker, went down the gambling route but is eight years clean now. 'I walked in off the streets to Gamblers Anonymous. I had a massive compulsion to compete. The competitive side of things doesn't leave you but the arena for the competitiveness does. It just spirals out of control. I was compulsive in everything I did. I had to kick the arse out of it. It's the all or nothing. You find very few people that can actually control it; if they can then they are special,' he said.

Watson admits that he's another that struggled to adjust to life as a retired footballer. He was awarded almost £1m in 1999 after a claim for negligence against Huddersfield Town's Kevin Grey for a tackle which broke his leg a year earlier. He retired a few years later through injury and warns that the time afforded by retirement can lead you down some dark paths.

'You do the same thing at 30 as you did when you were five – play football. All of a sudden that, and everything your body's been used to, is taken away. We have a thing called time, place and money. And when you have all three of them, it's an absolute recipe for disaster if you're searching to replace something that you've done all your life. A lot of retired players get into gambling or drinking because they can't adjust and get their kicks so they go searching for that high. There's a self-destruct button there.

'I certainly went down those paths. The first few weeks you're happy because you're having some downtime, you're having a rest. But then, all of a sudden, reality kicks in and it's almost like there's a bereavement there where your old life has now died.

'The biggest thing is having the support and understanding of family and trusted individuals around you. If you have that all the way through then it's easier to adjust. Football, for me, used to be a comfort blanket and also a form of escapism from the real world. Once that's taken away you're in a lot of trouble. I took myself away and, basically, tried to create a false world.'

Watson had been gambling during his career but the free time afforded by retirement exacerbated his problems. 'I think that it took hold all the way through my career. Time, place and money are the triangle of disaster. But I didn't have the time when I was a player. I was training or travelling or preparing for a match. But as soon as the lines of the triangle align, then it's just like a runaway train.'

He is another who didn't really plan for retirement until it hit him. 'I retired through injury but you almost think you're immortal, invincible if you like, that that day will never come. You do something for so long, you do take it for granted. It's just the way of life. You get up and do the same thing, day in, day out for the best part of 20 years.'

Watson explains that even the little things, like adjusting to life at home during the festive period, take a lot of getting used to. 'It is a big adjustment. Even Christmas and things like that. We used to go in the hotel Christmas Day so we wouldn't have the big roast dinners and things like that, and we'd get ready to play on Boxing Day. Or New Year's Eve we'd be in a hotel. And then you have more time at home and you've got no release for them things. Where does the aggression go? Where does the competitive side go? It just drives you mad.'

I sense that Gordon regrets not taking advice from others when he retired, but he's eager for others not to make the same mistakes. 'Remember HOW – have an Honesty about you, be Open-minded and have a Willingness to take on anything. Listen to others and trust your loved ones. Try and see the signs and don't be frightened to ask someone for advice. Because of that male bravado we wouldn't go up to someone and say, "I think I'm struggling with this, I think it's getting a little out of hand." But there are people there to help: don't wait until it's too late.

'It's awareness, making people aware of the pitfalls. Sometimes people get advice and don't listen to it. A lot of people think they're the arbiter, think they're the first one. But they don't realise that if they sat in a room with 60 others they'll all be like Churchill the dog nodding, "That's me, that's me, that's me."'

Watson had no preparation for retirement from his clubs, he was 32 at the time and 'it was a case of "off I go, and that's me"'.

He admits his immaturity when retiring hurt the ones he loved most. 'Maybe some people start wanting that little pat on the back, wanting to be loved. Because you've had the adoration of fans, suddenly that's been taken away, you're like, "How do I get that kick? How do I get that appreciation?" It's almost like a drug that you've been taken off but have been addicted to for 20 years, and then someone just says, "No, no more."

'The people you hurt are the ones who are nearest to you. And, all of a sudden, you've got other people when the money stops and their lifestyle then changes, they then change. It's just a domino effect of when one thing goes and you can't stop it.'

Watson has spent time as scouting coordinator at Leicester City and has worked in the media but nothing in the game has replaced the buzz from playing. The biggest enjoyment he has now is watching his son play golf or his daughter sing.

✳ ✳ ✳

A beautifully-flighted David Beckham cross was met by the head of Paul Scholes, who made no mistake from six yards out. The goal was possibly the most notable moment of a match featuring the talents of stars such as Ronaldinho, Luís Figo and Clarence Seedorf. It sounds like an epic Champions League clash from the late 1990s or early 2000s but was in fact the 2015 UNICEF Match for Children at Old Trafford. Beckham's involvement ensured massive publicity for the event, but several former footballers other than Adams and Beckham devote their retirement to causes close to their heart. Scratch beneath the surface and you will find that footballers have more foundations than a beauty counter in a typical department store.

Geoff Thomas enjoyed a relatively lengthy career, retiring at 37 after almost two decades in the game. Despite this, he was a late developer, signing his first professional contract at around 19, before going on to win nine England caps. He believes his late start helped him remain grounded when it came to retirement.

'I went straight into the workplace as an apprentice electrician from school,' he recalls. 'Playing part-time football and then being spotted on a park and then given the opportunity of earning a living playing something I loved doing, I think that way you appreciate it more. It was never a day's work for me playing football, it was great.'

He was relatively prepared for retirement, with an injury scare in his 20s prompting him to consider alternative careers. 'When I was 27 I had a serious knee injury when I'd just signed for Wolverhampton Wanderers. I thought it was the end of my career, really,' reveals Geoff. 'I invested some of the money I had into retail shops. I thought there was a chance that if I didn't get back I'd have another occupation to look forward to. Fortunately, I did get back and it lasted another ten years. So when I eventually finished at the age of 37, I chucked myself into that.

'Back in the late 1990s or early 2000s, money was just starting to come in where you could probably have survived for quite a while on the wages. But I think in our era you earned enough money to invest in something that could sustain your family and give you some sort of life after football. I was always aware that I'd have to do something else after football, for sure.'

However, nobody could prepare for what happened next. Just six months into his retirement from the game, Geoff was diagnosed with chronic myeloid leukaemia and given three months to live. This bolt out of the blue made him totally reassess his life.

'That totally changed my mindset of what I wanted to do for the future,' he recalls. 'When you come out of football you want to continue being a success, and I'd focused on being a successful businessman even though it was difficult. As soon as I was told my life was under threat, you re-evaluate everything and it made me realise what was really important – spending time with my family and making sure everything was right for them.

'In the process of going through the treatment, it made me look at everything totally differently. Ever since then I've been working alongside the doctors who saved my life and trying to fulfil what they're trying to do by helping fund their work, which is so important. It makes everything else I'd been trying to do before irrelevant.'

When he was diagnosed, the former Crystal Palace captain was told that there was no cure apart from going through a transplant, and that the chances of one were slim. 'I was one of the lucky ones as my sister was a really good match,' Geoff says. 'It took three months of intensive chemo and radiotherapy that got me prepared for the transplant, and a year to get into remission.'

He went into full remission in January 2005 and was determined to dedicate his life to improving research into the disease. 'That was really the start of me trying to pay back by doing different things like going on bike rides and organising football matches,' he recalls. 'I found that I had a voice after football and that it made a difference in getting different people to come on board. I've really tried to make that snowball and grow and accelerate the work that the tremendous doctors and professors in this country are trying to deliver. It's just an exciting time and I feel privileged to be part of it.'

He established the Geoff Thomas Foundation 'due to the lack of infrastructure that allowed potential life-saving science and that slowed that process down. Myself and a fellow patient, a businessman, and my professor Charlie Craddock, went out and spoke to Parliament, to Health Secretaries and MPs – various people we thought could make a difference. Eventually a bigger charity, now called Bloodwise, took up my cause and we linked up on the process that we were trying to put on trial, which is now flourishing. It's proving a great model for getting all the latest science out there an awful lot quicker in order to benefit patients.'

Geoff's new-found love of cycling was down to an unlikely source. 'When I was going through my battle I read Lance Armstrong's book, *It's Not About the Bike*, and like many back then it was an inspiration. That's sort of the reason I got back on a bike. In 2005, when I went through remission, myself and four journalists took on the Tour de France two days ahead of the Tour.' Geoff successfully completed the Tour and has said that riding down the Champs-Élysées in Paris towards the finish surpassed anything he did on a football pitch.

'I think that was the year Lance won his last yellow jersey,' says Geoff. 'There were various whispers about what Lance was up to but I was oblivious to that back then. But it was his influence that got me on a bike. My knees were shot so I couldn't play too many football games, I couldn't run too many marathons and the bike seemed a great opportunity of bringing so many people from different walks of life together and help raise money for the cause.

'So Lance was the spark and reason I got on a bike, but ever since then it's been clear to me that it's a growing sport, a great way of keeping fit and a great way of people doing great charity work. But at the same time you're giving them a message of what you're trying to do and raise money for and it really, really does work.'

Geoff returned to complete the 21 stages again last year, a day before the actual Tour, and courted controversy by inviting Armstrong to complete a few of the stages alongside him. He admits that this decision did have its downsides but helped put the cause on everyone's lips and raised over £700,000 for leukaemia research. 'Armstrong helped put the event on the map for good and bad reasons,' he concedes. 'It did stop us getting certain corporate partners last year. But the people who took part in it said they would remember it forever and that it was something special. We're going to go again in 2017 and the intention is to organise a few more cycle events. I've just started a campaign to bring more social awareness into the work I do, to try and get more funding without putting the NHS under any more pressure. I am still totally committed to trying to help make a difference to people in the future.'

The majority of former players I spoke to revealed that the thing they miss most about playing is matchday. The buzz, the preparation, the dressing room – it's what the whole week had been building up to. And why wouldn't they? No kid grows up dreaming of monotonous training sessions, working every Christmas and banal post-match interviews.

There's another thing, almost to a man, they also miss – the camaraderie. Former Republic of Ireland midfielder Matt Holland spent the first year of his retirement, from Charlton Athletic in 2009, visiting the gym virtually every day. It was his way of maintaining some sort of routine and fitness but also an attempt to try and relive the dressing room banter he missed. 'I was talking to people in the changing rooms in the gym, almost trying to replicate what it was like as a footballer. I think people were looking at me thinking, "What's he doing? What's he chatting to me for?"' he laughs.

It's easy to understand how this comradeship with former team-mates can be hankered after. You will have spent your entire life since childhood immersed in a group dynamic, spending a huge amount of your time with like-minded peers all striving towards the same goals. And then it ends. You're left at home alone, with often just memories to keep you company. Dr Steven Ortiz, who has studied the marriages of elite American male athletes for many years, agrees that this aspect of retirement can be difficult for sports stars to contend with.

He explains, 'All of a sudden, you've been cut or traded, or in some way your career ends, and that family of team-mates, that home away from home, is gone. It can be difficult for some players to process that change because they're no longer part of that close-knit brotherhood. The bonding process and feelings of solidarity among team-mates have become very important to them, and they don't find that sense of fulfilment outside of their team, or outside of their sport or career. And when you take that away from them, it can have a huge impact on their sense of self and identity. Also, because they are elite athletes, and considered celebrities, they may have developed an attitude of male entitlement and privilege during their careers, and this has been reinforced in the media and in interactions with fans and the public in general over the years. When suddenly deprived of this entitlement, some may feel neglected, ignored, and powerless.'

Former Republic of Ireland and Millwall striker Richie Sadlier agrees that it can be like coming out of a bubble when a footballer retires. 'Niall Quinn often uses the phrase, "It's like an adults' playground." It's quite juvenile actually, the whole set-up,' he admits. 'You're a load of grown men, playing football is the serious bit, and that's fun. You're cocooned in this little world where, for very good reasons, you keep non-footballers at arm's length because there's all sorts of pitfalls there. And, invariably, very few people around you will say no to you. It's a bonkers little world, it's a false little world. Johnny Giles uses the phrase that he was 15 when he went to England, and he was 15 when he retired. It's like arrested development as you're not really exposed to normal stuff. The challenge for everyone when they finish is that there's nothing that's going to happen on Saturday that's different to what happens on Monday or Tuesday.'

Some never let go. Richie has spoken to former players in their 50s and 60s who still see themselves as a footballer. 'Their conversations are totally around football, they still use the vocabulary of the dressing room, and haven't moved on one inch,' he says. 'All they've done is gotten older, but they're still in the mindset of a footballer. Which is kind of sad in a way. But the adjustment is hard. It's very difficult. It took years and years and years for me, a good bit of professional help and a load of really horrible moments along the way. It will always be difficult if you love it the amount that most people involved love it.'

Even for those who, on the face of it, seem to have it all, the prospects of retirement can be daunting. 'I've spoken to fellas in the last couple of years who are retiring and, on paper, they will tick every box,' he says. 'They're married, got children, are healthy, really wealthy, had a really good career, a load of Premier League appearances, caps – all the things that mean a fella should be able to put his feet up, breathe out and go, "That was great." And he's terrified and says, "I'm just shitting myself, I don't know what to do." Most people would brush that away and say, "I'd love to have your money, your memories, your wife, your kids, your house, your car." But very few people would want what's going on in his head, because it can be fairly bleak.'

Richie believes many strive to remain in the game, 'As they feel, "I better hang in here because if I leave the world of football I'm starting from scratch. If I leave, I'm nothing." A lot of people need support to deal with the emotional effects of transitioning. It's like a death. I remember trying to explain the enormity of the loss. Football was what I did to pay my bills, it's why I emigrated, it's why I left my family, it's what people talked about to me, it's how I saw myself, it's what I wanted to do, it's what I thought about, dreamt about, and then it's gone. It's a huge loss.

'There's nothing I'd change about my time though. Even knowing it ended how it did. It's an amazing experience, even the bad days. I was sent off one day, we won 2-0 against Stoke City at home and I felt like shit. But you feel alive. I was probably 19 or 20 at the time and thought, "What else could I do where I'd feel as alive as this?" What a memory! The good days are amazing. They're amazing.'

A common complaint I've heard, albeit not necessarily from ex-players, is that professional clubs fail to adequately prepare footballers for retirement or, indeed, assist them post-career. Most clubs nowadays employ a player welfare officer to take care of their players' needs. I've heard of many bizarre duties they've undertaken including organising somewhere for Les Ferdinand to land his helicopter and assisting players who've got lost on the Tube. One player was perturbed that his head was getting wet during the night and turned to his welfare officer for assistance. A plumber was sourced, who visited the player's bedroom to find the window above his bed was wide open. Nevertheless, player welfare officers provide an integral role in the modern-day game, often being the middleman between the player and club.

I spoke to one anonymously, who has been with their Premier League club for almost 15 years, to determine if clubs actually do prepare their footballers for the transition to a life after their playing days end. They revealed that while some players plan for retirement, others 'feel as if their career is going to go on for ever and need a lot of encouragement to consider planning for their futures'. Again many don't imagine they'll ever have to retire through injury, considering that 'it's always happened to someone else'.

'Many players, however, have started planning right from the start – generally through their agents and with the help of their families,' they continue. 'It is now accepted that a good agent will have started financial planning with him as soon as he begins playing.'

The club's academy also helps to prepare scholars for the fact they may not make the grade, which is all done in communication with the youngsters' parents. 'A financial advisor who specialises in this area comes to speak to them about this,' says the welfare officer. 'They are encouraged to develop other skills, and to continue their education – GCSEs, A Levels or equivalent qualifications if the player has come from abroad.'

Later on in careers, clubs tend to leave financial advice to players' agents and advisors but do 'generally provide advice, assistance and support to older players', says the welfare officer. 'Many players opt to undergo coaching or management courses, and this can sometimes provide them with a seamless transition into the next stage of their sporting life. Other players opt for the chance to pursue further education, and players here have gone on to study with the Open University.'

When players retire they are invited to join, and avail of the services of, a former players' association – which most clubs tend to have these days. This club's former players' association offers 'a wealth of advice, and employment often comes from contacts there – the association has links with business and industry in the city'.

The welfare officer works with the first team at the club and provides a crucial role, often acting as a Renaissance man to the players. The one I spoke to 'teaches English, sources properties, bank accounts, phones, childcare and schools – I am also their counsellor.

'I also work for the former players' association as a counsellor, and so am able to sometimes guide and support the player through this stage of transition. We have close links to organisations who provide professional help for any players who experience addiction problems, which can sometimes be the case.

'In my time working in football, I have worked with many players who experience difficulties – some who left many years ago – and suddenly have problems as their lack of confidence and their loss of a raison d'être become apparent.' In their experience, 'Divorce tends not to be the biggest problem – alcohol abuse and gambling are top of the list.'

Even when assistance is offered by clubs, the refusal to accept a pending retirement can often lead to players burying their heads in the sand. Again, it's not unique to professional football. Sociology professor Dr Ortiz asserts that elite American sports leagues and unions offer workshops and seminars to help the players ease into retirement. 'But many of the players may be reluctant to attend these workshops because they may be in denial, and reluctant to admit that there will come a day when they will have to leave the game they love so much,' he says.

'Consequently, they may put that off as long as they can and try to avoid any reminders that it's coming to an end. They're going to hang on to what they have as long as they can, even though there are institutional opportunities to prepare for retirement.'

During his spell as chairman of the PFA, Pat Nevin encountered the same problems. A large part of his time was spent organising outsourced education. 'But we always had the same problem. We never, ever beat it and I would suspect it's still never been beaten,' concedes Pat. 'You get those 20 young footballers, who are 16 or 17 years old, into a classroom after they've done their training for the day and sit with them for two hours. How many of them are actually going to listen? It doesn't matter how hard you try. They know what they want to be, they know what they're going to do. It's unbelievably hard. You can take the horse to water but you can't always make it drink. The opportunities, even from when I was a player, were there. Whether you took the opportunities, well that was a question for the young player.

'My thoughts, and very much the thoughts of the union, on this were make sure everyone gets an education as, a) it gives you something else to do, and b) you can think in a different way as well. That's easy to say; most people in our society admire at a distance people who "gave everything to it – he loved that, he lived just for that". Be it football, be it mountaineering or whatever. And we have an admiration for it.

'I have a slight admiration for it but I've an incredible fear of that because it's incredibly dangerous. If you live for one thing and that one thing is taken away for whatever reason, almost your raison d'être goes. We tried as a union to make sure that these educational possibilities were available.'

He believes that although some of these ideas are philosophical and that it's impossible to get through to every young player, there have been many success stories. 'What you do is put a base education in there for the next job, but also a method of thinking that hopefully gives them a chance. You hear about the players that fall off the wagon but there are plenty who actually didn't, because they got those educational possibilities. Some of them have done all right,' he adds.

One player whose education gave him 'something else to do' and helped him 'think in a different way' is former Norwich City and Northern Ireland striker Paul McVeigh, who retired at the age of 32 and believes it was the 'best decision' he ever made. He'd just won League 1 with the Canaries and decided to go out on a high.

He had given retirement some consideration during his playing career, but not overly so. 'I think it's very much an individual thing,' says Paul. 'Some people have the foresight or the understanding that it is a very real possibility rather than a theoretical concept that your playing days are going to end. You have other people who didn't think about retirement until the day they retired. It's quite a broad spectrum. I might have given a bit more thought to retirement than other players but, even still, I wasn't sitting there every year thinking my career was going to end soon and that I'd have to do something about it.'

At 21, Paul had started a Business degree but stopped after nine months when it began to impact on his playing career. As his career progressed he decided to return to university to pursue new interests. 'I got to 27 or 28 and re-evaluated things. It was getting closer to retirement so I decided that I was really interested in the physiology, sports science and the psychology in football. So I set myself a goal that I wanted to start my Sports Science degree before I was 30.'

He admits he made the decision to retire pretty quickly when he considered the other options available to him. 'I thought that I was going to continue playing, but then it came to the last couple of months of the season and I bumped into the guy who I went on to start a business with. He said, "You should come and work with me, I think you'd enjoy it." He had the same conversation with me a few months later and I took it a bit more seriously. I thought it might be time to go out on a high, we'd just won the league, and I was living back in Norwich where it felt like I was going to be settling. With all those things taken into the equation I decided to stop playing and go and work with Gavin Drake, who was a sports psychologist I'd worked with at Norwich ten years previously.'

A former player I spoke to commented that some footballers who retire are like '37-year-old newborns', wondrous at the new experiences open to them now they were no longer playing. It can certainly be the case that the transition from the cosseted nature of the game can offer new opportunities to footballers whose lives have been regimented for many years.

'Since coming out of football, the experiences and depth, quality and breadth of my life now is 100 times more than what it was in football,' Paul reveals. 'Not to say that I didn't love my days in football, because I did. But it was only one area of my life. Coming out of football is like taking the blinkers off. Suddenly you step into a world of opportunity and you become aware of all these things and experiences that you either weren't allowed to do, had no knowledge of or didn't realise you could do. That's why it was probably the best decision I've ever made.'

Since retiring he's certainly kept busy, delivering courses in the psychology of performance, becoming a keynote speaker, worked extensively in the media – including a stint reporting on Sky Sports's *Soccer Saturday* – written a book titled *The Stupid Footballer Is Dead* and established a sports psychology company called ThinkPRO, which has worked with Norwich City and Crystal Palace. He is currently studying for a Masters in Sports Psychology.

Pat Nevin also believes that clubs and organisations such as the PFA have a responsibility to be there for players should they encounter problems during retirement. 'There is an intrinsic set of problems there, so you don't beat yourself up about it. What you do is give the best opportunities, and if the opportunities aren't taken they're not taken,' he continues. 'But then you cannot ignore them when they fall off the wagon, for whatever reasons. Be it when you dump them at the age of 22 and they're on the scrapheap or whether they're 37, like I was. If they ask for help, you're there to give them help. It's not cash outlays, it's re-education and the monies within the game are there to do that.'

Pat was never your stereotypical footballer. While many 1980s players interviewed by *Shoot!* were citing Phil Collins as their favourite musician, Pat was writing for the likes of *NME* and *Art Review* under a pseudonym. His experience of retirement also differs from the majority, in that he encountered very few of the difficulties that we have seen are all too common.

'There was a tiny period where I thought, "Wait a minute, I've got a wee bit of time here." And then I thought, "Excellent news! I've got lots to read, films to see, things I'd like to do, other jobs I wanted to look at,"' he recalls. 'That kind of emptiness lasted for about ten minutes. Also, I had another job to walk into. I was player-chief executive at Motherwell, then stopped playing and became chief executive. And I was doing quite a bit of media work. So, I'd prepped for it for quite some time to make sure that I had other areas to go into.'

It has become obvious that preparation is the key to a healthy transition to retirement, but having passions outside of the sport is also crucial. 'My background was always look at it as a part-time idea anyway – to do football for a year, two years, four years, five years. I hadn't gone into it with the concept, "Right, this is what my career and life is going to be." This was a little stopgap on the way. It just happened to last 19 years, much to my amazement,' says Pat.

'So, my kind of attitude gave me a perfectly healthy way out, that I wasn't relying on that lifestyle, I was much more an outsider from within. That made me a real voyeur on the inside looking at what these other guys were suffering. And instead of just being a voyeur, what I decided to do was try and help. Hence my work with the PFA.'

Pat does concede, though, that he did struggle with some things. 'I loved fitness and I loved training. And that's a big miss because your body demands the adrenaline, it's a purely physical thing for some of us,' he reveals. 'And not doing it to that level was really hard to get used to. Little things like having to watch your weight, so what, you can cope with that. But the actual adrenaline kick, it's not unusual to go searching for that a wee bit. I did a bit of downhill cycling. I also got a little adrenaline kick because one of my other jobs was live television.

'Also, I just carried on running. I just decided that if I'm not training every day with the team, I'll just go running in the hills. And to this day I still do. That physical thing is something you need to deal with. But as long as you are self-aware enough to know what it is, you can deal with it. Not everyone is, to be honest. I missed the training and I missed a slight adrenaline kick. And I didn't think I'd miss that kick.'

While Pat got his buzz from running and live television, many seek theirs elsewhere, leading to addiction problems. He believes that the loss of identity also leads to problems. 'I can only guess, I've never really been the most addictive personality,' he admits. 'But, listening to the guys, talking to the guys and trying over the years – particularly with my work with the union – to understand the reasons for addiction, they're always much more complex than we'd all like to write down in ten sentences and figure out. It's always a mass of things together. It may be problems within the relationship, that's one thing. It may be who you actually are in the deepest sense.'

During his career Pat said, 'Being a footballer is what I do, it's not who I am,' a line that's often been used in books of quotations. It's something he still believes is crucial. 'I've been very strong on that since the age of about 19 – "Do not get caught into this, this is dangerous." And I could feel and see the danger of it. That's all very well for someone like me who comes from the outside, comes from an educational background, thinks about life in a different way. If all you've ever wanted to do – which many, many, many kids want to do – is be a footballer with all the trappings or many of the trappings, you succeed in that, you are treated in a certain way and then have that whipped out from underneath you.

'So you've got that aforementioned adrenaline kick taken away, you've got who you think you are to some degree taken away. You've also got who your partner thinks you are taken away. They married a "wow, superstar footballer, everyone loves you". And then it doesn't matter, you're not actually. Suddenly you're the guy who's doing the gardening again. Any relationship has that, it's kind of slightly multiplied within football sometimes.'

Pat laughs when I ask him what advice he'd give a player about preparing for retirement, as during his tenure as PFA chairman he 'cannot remember one player coming up and asking for advice on what they should do when they finish. Not one. So the concept of someone coming and asking for my advice is so odd, so strange.'

However, he does insist on one thing. 'Try and have a hinterland,' he advises. 'Try and have something else so it's not just family and football. If that's all your life is, if either or both finishes – you're stuffed. So my best advice would be to make sure you have got another interest, hobby or pastime or something you want to study, that you actually like as well. You need to find another interest. And I would suggest to most people that when you find that other interest, it'll a) make you a wider person, b) help you in later life and, c) and this is the killer, it'll make you a better footballer because you won't be playing through fear all the time, because you're not scared to lose what you've got.

'You'll play because you remember why you love doing it. This is the healthy part of it. If you've got something to fall back on, then you're not fearful, playing through fear, worrying about the end, scared of the end, scared of what the difference will be. You actually are that other person as well, who's running concurrently.'

Despite all the problems retirement can bring, the general public still seems to be ambivalent towards the difficulties former footballers can go through. While this might be due to the sweeping generalisation that they're overpaid during their playing days, Dr Ortiz has another theory.

'The public really doesn't want to know about the off-the-field issues their heroes have to confront. They want to keep them on a pedestal — they want to worship them as heroes,' he maintains. 'They really don't want to know their heroes have feet of clay, that they have bad marriages, that they make poor life or financial decisions, or that they feel lost and hopeless when the game is over. They want to keep those memories of when they were great athletes and of great moments during a game that they shared with others. They don't want to know that some are going to struggle for the rest of their lives when the game is over. They don't want their heroes to get old and wither away. They want them to always remain young, vibrant and talented.'

As I came to the end of writing this book, I began to wonder how I'd spend my time immediately afterwards. It had taken up a large chunk of my life for a long time and I got the feeling that I might feel a void when it was finished. So I can only imagine the feelings of a footballer, who has played for maybe 20 years, when they finally hang up their boots.

I could have written a book about the household name football stars living happily ever after in retirement. But, you could pick up many ghostwritten autobiographies for that. The likes of Karl Fredrik Ljungberg, born the same week as me, may well be enjoying his retirement. But then again, maybe he isn't. Certainly, for the 60,000-plus retired footballers scattered across the British Isles, their lives are not the ones of luxury that many imagine. Are the highs of a football career a welcome trade for the many problems that a life away from the game can bring? Can the memories of goals scored many years ago assuage a retirement riddled with problems such as divorce, financial ruin, mental health issues and career-related injuries?

And would I still like to have been a professional footballer? Of course. A retired footballer? My initial reaction would have been, 'Probably not so much.' But then I think about the former players I've spoken to and the majority have been articulate, engaging and honest men who just so happened to play football earlier in their lives. They were lucky enough to enjoy a career that millions of kids around the world can only dream of but now lead new lives, with new hopes and have their own problems to deal with.

To football fans they may always be associated with a goal, a Panini sticker, an injury, a sending-off, an off-field controversy. They may want them to always remain young, vibrant and talented. But to those who matter, they are a husband, a father, a brother, a son, a colleague. And that's what they will always remain.

To paraphrase Pat Nevin, 'Being a footballer is what they did, it's not who they are.'

12   186000